PENGUIN BOOKS
RUDE FOOD

Vir Sanghvi is probably the best-known Indian journalist of his generation. In 1978 he became the youngest editor in the history of Indian journalism when he was appointed editor of *Bombay* at the age of twenty-two. He became editor of *Imprint* at twenty-six and of *Sunday* at thirty.

From 1999 to 2004 he was editor of the *Hindustan Times*, where he is currently editorial director. He is also one of India's leading television anchors and has hosted several programmes for the Star TV group.

# rude food

the collected food writings of

Vir Sanghvi

PENGUIN BOOKS

An imprint of Penguin Random House

PENGUIN BOOKS

USA | Canada | UK | Ireland | Australia
New Zealand | India | South Africa | China | Singapore

Penguin Books is part of the Penguin Random House group of companies whose addresses can be found at global.penguinrandomhouse.com

Published by Penguin Random House India Pvt. Ltd
4th Floor, Capital Tower 1, MG Road,
Gurugram 122 002, Haryana, India

Penguin
Random House
India

First published by Penguin Books India 2004



The pieces in this collection first appeared, in somewhat different form, in the Hindustan Times. 'A Rendezvous with Fine Dining' First appeared in The Taj Magazine: The Centenary.



12 11 10 9 8 7 6

ISBN 9780143031390

Typeset in Garamond by Mantra Virtual Services, New Delhi
Printed at Repro India Limited



www.penguin.co.in

FSC
www.fsc.org
MIX
Paper from
responsible sources
FSC® C047271

This is a legitimate digitally printed version of the book and therefore might not have certain extra finishing on the cover.

*For the Petit Fromage and*
*the Significant Other, with*
*love and gratitude*

# contents

## *desi* delights



## going places



## are you being served?

## we are what we eat



## what's cooking?

e are What We Eat



What We Cook

# introduction

# a fragment of autobiography

For as long as I can remember, I have denied that I am a food writer. And yet, I have been writing about food since 1979.

My defence is that all my food pieces were written by accident. The story begins with the launch of *Bombay* magazine in 1979. As managing editor, I thought it important that the magazine reviewed the city's restaurants.We had long discussions about how the reviews would be done. As the magazine was vaguely modelled on *New York* magazine we considered copying *New York*'s reviewing style: its iconic food critic (at the time, Gael Greene) would go to new restaurants and then take them apart over 2000 words or so.

We had two problems with that approach. First of all, who, in Bombay, would bother to read 2000 words about a restaurant? And secondly, even if we could get readers interested, who would write the reviews?

In those days, there were only two food critics in Bombay (read the piece on page 197), and neither was willing to be rude about restaurants. It was not because they always got free meals (that trend began later with the start of the magazine boom, heralded, ironically enough, by *Bombay*) but simply because they defined their jobs differently. They liked the people who ran the restaurants and the restaurant owners liked them. Their role was to serve as a bridge between the catering industry and the eating public.

This was great for them but no good for me. I wanted somebody who would burn the bridge, not strengthen it.

You can look at restaurant reviewing in two ways. You can treat it like film reviewing in which case it doesn't matter if the film director knows the critic. He's already made the movie, probably has some respect for the critic's judgement, and the critic's job is to treat it like a work of art.

Or you can treat it as a consumer test. In this approach, the food critic must, almost by definition, be knowledgeable. But he's not an art critic. Rather, he is a consumer inspector. Each time he goes to a restaurant, he represents his readers. Ideally, he must be anonymous so that his dining experience most closely approximates what his readers are likely to get. He must not care about offending the chef (or the hotel PR person), he must pay his own way (unheard of these days, alas), and he must be categorical: should his readers go to that restaurant or not?

Nobody I met seemed to agree with this approach. But because I was convinced that a city magazine must have restaurant reviews, we decided to evolve our own format. Each issue would contain a round-up of restaurants by category (Sichuan one week, cafes the next, and so on) and the reviews would be written anonymously by members of our staff.

Which, of course, meant me.

How good was I as a critic? In retrospect, I would imagine that I was far less knowledgeable than I should have been. But then, to be fair, Bombay restaurants weren't as good as they should have been either—at least not in that era.

My strength, if you could call it that, was my anonymity. I had just moved back to Bombay after several years of living in England, and nobody in the incestuous journalistic world (even smaller and more incestuous than it is today) had any clue as to who I was. Nor could restaurant owners get accustomed to the notion of a food critic who would pay his own bill. Many actually complained that I had been unfair to them by not announcing my presence. ('How were we supposed to know that he was going to write about the food? *Agar pata hota to* we would have done something special.')

When the restaurant business finally worked out that some snot-nosed twenty-three-year-old was making fun of their food, they were all outraged. What did I know about food, anyway? I was no better than the average person who came to eat at their establishments.

My point, exactly.

*

All through this storm in a wonton, I treated restaurant reviewing as nothing more than an enjoyable sideline. It was good for the publication—nobody had ever read a restaurant review which tore the food to shreds before. But my primary job was to edit the magazine, not to compare restaurants.

In 1981, I left *Bombay* magazine and went abroad. When I returned to journalism as editor of *Imprint* in 1983, I found that the restaurant scene in Bombay had changed almost beyond recognition. Not only were there many more restaurants but food criticism had become established as a journalistic form. Newspapers and magazines were willing to be rude about restaurants and the big hotels had hired PR people whose principal role seemed to be to take hacks out for large free meals. But at *Imprint*, a monthly magazine dedicated to long feature stories, there was no scope for restaurant reviewing, and so I concluded that my little stint as a food writer was now over.

Then, one evening, I ran into Vinod Mehta at a dinner party. Vinod had just launched the *Sunday Observer*, hailed as India's first Sunday newspaper, but more accurately described as India's first modern newspaper—even *The Telegraph*, which usually merits this distinction, was launched after the *Observer*.

Vinod asked if I wanted to review restaurants again. I don't know why I said yes, but right there, on the spot, I even told him how I wanted to do it. First of all, I said, Bombay was now ready for full-fledged restaurant reviews which tackled one place at a time. We no longer needed to do the category-wise breakdowns of the *Bombay* magazine days. And secondly, I said, I didn't want to join the club of freebie food writers. I would use a pseudonym for the pieces (Vikram Sinha) and my identity would remain our little secret.

Vinod agreed, and so from 1983 to 1986, when I left Bombay for Calcutta, Vikram Sinha became India's first proper food critic, reviewing a new restaurant each week, awarding stars for food and service, and yes, earning the ire of the restaurant owners.

By the time the restaurant business found out that Vikram Sinha was Vir Sanghvi, I was gone. I had left the city. And my career as a food writer was over.

*

I went to Calcutta to edit *Sunday*, then India's largest-selling weekly news magazine. Because I was thirty years old, from Bombay, and not on first-name terms with Chandra Shekhar or Devi Lal, many of my colleagues took the perfectly understandable line that I was an odd choice to edit a national news magazine. 'So, Aveek,' one distinguished business editor asked Aveek Sarkar, *Sunday*'s owner, 'you've decided to appoint a Bombay-type as your new editor?'

Conscious of the controversy that my appointment had generated, I began spending two days each week in Delhi, and made the rounds of politicians' homes, trying hard to act less Bombay and more Hindi heartland.

In the circumstances, the worst thing I could have done was to resume my career as a food writer. It was just what the sceptics needed: 'The fellow writes about cocktails and canapés, not about the things that really matter.' (Like booth-capturing, rent-a-crowd rallies and the CIA's plans to destabilize India, presumably.)

So I learnt all about Bofors, the need to amend Muslim Personal Law and the negative effects of Mandal and masjid. It was not, as I had suspected, all that difficult to do: how much of a genius did you need to be to figure out that V.P. Singh was about to stab Rajiv Gandhi in the back? Or that L.K. Advani's symbolic Ram Rath was really an adapted Toyota? Or that a newly retired Narasimha Rao, who had only agreed to be Congress president with a great show of reluctance in the aftermath of Rajiv Gandhi's assassination, would eagerly grab the Prime Ministership if the Congress won the election?

But because editing a news magazine is a full-time activity and because most of my writing in those days consisted of rewriting other people's copy, I more or less abandoned my own career as a writer for five years or so. I gave up my column in *Debonair* and lacked the time to start a new one in *Sunday*. I rarely wrote under my own name. And there was no time for anything that sounded at all like fun—especially for food writing.

*

I can't remember if I did any food writing at all between 1987 and 2001. There may have been the odd piece for *The Taj Magazine* or the occasional article on a restaurant I liked, but that was about it.

And yet, somehow, the food world seemed to treat me as an insider. I was invited to speak at the first Chefs' Conference in Bombay in 1996. A year later I was asked to join the panel of judges at a contest to find the best chef in South India. The following year, I was among those who presented the Hotel and Food Service Awards and moderated a session at the Food and Beverage Summit.

I could never work out why this should be so. Partly I suspect it was because I ate out at restaurants a lot, so most people in the food business knew me as a customer—if not as a writer. Partly it was that I was interested in food. Unlike most diners at Indian restaurants, I would actually ask to meet the chefs and had strong views on what I liked and how I wanted my food cooked. And partly it was because, as the food business exploded in the 1990s, chefs and restaurateurs were grateful to come across even moderately known journalists or TV presenters who took food seriously.

It helped also, I think, that I remained a dedicated foodie. If I went to a foreign country I made it a point to try the local cuisine. When I went to New York or London I would seek out all the new restaurants and track the new food trends. I had—and continue to have—friends in the food business: people like Rohit Khattar of Delhi's Habitat Centre and London's Chor Bizarre and the Panjabi sisters of the Taj group (Camellia) and Chutney Mary group in London (Namita).

But food remained a hobby. Whenever I was invited to speak at a conference (and I accepted something like one out of every ten invitations) I always took care to make it clear that I spoke from the customer's side of the business. Put me in a kitchen and I would be the worst chef in the world. And as for running a restaurant, I would make a complete hash of that. My perspective was always the perspective of the enthusiastic amateur.

Food writing was never something I seriously considered. Yes, I had once reviewed restaurants. But that was a long time ago. And both food journalism and I had moved far beyond since.

*

In the fourteen or so years that I avoided writing about food the world had changed, or so it seemed.

In 1979, my willingness to slam chefs had seemed novel and outrageous. In the early 1980s, my enthusiasm for awarding stars to Indian restaurants had seemed like a daring innovation imported directly from the pages of *The New York Times*.

But now, everybody was a food writer.

Beleagured airline employees always complained that every Indian who travelled by Air-India immediately considered himself an expert on aviation. Something similar happened to the world of food.

In the beginning, anybody who went to a fancy restaurant or shook hands with the chef declared that he was a food critic. Then, it got worse. Any trainee journo who went to a freebie lunch thrown by a hotel PR decided that he or she was competent to rate restaurants and to advise diners where to go.

Some of this had to do with the liberalization of the 1990s. In the 1970s and the 1980s we were still shackled by the licence-permit-quota raj. Five-star hotels were treated as islands of privilege by the government. Relatively few people travelled abroad not because this was difficult to do but because such was our mindset. (In 1988 I pointed out in *Sunday* that it was cheaper to go to Bangkok from Calcutta than it was to get to Bombay. And Bangkok hotels were less than half the price of their Indian counterparts. This revelation was greeted with disbelief.)

After Manmohan Singh liberalized the economy we began at last to think of ourselves as consumers. New goods appeared in the shops. International brands were available in our local markets. Foreign hotel chains began to open fancier hotels in Indian cities. Swarms of foreign businessmen investigated opportunities in India—and naturally, they needed hotels and restaurants.

At about the same time, the satellite TV revolution hit middle-class homes. Western lifestyles suddenly seemed more accessible. Indian TV channels began turning such chefs as Sanjeev Kapoor into stars. Andy Verma and Rita Gulati became staples of breakfast shows. Karen Anand seemed to crop up everywhere.

And then there was the print explosion. As advertisers searched for colour media to flog their new products, such previously staid and stolid newspapers as *The Times of India* and the *Hindustan Times* introduced colourful city supplements that were all about consumption: which designer should you patronize; which mobile phone should you buy; which brand of make-up made you fairer? And then, almost inevitably, which restaurant was trendy? Or, what's the hip wine? Or, who serves the best pasta?

The economic boom led to a growth in what I sometimes regard as the bullshit professions of the 1990s: the PR adviser, the event manager, the design consultant, the marketing expert—and, yes, the food and wine journalist.

*

The city supplements and the Saturday supplements were perfect for restaurants to promote themselves or to plug food festivals. Because these supplements were personality-based (or as personality-based as is possible when the average piece is 250 words in length) journos needed new people to write about on a daily basis. Following international practice, they turned to chefs and restaurant owners to provide copy.

By the end of the 1990s, the formula had become set. The supplements would have a varied front page, page two would be listings, page three would be parties (hence the term 'Page Three People') and then, from page four onwards, it was plugs, promos, celebrity profiles, celebrity columns and movie gossip.

Such was the hunger for copy that any restaurant that wanted to be written about could throw a journo lunch and the free meal alone was enough to guarantee a colour picture and two hundred words of text. As the supplements were usually staffed by very young people just out of college, the articles generally consisted of stenography: the journos faithfully reproduced whatever they were told over lunch.

Articulate chefs found themselves being treated on a par with film stars. Hemant Oberoi and Ananda Solomon became staples of the Bombay supplements. In Delhi, Bill Marchetti, Imtiaz and the Italian chef of the moment at La Piazza all became stars. Restaurant owners fared nearly as well: A.D. Singh, Baba Ling, Rahul Akerkar, Ritu Dalmia and Nelson Wang became household names in newspaper-reading homes.

Even as the food boom was under way, a wine boom began. European wine merchants who had seen profits skyrocket with the opening up of the East Asian market positioned themselves for the profits that they were sure would eventually flow out of the Indian market. Soon New World vineyards also saw the potential in India.

The wine boom remains a media phenomenon as of now (I've dealt with it on page 74) but certainly there are almost as many journalists writing about wine in Delhi as there are people buying the stuff.

*

All this leads us to 2002 when the columns published in this book began to be written. I have to say that none of it—the book or the columns—was my idea. But first, the background.

In 1999, fearing that people had begun to forget that I was a journalist and started to regard me as a TV presenter, I abandoned the salaried security of a cosy consulting editorship with ABP and decided that I needed—for want of a better term—a big-ticket journalistic job.

The editorship of the *Hindustan Times*, for seventy-five years Delhi's biggest and most influential newspaper, had fallen vacant in unhappy circumstances—the editor had been forced to resign after being accused of plagiarism.

I wanted to edit the *HT* and at forty-three I knew I had the energy required to take it into the twenty-first century. But I was also unwilling to give up the successful TV career that my comfortable consultancy with ABP allowed me to pursue.

I knew that if I pushed my luck, the *HT* would let me do some television. My confidence was based on friendship. I had known K.K. Birla, the paper's chairman since 1987, and was sure that I could take advantage of his good nature. Besides, his daughter Shobhana Bhartia, who actually ran the paper, was one of my closest friends. (It's time to come clean. She is the person who is described as the Princess in these columns.)

But could I find the time to do both—edit a national newspaper and run two weekly TV shows? The *HT* required a lot of hard work, and besides, it was poised for the biggest expansion in its history: eight new editions over the next eighteen months. And even if I pulled both those rabbits out of my hat, could I still find the time to write 'Counterpoint', the weekly column that I had started in *Sunday* in 1993 before shifting it to *The Telegraph* in 1996?

I decided that time would provide the answers to those questions, took a deep breath and plunged into the *HT*. After a couple of months of wondering if I had done the right thing I discovered that I loved everything about my new job. I loved the *HT*, I loved the people (surely the best staff that any editor could pray for), I loved my proprietors and I loved the thrill of editing a national daily.

If I have sounded sniffy about the city supplements then let me put this in perspective for you. As editor of the *HT*, I took *HT City*, our two-days-a-week supplement, and turned it into a daily publication. I switched editors, bodily lifting Sourish Bhattacharya from the Sunday magazine and placing him behind the wheel of *HT City* with the specific brief of making it the top food and wine publication in New Delhi, if not India. As any fair-minded observer will concede, Sourish succeeded admirably and also ended up as one of Delhi's best-known food writers himself.

The success of *HT City*, the spurt in the *HT*'s circulation, the largely successful launch of many new editions and, in particular, the change in the *HT*'s image, pleased me no end.

But I still felt that something was lacking.

*

Perhaps because I come from the world of magazines I am always dissatisfied with very short articles. As somebody who has been on TV every week for a decade I'm only too aware that it is essentially a superficial medium, great for creating an immediate impact but lousy at communicating anything at the level of ideas.

As the magazine boom has wound down, as sound bite TV has taken over and as newspapers have begun dealing in itsy-bitsy stories, I've taken to worrying that we are turning into a nation of browsers with the attention spans of seven-year-olds.

I've always struggled to get longer articles into the paper (the *HT* is justly proud of the strength of its editorial page at a time when other papers are replacing editorials with sponsored spiritual crap), and maintained that even light subjects—film, food, fashion etc.—would benefit from a slightly more in-depth approach.

The *HT City* formula was set and it was working so I was reluctant to tamper with that publication. But I felt that we needed a supplement that had room for longer articles on lighter subjects. A Sunday section is the logical place for such features but India is possibly the only country in the world where advertisers fail to recognize the merits of advertising in a Sunday supplement.

In 2001 the *HT* decided to take the plunge. We would revamp and redesign our Sunday supplement, we announced. And if the product became an editorial success (never mind the advertising) then we could consider a full-fledged magazine.

*

It was while we were designing and reinventing the new Sunday supplement that the idea of a food column first emerged. My views on city-supplement-style food writing were well known around the office. I loved the fact that food had become so much a part of our lives but I resented that journalists had surrendered our right to decide how food was to be covered. Now PR companies, wine importers and hoteliers were setting the agenda—they decided what would be written about by choosing which events to stage and which foods to promote.

There was another problem. Because all food journalism

anywhere in the world is basically incestuous (the same journos write about the same chefs), it is nearly always full of camps and intrigues. Moreover, because many journalists are routinely fed free meals and drink bottles of wine that cost more than they earn in a month, they consider themselves beholden to their benefactors.

And so a nasty, bitchy ambience can develop. Who gets invited to which wine dinner? Who gets the free holiday in one of the hotel chain's resort properties in return for hyping the asparagus festival? Why invite him when I am so much more influential? Inevitably, the journos become creatures of the industry they seek to write about. Sometimes it is hard to tell where the PR ends and the journalism begins. Often, to please their benefactors, they invent a snobbery around places and restaurants. ('Can't get past the velvet rope at Djinns? Well, that means you are not part of the in-set?' Yuck!) They brag about having consumed expensive foods (though they rarely mention that they got them free), they drop the names of first-growth wines and they try and seem part of a charmed foodie circle of which the reader (to say nothing of their fellow journalists) is not a member.

*

My intention was to launch a food column that cut through all the crap, swept away all the bullshit, treated the snob nonsense with the contempt it deserved and did not take sides—of hotel chains, chefs, wine importers, head waiters and God alone knows who else.

The idea would be to demystify food, to make all the wonderful new dishes that were now available at our restaurants accessible to everybody and to tell our readers how to find the truth amidst all the hype.

Sourish Bhattacharya was the obvious person to write it but he already had his hands full with *HT City*, Marryam Reshii was already our restaurant reviewer and we thought she would be overextended if we landed her with a Sunday column as well.

I asked Poonam Saxena, the editor-designate of the new Sunday supplement, to think of non-journalists who had no axe to grind, who paid for all their own meals and who knew about food. We looked and we looked but we soon came across the Pompous Old Fart phenomenon. The best example of it is Michael Winner, the British film director who has written a food column for *The Sunday Times* (London) for years and years.

When the column first started Winner was best known as a film director (he made the *Death Wish* movies starring Charles Bronson). But because he was very rich, and had been eating out regularly for years, he didn't need to ingratiate himself (or even socialize) with the food industry. In the early years he cut through all the hype and bullshit and heaped well-deserved scorn on celebrated chefs.

Then, a funny thing happened. People forgot that Winner had ever been a film director. The few movies he made bombed. He became best known for his food column. And in no time at all the column became a rather tiresome listing of expensive restaurants, plugs for pals and silly little vendettas.

That's happened to people in India too. I will be kind and not take names. But basically, my conclusion is this: allow a rich man to hold forth on restaurants and sooner or later he becomes a Pompous Old Fart. People forget he ever did anything else. And sadly, so does he.

*

I suppose I should have seen it coming. With two weeks to go before the launch of the new Sunday supplement, we had a name for the column ('Rude Food', which I stole from a 1970s' book of dirty photographs) but no columnist. Worse still, we didn't even have a shortlist of potential columnists.

When Poonam asked me if I would start the column off—'only

for the first few weeks,' she said—I was torn between conflicting emotions. I wanted the column to happen; I was committed to demonstrating that it was possible to write about food with affection and without corruption. But I knew that there was no way I was going to do it.

To begin with, there was the problem of time. In 1999 I had agonized about my ability to juggle two TV shows, a weekly column and the editorship of the *HT*. I had managed that (highly stressful) balancing act so far. But I feared that if I agreed to do one more column I would finally tip the balance and fall off my tightrope.

And then there was the problem of knowing what to write about. A columnist must be plugged into the environment he covers, even if his connection is entirely dispassionate. I was friends with a few chefs, read a few food books and ate the odd good meal but I really did not know enough about food to sustain a regular column.

But the column had to be written. And the launch of the new supplement was scheduled for early 2002. So, finally, I agreed to a compromise. 'Rude Food' would appear as planned. I would write the first few pieces. But they would appear without a byline so that when a regular columnist was found, he could take over.

The first piece to appear was the one on the Nizam's Roll (page 97). I was in London when it came out, but just before the paper went to bed I received a panicky call from Delhi. The designers were saying that their layout required a byline.

Fine, I said, you can use the byline 'Cochon'. It's French for pig, and that's all I really am.

So the Nizam's Roll was written by 'Cochon'. The next piece also used the same byline but for reasons best known to Poonam she changed the spelling to 'Couchon' which is not 'pig' in any language, and certainly not in French.

I have an unreasonable aversion to spelling mistakes in my own copy (I am much more philosophical when the *HT*'s subs screw up other people's copy). So the appearance of the spelling mistake coincided with a certain amount of screaming and shouting on my part. There may even have been a bit of a sulk. ('I don't want to do this fucking column, anyway.')

Eventually, a new name was found. The column would be signed 'Grand Fromage'. Literally, it means 'large cheese' in French but the idea was to treat it as an in-joke for the office. The Grand Fromage was of course the Big Cheese—the paper's editor. (Heh, heh, heh. No, I didn't find it very funny either.)

What I did not recognize when I agreed to the silly pseudonym was that even though my colleagues kept the fiction of a temporary arrangement alive, the nature of the name suggested that they intended this to be the editor's second column in the Sunday paper—every Sunday.

For a while I fretted, fumed and fussed. But then, after two months of complaining, I reconciled myself to churning out yet another column every week.

The mouse of regularity had snapped up the Big Cheese.

*

Initially, the column was supposed to be about 800 words long. Then we found that this was an awkward length: too big to slot on the side, too small to carry properly. Given that I was unwilling to drop the length below 800 words—I was the chap who had made the case for long articles, remember?—we settled on 1200 to 1400 words.

Effectively, it ended up being the same length as 'Counterpoint'. But fortunately, the deadlines were far apart. 'Rude Food' went to press first, on Tuesday (which meant that I had the weekend to write it), while 'Counterpoint' was due on Friday.

While the response to the new Sunday supplement was so good that we immediately planned a full-fledged magazine (*Brunch*—it first came out in Calcutta and then in Delhi), it was Poonam who got all the well-deserved credit. Nobody said very much about 'Rude Food' for the first two or three months or so. I began to wonder if the column was being read at all.

Then slowly the feedback started filtering in. At this stage nobody outside the office—and not even that many people on the inside—had any idea I wrote it, so the responses I received were as editor of the *HT* rather than as the author of the column. The name 'Grand Fromage' seemed to pose a problem for many readers—the column was forever being called 'Rude Fromage' which, I suppose, was true enough in its own way.

Because the early pieces focussed on food (Nizam's Roll, *bhelpuri*, how to cook a Thai curry at home etc.), the hotel industry had no real interest in the column. Then a couple of pieces about eating out in Delhi—not included in this book because they were topical in nature—made hoteliers and restaurateurs sit up and take notice and 'Rude Food' began finally to have a certain influence within the industry.

*

The original brief for 'Rude Food' had been to demystify the whole business of fancy food and fine wine and to take all the snobbery out of going to expensive restaurants.

Many of the pieces collected in this book (on wine, on olive oil, on coping with bad service at restaurants etc.) reflect that early missionary zeal. But by the time I was writing about foie gras and caviar (both included here) I realized that the column had moved away from its original intent. I hoped that the pieces would deal with foie gras, caviar and truffles without seeming pretentious, but it was clear that I had wandered far from the original brief: how many of my readers actually shaved truffles over their pasta and how many needed to know the difference between beluga and sevruga?

Partly this was because, as the months went on, I never quite knew what each week's column was going to be about when I sat down to write it. Sometimes it was easy. If I went to Moscow or

Shanghai I was sure I would get a column out of each trip. If I learnt something interesting (Nelson Wang telling me the story of how he invented Chicken Manchurian), then I knew it would end up in 'Rude Food'. If I was outraged by something ('At Your Service', page 168, was written at the Maratha Sheraton in Bombay where I was gobsmacked by the prices), then the column tended to write itself.

But these were exceptions. Most weeks I would not have had the time to think about 'Rude Food' till Sunday. If I had a relatively free day I would do a certain amount of research: on the origins of kedgeree, for instance, or the various recipes for bread-and-butter pudding. My concern then would be with ensuring that I didn't do a Narayanan—my predecessor at the *HT* who had to leave after a plagiarism scandal—and would find enough to say that was not contained in any one book. (My obsession with avoiding Narayanan's fate explains why so many books are mentioned in the text. As much as possible, I wanted to come clean.)

But many of the pieces were written on busy Mondays in the office with the deadlines looming and with no opportunity to do very much research. Almost all of them came off the top of my head. If they were vaguely autobiographical in character—such as the one about travelling on the PM's special plane—then this was not difficult to do. But when I had to rely on my memory then I was on much less sure ground. As you will see when you read further, these are the columns with the most jokes and the least information.

*

This book was not my idea. I once toyed with the possibility of doing a collection of my 'Counterpoint' columns. In the late 1990s I had had several meetings with David Davidar and V.K. Karthika of Penguin who thought that if I put my 'Counterpoint' columns together along with profiles and a few other pieces I had written in the nineties, we could compile a book that was a snapshot of India in that decade.

I thought it wasn't a bad idea, and went off to dig out photocopies of my old columns from the ABP library. David and I agreed that because journalism is written for the moment and not meant to be read months afterwards I should be ruthless in throwing out those columns that were past their sell-by date. The columns could be reorganized into sections and I would do a fresh intro for each section.

I spent about a month on the project (the unused introductions to many of the sections are still lying at the bottom of my cupboard) before abandoning it and returning the contract to Penguin unsigned.

My problem is that I nearly always hate everything I have done when I come back to it. Show me a column I wrote last month and I'll show you all the awkward sentences, all the badly chosen words and the all the half-baked ideas. Similarly, I find watching myself on television an intensely masochistic business. I focus on the banality of my questions, my quivering double chin, the bags under my eyes and my tendency to spout inanities ('Really', 'How did that feel?'). When I get tired of being hard on myself I blame everything else: the editing, the lighting, the shot-taking etc.

So it was with the 'Counterpoint' collection.

Why would anybody want to read this crap, anyway, I thought to myself. It is all so dated and so badly written that I will be embarrassed to see it collected in a book.

*

So a 'Rude Food' book seemed out of the question. Then Diya Kar Hazra, my editor at Penguin (and the wife of a colleague at the *HT*), managed to persuade me that because food pieces—unlike 'Counterpoint'—were relatively undated, they might work as a collection.

My views on books of columns had not changed much. I had

seen several such collections being published over the years and the pattern was nearly always the same. The book would be launched with a great deal of publicity: there would be launch parties, panel discussions about its contents and favourable reviews by friends in other papers.

And then, of course, the book would sink without a trace.

I kept telling Diya that a collection of 'Rude Food' columns would probably end up as an ego trip for me but Penguin would have two problems. First of all, I'm not big on launch parties (none of my TV shows have ever had formal launch events) and secondly, Penguin would probably have to pulp most of the print run as the unsolds mounted. People may be willing to read a food column for free in a newspaper or a magazine. But would they actually pay good money to buy a book of columns?

I think not. But, of course, we shall find out the hard way.

*

My first contact with the book came in February when Penguin sent me page proofs. I told Diya how I wanted the pieces arranged and she came up with the clever section heads. My responses when I read formatted proofs followed what are for me the predictable paths. I was shocked that I had actually written so much over two years. And I was appalled by some of the pieces I had written.

When you write a piece about Thai food in February 2004 you do not think it likely that your readers will remember a similar piece you wrote in July 2002. So you take it upon yourself to repeat some of the info, recycle a few of the anecdotes and perhaps tell one or two of the jokes again.

Because the reader genuinely doesn't remember the piece you wrote nearly two years earlier, you get away with this. And in fact your second piece is stronger for all the background that you've decided to recycle.

But then the two pieces appear in a collection with nothing to indicate that they were written twenty months (and eighty columns) apart. My God! you think. Readers are going to believe that I'm the sort of fraud who has only two jokes and repeats them week after week!

My first response when I read the proofs of this book was that I should rewrite parts of it. Not only was there a certain amount of repetition but the same cast of characters often appeared again and again: the pages seem to be full of the Bombay chef Ananda Solomon and Delhi's Ritu Dalmia, and the Bombay Taj is treated as though it is the most important hotel in India (which it probably is, anyway).

Then there's the language. When you write a column, certain flip phrases become your trademark. And because the reader sees your stuff after a gap of several days, he recognizes your style from these catch phrases. But when the columns are collected and the hapless reader is expected to read them together, the phrases seem to grate.

And finally, there's the matter of the info.When the caviar piece first appeared, for instance, Jug Suraiya, the editor of *The Times of India*'s edit page, wrote a letter to the editor to make the valid point that if caviar had only reached Europe in the nineteenth century then why was Shakespeare familiar with it? (Shakespeare used the phrase 'caviar to the general' in *Hamlet*.)

There is a good answer to Jug's question. While caviar reached Europe in the nineteenth century, some of the English were certainly aware of it long before. But because it was so rare and little known, Shakespeare used it as a metaphor for obscurity. When Hamlet says that his play was 'caviar to the general' he means that it was something that the general public did not understand or recognize.

In my caviar piece I meant that most Europeans only became aware of caviar in the nineteenth century, not that nobody in sixteenth-century England had ever heard of it. When I reread the caviar piece my first instinct was to amend it to take note of Jug's objections. At the very least, I thought, I could do a footnote explaining the apparent anomaly.

But then I changed my mind. If I was going to change the caviar column then where would it stop! Because the first pieces in this book were written over two years ago, they also represent something of a journey for me. I did not know everything I do now when I started writing the early pieces. For instance, until I met Nelson Wang in Delhi in February 2004 I did not realize that he had invented Chicken Manchurian. I had imagined that the dish had developed at one of the new Sichuan restaurants that had opened in the 1970s. So was I to go back and rewrite the piece on Sino-Ludhiana food to take account of what I know now?

*

Finally, I decided against rewriting. This is not a book on food; it is a collection of columns related to food (though some of the pieces—'Rooms at the Top', for instance—have only the slightest connection to food) and must be judged as such. Sometimes two chapters may echo each other. Sometimes each may actually contradict the other. Often, some of the phrases will seem tiresomely familiar.

But that's the difference between a collection of columns and a proper book. You write a book for people to read all at once. You write the columns to make each complete in itself.

How you read the book is, of course, up to you. But my advice is not to worry about starting at the first page and reading it straight through. Treat it as a moveable feast, a buffet table groaning under the weight of appetizers and main courses. Dip into it as you wish; read what you like first; pick any order that makes sense to you.

As for myself, the book has made one definite difference to my life. Because Penguin would not publish a book under the name 'Grand Fromage', Diya has, effectively, outed me. There's even a picture of me sucking my stomach in on the cover, and at the *HT*, Poonam's killed off the poor old Grand Fromage, borrowed the Penguin picture and started carrying 'Rude Food' under my own name.

The outing of the Fromage coincided with my stepping down as editor of the *HT* (I'm still there but as editorial director), so perhaps I'll now have more time to devote to my writing.

But, enough already. You have a whole book to read and I've gone on and on about myself for too long.

# enter the dragon

# shanghai wok

Before I went to China, nearly everybody who had been there said two things about the food. One: 'Oh my God! Real Chinese food is so strange that you'll give up on it and eat hamburgers instead!' And two: 'Forget what you know about Chinese food. Real Chinese food in China is so, so different that it bears no relation to anything you've eaten outside China thinking it is authentic Chinese.'

To both these observations, I have only one response.

Crap.

Real Chinese food is fine. I couldn't eat enough of it while I was there—so much for all the 'you'll go hungry unless you eat Big Macs' rubbish. And no, frankly it is not all that different from the Chinese food you get outside China.

All right, I admit that I was there only for a week and went to only two cities (Beijing and Shanghai) and that this limited exposure is probably not enough to make any kind of reasoned judgement.

But, on the other hand, except for one day (Tuesday) when I was vegetarian, I ate only Chinese food for six days. That makes twelve meals. (Actually more, if you count the times I sneaked into restaurants for snacks before and after dinner—blame it on having to get used to the time difference.)

And I ate at all kinds of places. I ate at fancy restaurants in Shanghai where hotshot Chinese businessmen were knocking back the cognac; I ate at street stalls in open markets; I ate at branches of Chinese chain restaurants where shop girls stared at me through their chopsticks, astonished to find a non-Chinese person in their midst; I ate at buffets at five-star hotels. I pantomimed my instructions to pretty Chinese waitresses in barbecue restaurants as they cooked my beef for me on my table. (How do you use your hands to indicate that you want your meat medium-rare when the pretty girl cooking the steak speaks no English? That's my secret and I'm not telling.)

I went to dry markets where they tried to sell me ginseng roots ('Make you strong', the only English phrase they knew—it only made sense when you took in the lewd gesture that usually accompanied it) and wet markets where the vegetables were laid out for Chinese housewives to press each straw mushroom and check how fresh it was. I went to seafood restaurants where the language problem was circumvented by pointing at a live lobster lazily swimming around in his tank till—whoosh!—end of lobster life, beginning of very nice Lobster with Black Beans.

So, yeah, I'm no expert. But believe me, I've been around.

So what is real Chinese food like? Hard to say. For a start, there's no such thing as 'Chinese food'. Just as a masala dosa has nothing in common with a tandoori chicken and both have even less in common with *chingri malai* curry, the food of China has enormous regional variations. Some of them we know well: Peking, Cantonese and Sichuan. Some, we dimly understand: Hunan and Mongolian for instance. But there're many, many, more variations from the native cuisine of Shanghai to the Muslim food of Xinjiang province (yes, I tried it and no, it will not go down in history as one of the world's great cuisines).

But once you work out the regional variations, it is not that difficult to crack the cuisine. Of course it's different from the native cuisine of Ludhiana (known to us all as 'Indian-Chinese'), but then you already knew that. But it's not so different from the stuff you get at expensive Chinese restaurants in India and pretty much the sort of thing you get at most Chinese restaurants in New York or London.

So what makes Chinese food in China so special? Why is it worth going to Shanghai for a good meal if the food is not that different?

I don't know the answer to that one. All I do know is that nobody who loves food can fail to love China. At least, I'm still tingling from the experience.

I'm still not terribly coherent about my Shanghai dinners. So, here is a brief rundown of my mental notes about the food.

- Nobody stir-fries meat like the Chinese. No matter where I went, the pork, the chicken and the beef were cooked so spectacularly well that the food just melted in my mouth. There was no trace of fibre in the meat, and no chewy bits at all.
  This is simply not true of Chinese food outside of China, no matter how expensive the restaurant in New York or London.

- Rice is not an integral part of Chinese food in Shanghai. One popular chain restaurant (six branches including a very fancy sidewalk cafe on the upmarket Nanjing Road West), actually did not serve rice at all even though the menu listed 130 items. (I know this because they had only one tattered English language menu and, as nobody on the staff could read or speak English, I ordered by numbers, rather as one would at a takeaway dive in the Western world.)
  If you order fried rice, it is a dish by itself and is served after you've finished all the other food. If you are the sort of chap who can't eat his Chinese food till the Egg Fried Rice is on the table, then, tough titty, partner, you'll grow old waiting for the rice.

- There is usually no need for rice because of the way that all Chinese people approach their meals. Rarely will you get a dinner plate—usually you'll get a small saucer (or a sort of quarter plate) and a bowl.
  The food will be laid on the centre of the table and everybody

will eat it directly from the serving dishes with chopsticks. This makes it difficult to mix it with rice so you probably won't miss the rice anyway. Everybody eats like this.

I heard about an Indian diplomat who discovered that the best way to taste Chinese home cooking was to travel by train. During meal times, people would go into the dining car, find a table, take out the food they had packed from home, put it in the centre and share it with the four or five other strangers who happened to occupy the same table. Everybody ate everybody else's food. (Needless to say the Chinese are not big on the Hindu concept of *jhoota*.)

- If you are used to Indian Chinese restaurants with their bowls of chopped chillies in vinegar and bottles of soya sauce, you might be surprised to discover that at no Chinese restaurant that I went to were there any condiments on the table. Some dishes (dim sum for instance, or Tea-Smoked Duck) came with their own little bowls of sauce. But, given the language problem, it was hell to get anyone to understand that I wanted chilli sauce.

- There is absolutely no logic to the pricing. The best meal I had was at the relatively fancy Jade Garden restaurant in Shanghai. Some starters on the menu cost 68 yuan (Smoked Sausage with Prawns) while an enormous main course (Beef with Onions) cost 20 yuan.

  Is there a method to this apparently random pricing? I don't know. I certainly couldn't work it out. Yes, seafood is more expensive, but that doesn't explain the huge discrepancies I came across. These extended across categories of restaurants—I spent nearly as much at Jade Garden as I did at my chain restaurant.

- As for the snake/scorpion factor, well, yes, it is true that there are many dishes on a Chinese menu that you and I might be squeamish about. It is said about the residents of Shanghai that if something crawls, walks, or flies, they'll eat it.

At the dry market, a shopkeeper tried to interest me in dried bats strung up on sticks and an enormous snake, its tail stuffed into its mouth, rolled up inside a jar. (The snake had the same sales pitch: 'Make you strong.' Thanks pal, but I'd rather be limp than eat that.) At the wet market, along with the cages of live crabs and buckets of prawns swimming the last laps of their lives, were also crates of wide-eyed live frogs, their skins so green and shiny that they might as well have come from Mars.

And the average menu will include things like Pig's Intestines with Bamboo, or Cow's Stomach with Mushrooms, or even that great favourite, Chicken's Feet in Bean Sauce. There will be many more such dishes—animal blood, for instance, is the principal ingredient in an authentic Hot and Sour Soup—but here's the thing: you don't have to eat this stuff.

There's always enough on the menu for you to steer clear of the snake/scorpion factor. If, like me, you can't even eat liver or kidney (let alone lizard), there's still more than enough choice.

- The Chinese love eating. In only two cities of the world (New York and Bangkok) have I seen as many restaurants. Every three shops or so, there's a restaurant. Because the SARS scare is not over, China was bereft of foreign tourists but not only was every restaurant full, many also had queues of locals waiting for tables.

  Though there were a distressing number of fast food outlets (I counted three McDonald's, two KFCs and one Pizza Hut on a single popular road), something like 90 per cent of all the restaurants served only Chinese food.

  This, to me, was further evidence for the theory that a great cuisine only evolves when people go to a restaurant to eat their own food. (Not true of India, alas. When we go to an

Indian restaurant it is to eat things we would usually not cook at home—tandoori chicken for instance.)

- Many of the popular restaurants are new. The plush ones have come up after the economy liberalized. But some of the best food is at the old restaurants. The single best meal I had in Beijing was at the State-run Sichuan Restaurant, famous for being the favourite of Deng Xiao Ping (who was from Sichuan) and the location for State dinners hosted by Chou En Lai in the 1950s.

  On the subject of Sichuan food, though, if you don't like the tingly, mouth-puckering taste of Sichuan peppercorns, you probably won't like Sichuan food in China. These seemingly mentholated peppercorns dominate everything and there's not always as much chilli as you find in Sichuan food outside of China. The heat comes from the pepper.

- There's obviously a law governing street vendors but I couldn't figure out what it was. I saw a policeman chasing away a woman selling strawberries on the street and the fancy parts of Beijing and Shanghai were almost completely bereft of any street food. But I did see some street food at less fancy places: people grilling satay on charcoal stoves, or large metal pots filled with boiling stock into which they tipped masses of noodles.

But, on the whole, Beijing and Shanghai do not have a street food tradition like Bangkok (on every corner) or Singapore (at a numbered hawkers' centre). At the famous Gifts Market in Shanghai, there were stalls selling cold bean desserts (I tried one in the line of duty, but next time I'll stick to Baskin-Robbins) and an amazing cold rice noodle salad. It was freshly mixed in front of me and used dried shrimp but still managed to avoid the fishy taste that spoils authentic Pad Thai (for me, at least). The seasoning was a mixture of sesame oil and a hot chilli sauce. Logic suggests that the chilli should murder the delicate sesame flavour. But no, both tastes came across perfectly. I could happily live on that salad for weeks.

I could go on. I could tell you why Tsing Tao is the only beer to drink with Chinese food. (On the subject of liquid refreshment in China, I'm one with W.C. Fields who said, in a different context of course, 'Never drink water; fish procreate in it'—actually, he was more alliterative and did not say 'procreate', but you get the general idea.)

I could tell you what to steer clear of (Sweet and Sour Pork which every hotel will try and push because Americans like it). And I could give you the menus of every meal I had—yes, I remember them all.

But enough for now. I'll wait till I go back to China—and that will be soon, I hope—to list all the new things I've learnt about one of the world's great cuisines. I just covered Beijing and Shanghai this time and there's at least another fourteen regions left to try. In China, fourteen regions equals another fourteen cuisines.

In the end, the best reason for going to China is not to mourn the death of Communism or to celebrate the resurgence of capitalism.

You go to China simply to pamper your stomach.

# the thai food fast track

Because we associate the term 'fast food' with Ronald McDonald we are reluctant to use it to describe anything that isn't served by a branded chain restaurant. But any food that's inexpensive, quickly prepared, and served by a restaurant or an outlet that does not care too much for waiter service should fit the bill.

If you use that definition, then the best fast food in the world is not the rubbish that the American chains churn out. The best fast food is Thai street food.

Almost anywhere you go in Bangkok you'll see a man cooking something behind a roadside stall and serving it up to people who sit on plastic chairs in front of a table on the pavement.

If you stop and see what's being cooked, you'll notice charcoal-grilled chicken, fresh and spicy non-vegetarian salads, Khao Man Gai (a Thai chicken rice closely related to the Hainanese Chicken Rice which is Singapore's national dish, though the best Thai variation uses batter-fried chicken), skewers full of pork satay, spicy squid on sticks, pungent fermented sausages (from Chiang Mai, also in the north), and even, if you are prepared to wait for three minutes, rice freshly fried in a wok in front of you with chicken or pork, a little stock, some soya paste, a small quantity of sugar and chilli and large, crunchy chunks of onion. The Thais use no salt so that flavour comes from *nam pla*, a fermented fish sauce without which no Thai food tastes right.

You could call all this street food. But if you are squeamish about sitting on PVC chairs in the Bangkok sun, then you can head for one of Bangkok's many air-conditioned food courts, where nearly all of the above are readily available. Generally, you buy coupons from the counter and then order what you want from a variety of stalls.

It is hard to have a bad or unauthentic meal, the food takes less time to be served than it does to order a *channa-tikki* burger or whatever it is that McDonald's now serves, and it is much cheaper than Domino's or Pizza Hut. My favourite food plaza is at the upmarket Siam Centre shopping complex, and despite the relative luxury of the surroundings, two people can eat all they want for under 200 baht (just over Rs 200). Try doing that at Pizza Hut.

I often wonder if Thais bother to cook at home. There is a food cart at every street corner and all the carts are always crowded with customers. Unlike Singapore, where the food courts (though perhaps not the hawker centres) thrive on tourist business, the Thai courts are full of locals. Go to Emporium, Bangkok's second most expensive mall (now that the new Gaysorn Plaza with its Gucci, Armani, Dior, Prada and Louis Vuitton concessions is number one), and you'll find the food court crowded with Thais. At the fancy new food loft at the Central Department Store in Chidlom, the stalls don't even have signs in English. It isn't tourists they cater to—it is their own people.

Often, I trudge from one end of Bangkok to the other, just to eat at a particular stall. I love the clams with basil at a street stall on Petchburi Road (I'll give you the recipe later), the Gway Tiew Nam (a sort of noodle broth with meat and vegetables), at Soi Nana off Sukhumvit Road, and I keep coming back to the food court at Siam Centre to understand why the fried rice is so special.

Some of the dishes are the kind you can't really make at home. The noodle broth is what most Thais eat as fast food (though you'll hardly ever find it on restaurant menus which boast of 'Royal Thai' cuisine). The basis of the dish is a rich stock made usually from meat bones, soya, 'red whisky', galangal, garlic, and assorted herbs.

Nobody who runs a noodle stall will ever tell you exactly what's in the stock. And once they get it right, it keeps on simmering: they just keep adding more as time goes on. At some places the stock has been bubbling for fifty years. So, it is foolish to try to copy it at home.

To order the noodle broth, you tell the stall owner what ingredients you want: chicken, fish, meat balls, shrimp, seaweed, bean sprouts. Then you choose the rice noodles: thin, thick, fat etc. Everything you choose is put into a wire basket which is dropped into a pan of water, sitting on the stock. After 30 seconds, the meat is cooked, the basket is emptied into a bowl and the cook spoons some stock over it. You eat it like a rich, nourishing soup.

The fried rice is more difficult to explain. I'm not much of a cook, but my Significant Other, a woman with magic fingers who learned her craft with Thai cooking, admits that she is baffled by the flavours of Siam Centre's fried rice. We order it again and again to learn what the trick is, but we still can't crack the secret. (Is it the soya bean paste they use rather than the normal soya sauce? Is it the ladleful of stock? We can't work it out.)

The clams with basil from the Petchburi Road vendors are easier to figure out. Here's a recipe by Alex Renton (from London's *The Observer*) which, he says, comes from the Popular Restaurant on Soi Nana but it sounds about right even for the Petchburi Road version.

You need about 30 clams in their shells (that's the small Indian clams that they call cockles in England) and they must be fresh. You also need Thai chilli paste (*nam phrik*) and fish sauce (*nam pla*), all of which are now easily available in India.

First, you heat two tablespoons of vegetable oil in a large wok at high heat. When the oil is smoking, add one large tablespoon of chopped garlic. Add half a cup of stock (chicken is best) and reheat (the temperature will have come down when you added the stock). When it all seems very hot, throw in the clams. Stir for 90 seconds and you'll see the shells opening (throw away any clams that don't open).

With the pan still hot, add two small spoons of chilli paste, two chopped red chillis, a tablespoon of fish sauce and one finely chopped (or two, if you like) spring onion. Cook for another 30 seconds.

Put off the gas. Now throw in a whole cup of hand-torn basil leaves. Leave in for 30 seconds so that the basil flavour is absorbed.

Serve.

Like all good fast-food dishes, it won't take more than three or four minutes to cook. And you can eat it with boiled rice.

The great thing about the dish, as Renton points out, is that you get three distinct flavours. The chilli, the basil and the delicate clams. In most countries, this would be haute cuisine. In Thailand, it is fast food.

Because the fast food is so good, I'm always sceptical of the claims made by fancy Thai restaurants. None of the hotel restaurants I've eaten at in Bangkok have been very good (though I did once have a great meal at the Oriental's Sala Rim Nam) and the stand-alone places (with the possible exception of Thanying, off Silom Road—though I haven't been there for years) serve food that's good but not significantly better than the street food. (One other exception is the original Baan Khanitha in Sukhumvit.)

Strange to say, the best and most unusual Thai meal I've had in a restaurant has been in London, at the Michelin-starred Nahm where the chef, David Thompson, is Australian. Thompson loves Thailand (the Thai government has asked him to open a cooking school in Bangkok) and is confident enough to take chances with the cuisine (his Thai take on foie gras still lingers in my mind) though Nahm's prices will burn you even before the chilli does.

Otherwise, my advice to anybody who wants a good, cheap foodie holiday is to go to Bangkok. Stay away from the hotel restaurants and the tourist traps. Eat on the streets, look for the snack bars and frequent the food courts. You'll realize then what crap American fast food is. And how Thai is not just one of the world's great cuisines, but that Thai fast food is also the world's best.

# the tale of sino-ludhiana cuisine

There's a restaurant in the centre of Bangkok called Copper Chimney. The name suggests a partnership with the successful Copper Chimneys in Bombay but the food is so dire that I doubt if it is a branch of the real thing. Its claim to fame, however, is not that it serves greasy Indian food but that it also serves Indian-Chinese.

Indian-Chinese? Who would have thought it? In just twenty-five years, our bastardization of Chinese cuisine has become a school of cooking in itself. In the late 1980s, when Rajiv Gandhi paid a state visit to China, Chinese officials asked the PM's delegation if we had Chinese food in India. Oh yes, we did, they were assured. It was very popular.

And what kind of Chinese cuisine did we have? Cantonese? Hunan? Peking? And so on.

Oh, we have our own, Mani Shankar Aiyar, the most voluble member of Rajiv's delegation, assured them.

Really? asked the Chinese.

Oh yes, said Mani, we call it Sino-Ludhiana.

End of conversation. The Chinese retired gracefully, their faces masks of bemused incomprehension.

It was meant as a joke, but Aiyar was right. No self-respecting Chinese person would recognize much of what passes for Chinese food in this country.

Try ordering Chilli Chicken at any Chinese restaurant anywhere in the world (with the notable exception of the likes of Bangkok's Copper Chimney) and you will be met with looks of total bemusement. (If you ask for Chilli Gobi, the head waiter will probably pass out.)

Blame it on Camellia Panjabi and Arvind Saraswat.

Till 1973, we had lots of Chinese restaurants in India (Nanking in Bombay, Waldorf in Calcutta, Café Chinois in Delhi, etc.) but they all served a cuisine that most Indians would not recognize today. It was based on Cantonese cooking (though many of the Calcutta Chinese came from other parts of China, they recognized that restaurant cooking concentrated on Cantonese principles) as adopted by early Chinese immigrants to the US (the inventors of American Chop Suey). The food was popular enough, but it was no craze.

Then, Camellia Panjabi discovered Sichuan cooking.

She first tried the fiery favours of Sichuan in New York in the early 1970s but only got into the cuisine when she went to a restaurant called Red Pepper in Hong Kong.

At the time, Panjabi was a vice-president of the Taj Group—which had never opened a Chinese restaurant before—and she recognized that here, at last, was a school of Chinese cooking that would appeal to Indians. In a moment of inspiration, she hired the maitre d' hotel and several chefs from Red Pepper and told them to open a restaurant at the Bombay Taj.

Thus was born Golden Dragon, India's first Sichuan restaurant. It was an instant hit, and within a year all the existing Chinese restaurants had quickly overhauled their menus to include spicy dishes copied from the Dragon's menu. (Don't forget: the farthest East that most Indian Chinese have been is Chowringhee.)

As popular as the Dragon was in Bombay, the real breakthrough came when the Taj opened in Delhi. The chain was determined to open North India's first Sichuan restaurant but was wary of trusting the Red Pepper chefs who had proved to be temperamental, frequently storming out of the kitchen and leaving it to their Indian juniors to actually cook the food.

So, a delegation of Taj chefs led by Arvind Saraswat, then India's leading Continental chef and slated to become Executive Chef of the new Taj on Delhi's Man Singh Road, was sent off to Chengdu (the capital of Sichuan) and to other Chinese cities. They were thrilled by what they discovered—in particular, it was the Sichuan peppercorn with its tingly taste that really got them excited—and returned to India to open the House of Ming.

Frankie Lok, the original maitre d' from Red Pepper was shifted from the Dragon to become House of Ming's first manager as was a chef called Michael, but the real cooking was done by Saraswat's boys.

Almost from the day it opened in 1978, the House of Ming became Delhi's most successful restaurant. Not only was the food excellent, it was also different. Delhi Punjabis, used to bland, cornfloured Chinese food at Fujiya, Ginza and Akasaka (why do so many Chinese restaurants have Japanese names?) made a huge discovery: Chinese food could be HOT! Better still, there were Chini Pakoras! The House of Ming introduced Golden Fried Prawns to Delhi, and despite the high price, it became the single most ordered starter at the restaurant.

Though the Dragon had opened four years before the House of Ming, it was the latter restaurant that changed the way we eat Chinese food. Punjabis who had, till then, stuck to ordering Butter Chicken and Saag Paneer at restaurants suddenly realized that there was now an alternative: you could eat *masaledar* Chinese food.

Though neither Panjabi nor Saraswat would admit it, by the 1980s the Taj's tradition of personalized service meant that the House of Ming cooked what the guests wanted. So, every dish had to have a gravy (how else could you eat it with Mixed Fried Rice?), and ideally, this had to be a thick red gravy. All starters had to be deep fried. And so on.

This soon became the standard Chinese food at every restaurant. The delicate flavours, the steaming techniques and moist but gravy-less dishes of Cantonese cuisine were forgotten. Everything was fried—ideally it was first deep fried and then soaked in a congealed red sauce because mere stir frying seemed too healthy.

Today, it has got to the stage that no matter where you go in India, most restaurants will offer you this kind of Chinese food. Even if you don't want to go to a restaurant, there will be a *thelawallah* who will make 'Chinese food' with soya sauce, chilli sauce and tomato ketchup. New dishes that the Chinese have never heard of—Chicken Manchurian is just one example—were introduced to menus to tickle the North Indian palate.

Both Panjabi and Saraswat disown Sino-Ludhiana cuisine but they are honest enough to admit that had the Taj never shown Indians that Chinese food could be spicy, we would still be eating American Chop Suey. As for the future of Sino-Ludhiana cuisine, I've even found an Indian vegetarian restaurant in Singapore's Little India that has a menu full of Gobi Manchurian and Golden Fried Potato-kind of dishes. So who knows, maybe it deserves recognition as a cuisine of its own.

I still won't eat it.

# the nelson wang story

Few dishes have fascinated me as much as Chicken Manchurian. It is a dish that is unknown outside of India—certainly nobody in China has ever heard of it—but is, nevertheless, possibly the most ordered dish at Chinese restaurants in this country. You'll find it on the menu of nearly every Chinese eatery—outside of the five-star hotels where expatriate chefs are employed—and now, even McDonald's does a Manchurian-style burger.

For years I believed that because Chicken Manchurian (and now Bhindi Manchurian, Gobi Manchurian and God alone knows what else) first began appearing on restaurant menus in the late 1970s, its rise to fame was linked to the introduction of Sichuan cooking to Indian shores (first at Bombay's Golden Dragon and then at Delhi's House of Ming).

But all chefs I spoke to denied that Manchurian had any connection with the early Sichuan restaurants. They conceded that because it was spicy, it had little in common with the Cantonese food that was served at most Indian Chinese restaurants till the mid-1970s but argued that perhaps some enterprising chef had sensed that spicy Chinese food appealed to Indian palates and imported this dish. But where could he have imported it from? Just as Chicken Tikka Masala, the UK's most ordered Indian restaurant dish is unknown in India, so Chicken Manchurian does not seem to have had an existence anywhere in the world prior to 1974-75.

And besides, who was this chef who first put it on the menu?

I think I finally found the answers to those questions in February this year.

If you are familiar with Bombay, you've probably heard of Nelson Wang and his China Garden, possibly the most famous Chinese restaurant not to be located in a deluxe hotel.

Nelson's heyday was in the late 1980s and the early 1990s when China Garden hosted the Bachchans, the Kapoors (as in Raj Kapoor and family), the Ambanis, and much of Bombay's swish set. Then, he was forced to abandon the original China Garden (which ran afoul of building laws), opened a new version at a shopping mall, and now, he's finally come to Delhi with a 200-seater China Garden in Greater Kailash II.

But long before he became famous or served champagne to Parmeshwar Godrej, Nelson had already done the one thing that will survive him and his restaurants.

He had invented Chicken Manchurian.

The way Nelson tells it, he began in the kitchen of the old Frederick's restaurant in Bombay's Colaba district. Nelson was not from Bombay, of course. Like all good Indian Chinese restaurateurs, he grew up in Calcutta. His family was from China but they'd been three generations in India so he says he doesn't even know which part of China his ancestors came from.

In the 1960s, Nelson's father decided to emigrate to Canada. Naturally, he took his family with him. But there was a problem. The young Nelson was in love with a Bengali girl and declared that he wanted to marry her. While his family had spent many decades in Calcutta, their love for India did not extend to marrying the local population. So the senior Wang told Nelson that there was no question of marrying a Bengali.

All right, said Nelson defiantly, if I don't get to marry her then you'll have to go to Canada without me.

His father shrugged, said this was fine with him and the Wang family departed for Canada leaving behind one lovesick Chinaman.

Forced to rely on his own resources, and fond of the good

things of life (chiefly, gambling—the usual Chinese hobby), Nelson went to Bangalore and Madras to make a living. Because he didn't really have very many skills, he ended up working at nightclubs, not as a chef but as a performer.

'I was very acrobatic,' he recalls. 'So I became the best limbo dancer in India.' Older readers may remember the limbo. It was a staple of nightclub cabaret in the 1960s. Calypso-type music would be played and bare torsoed young men would wiggle under a horizontal bar (like the kind of bar you see at high jump competitions), moving forward, crotch first, bending backwards so that their chests just narrowly missed the bar. (By the way, Wang never married the Bengali girl. He opted for an arranged marriage with a nice Chinese girl.)

It was a silly way to make a living and by the early 1970s, when Nelson made his way to Bombay, he'd given up on cabaret and ended up on the food side of the restaurant business. His first real job was at Frederick's, an old-style Chinese restaurant with booths where menu staples were American Chop Suey, Sweet and Sour Pork and Chicken Sweet Corn Soup.

But Chinese food was changing. The Taj, a few minutes away from Frederick's, had just opened the Golden Dragon and the punters wanted spicy Chinese food.

The problem was that while the Golden Dragon had real Chinese chefs imported from Hong Kong, Nelson and his compatriots were as authentically Chinese as Bipasha Basu. They knew two styles of Chinese food: the simple, relatively bland stuff they ate at home and the Americanized Cantonese fare they dished out at their restaurants. None of them had heard of a Sichuan pepper, let alone seen one.

So, Nelson decided that he would spice up the Frederick's menu using the only techniques his cooks knew well—the techniques of Indian cuisine. They would deep-fry everything to produce *maida* pakoras (no cornflour for their deep-frying) and make thick *masaledar* sauces.

'I thought to myself,' he remembers, 'why not use all chilli, garlic, *dhania*, things that Indians like?' He made a sauce of these ingredients, added chicken pakoras to it and suddenly, a new dish was born.

'My boss asked me what name to give it,' says Nelson, 'because you know, Chinese people, they had never seen anything like it. In China, we regard the people from Manchau as barbarians. And this was really a dish for barbarians—all *dhania* and everything—so I told him that we would call it Chicken from Manchau or Chicken Manchurian.'

The dish was an instant success. It was easy to make, required no ingredients not available at your local grocer, and Indians just couldn't get enough. In no time at all, other restaurants were copying it and within two years it was on every menu.

'Now when I see it at McDonald's, I feel really proud,' says Nelson. 'What is Manchurian? Nothing! I made it up. There is not even a proper cuisine called Manchurian. Manchau was a part of China that the Japanese had colonized. When the Japanese left, the name Manchau disappeared. I want to tell all these fancy people who say that the dish is from Manchuria: "find me Manchuria on the map!" You will see, there is not even a Manchau region on the map of China any longer. The only Manchurian thing that remains is my creation, Chicken Manchurian!'

Okay, so he's saucing it up a little bit. But he's probably entitled to boast. How many chefs (or limbo dancers, for that matter) can claim to have invented a dish that is on every menu?

Nelson takes the credit for introducing Hot and Sour Soup to Indian menus as well. He is on slightly dodgier ground here because this is not a made-up dish. You'll find variations of the soup in Singapore and Hong Kong (sometimes called Sour and Pepper) though usually, the recipe will differ substantially from the way it is made in Indian-Chinese restaurants. (One version, for instance, requires litres of chicken blood.)

Nelson concedes that he didn't actually invent the soup; he just reinvented the recipe so that any cook with no talent and no access to ingredients could turn out an acceptable version. 'Until I put Hot and Sour on the menu,' he brags, 'they used to all order Sweet Corn. Now they order Hot and Sour.'

Nelson's success at China Garden came from his ability to take dishes that were vaguely Chinese in origin and to reinvent them in a style that suited the Indian palate. By the 1980s, when he had made a little money (he started running Chinese restaurants at Bombay clubs), he began to travel to South-East Asia. Each trip yielded more dishes.

By the time he opened Chinatown in 1982 and China Garden in 1985, he had begun to do things that would have him arrested by any self-respecting Chinese food inspector. He would put butter on vegetables. He would pass Tom Yam Soup off as a Chinese soup. He treated Korea as a part of China on his menus. He invented vegetable dishes that would not have seemed out of place on a Sindhi menu. And whenever possible, he deep-fried everything.

But it worked. China Garden was an instant success with people who either knew nothing about Chinese food or who wouldn't have liked the real thing if it had been served to them. Other fancier restaurants that served authentic Chinese food had to cope with angry guests who kept demanding China Garden-style food. At the Golden Dragon, for instance, waiters had to memorize the phrase 'Sorry, sir, we do not serve Tom Yam Soup. It is not Chinese. It is a Thai soup.'

Nelson laughs now at the inauthenticity of it all. It was bogus but—what the hell!—people enjoyed it. Besides, it made him rich and famous.

Nevertheless, he insists that it isn't as though his chefs can't make the real thing. 'That is the job of the manager,' he says. 'He should look at the guest and decide if the person wants Manchurian Chicken or real Chinese food. If he wants authentic food, we will make the best.'

I'm sure they will. As for me, I still prefer to think of Nelson Wang as the limbo dancer who invented Chicken Manchurian.

# salads: the way of the rabbit

While I'm quite willing to eat most things, I do draw the line at rabbit. No matter how you cook it the meat is always too strong and too sharp for my taste.

Of course, many otherwise sensible people refuse to eat rabbits because they are such warm and floppy characters that it seems a shame to put Peter Rabbit in the oven or to chop Bugs Bunny into little pieces for a fricassée.

I have to say that I am not among these people.

Not that I have anything against rabbits—most of us would kill for their sex lives—but it seems to me that if we were to refuse to eat cute and cuddly animals (Porky Pig, Chicken Little, Flossie the Cow, Donald Duck etc.) we'd end up on a diet of skunk and crow.

My favourite rabbit story concerns an English butcher who was prosecuted in the 1970s (this is a true story) for trying to encourage his customers to buy more rabbits on the basis of the terminally cute, grotesquely successful movie *Watership Down* ('Bright Eyes, burning like fire, bright eyes' etc., etc.) about a colony of bunnies.

The butcher happened to own a shop near a cinema that was showing *Watership Down*. So, he, quite reasonably, put up a sign that said 'You've read the book. You've seen the movie. Now, eat the cast.' Some humourless animal lover sued the poor fellow.

The closest I've come to rabbits though, is in the excuse I used to offer for not eating salad. 'I'm sorry. I've no desire to become a rabbit or to copy the eating habits of that species.' This was a suitably cutting and moderately witty way of saying, 'I hate salad.'

Then, my waistline caught up with my wit. No, that's not quite true. What happened was this: my waistline began to exceed my wit by a considerable margin. Suddenly, I had to consider low-fat options. And inevitably, these included adopting the eating habits of a bunny rabbit. So, still snarling at the lettuce, I was led to the salad bar.

It's been five years now and I've more or less abandoned my old objections to leaves. After all, the only thing worse than eating rabbit food is to eat the bloody rabbit itself.

But no, I'm still not a salad-eater by choice. I'm not the sort of chap who orders my steak with salad rather than potatoes; the sort of health freak who foregoes lunch so that he can have 'a small green salad, please'; or the sort of gastronomic illiterate who considers a lettuce leaf to be the high point of our foodie heritage.

But yes, I've softened. I have learned the Way of the Rabbit. One reason is that I've discovered warm salads. Another is that I've found leaves and vegetables I like. And a third is that I've discovered the salads of Thai cuisine.

Of these, the third is the most compelling. A Thai salad is a wondrous creation, full of coolness and heat, of crunchiness and meat, of sourness and sweet. It has as much to do with the 'small green salad' of Western restaurant cuisine as Phuket has to do with Dusseldorf.

There are fancy and famous Thai salads. Top of the heap is the Som Tam from the Northern Isaan region which is a mixture of thinly sliced raw papaya, prawns (ideally) and ground peanut. Properly made, this is a delicious, low-calorie feast.

But once you understand the basic principles of a Thai salad you don't really need to stick to the famous recipes or the big names. Thais make salads out of everything: winged bean, snake gourd, squid, shark and frog. All you need to learn are the principles:

1. Serve the main ingredient (fish or mushroom or whatever)

along with cucumber and onion or a few other side vegetables.

2. Mix hot ingredients (chillis, raw garlic) with cool herbs (basil, coriander etc.).
3. The final taste must combine yin and yang; cool and hot, sweet and chilli etc.

Let's take a typical Thai salad of prawns. You need first to get lots of small prawns and lightly boil them (but not so much that they become tough). Next slice a couple of cucumbers thinly so you have lots of slender slices. Take an onion and cut into pieces each the rough size and shape of a 50 paise piece. You can add more vegetables but these will do. I add a few chunks of chopped garlic and like spring onions, but these are personal preferences.

Next, get the herbs ready. Use mint, coriander (both easily available) and Thai basil (more difficult but appearing at sabziwallahs everywhere these days) and hand-tear the leaves so that they complement but don't overwhelm the prawns and vegetables. (In terms of quantities: two parts prawns, one part herbs and four parts vegetables.)

Finally, the most important part: the dressing. The secret of a good Thai dressing is the balance you get of four flavours: sweet (sugar), spicy (red chilli), sour (lemon juice) and salty (*nam pla*, Thai fish sauce, now easily available everywhere). Western chefs refer to Thai dressings as having a chilli-lime flavour which pretty much tells the story.

If you are making a salad for two or three people (as a main course), then here are some quantities: mix three small red chillies (finely chopped), juice of two lemons, two spoons sugar, one spoon light soya sauce and two to three spoons *nam pla*.

Ideally, you pour the dressing over the prawns as soon as they are boiled, wait till they cool, then add all the other ingredients and mix well. But frankly, you can just add it all in one go.

That's the basic recipe and you can adapt it to anything. I've made Thai salads with mushrooms (increase the quantity of the onion slightly), sliced steak (increase dressing by half), Chinese sausage slices, and roast pork. I've added little variations to tart it up: green onion leaves, chopped lemon grass, finely chopped *galangal* (a Thai ginger), a little parsley and a few Kafir lime leaves.

It has never failed—as long as the dressing has been right. I've become so confident of this recipe that I've even taken the ingredients of a normal Indian *kachumbar* (tomato, onion and cucumber, chopped into small pieces), mixed them with the herbs and the dressing and served the Thai-style *kachumbar* as a side dish with a Thai curry and rice. (But then I also serve papad with Thai curry, which is perfect but totally inauthentic.)

I doubt very much if the cast of *Watership Down* would enjoy a Thai salad. It would probably burn the mouths off all those ghastly bunnies. But a Thai salad is a grown-up salad, a salad that isn't afraid to mix cooked ingredients with raw, and one that understands the herbs and spices of the Orient.

# durian: the fruit with the smell from hell

Writing a weekly food column can be an enlightening experience. The first thing you learn is that the old cliché about taste being 50 per cent smell is true. I discovered this some time ago when I wrote about truffles (or more properly, about the white truffles of Alba). Somewhere within 1,200 words or more of copy, I mentioned that it was the smell of truffles that many people considered more distinctive than their taste. It was a smell, I said, that had sometimes been compared to the smell of old socks. On the other hand, some people also thought that truffles smelt of sex.

Cue: complete chaos.

It is a sobering thought for a food writer to recognize that after hours of research trying to track down the first tandoori chicken (Lahore before Partition but after World War I), find the original medu vada (in the Karnataka town of Meddur where it was invented), rate the service at city restaurants, and expose the mysteries of foie gras (now even more widely available) to my vast readership (all four or five of you), the only thing that really touched a chord was my characterization of the smell of the truffle.

'Smell of sex?' 'What does sex smell like?' 'How can a mushroom smell of sex?' 'Sex from the male point of view or the female?' And so on. The comments and questions just kept on coming.

There's even been some outrage expressed. At least two people have written letters to the editor to complain about the food critic's desperate attempts to drum up interest in his pathetic column by drawing sex into it. Disgusting! Not fit for a family newspaper! Shameless! Vulgar! etc. etc.

So you will forgive me, dear smell-sensitive, olfactory-aware readers, if I do not attempt to drag you off the straight and narrow by seducing you with the scent of expensive mushrooms.

This piece is about smell. But no, it is not about the smell of sex. In fact, it is about a smell so disgusting that it has often been compared (inaccurately, I think, but then, what do I know—I'm clearly the sort of chap who gets turned on by mushrooms!) to another, altogether more vital, bodily function.

If you've travelled in South East Asia then you'll know the smell already. You can sense it wafting past you as you near a vegetable market or a fruit stall. And if you've bothered to try and trace this smell then you will recognize the large, green, menacingly spiked fruit that it originates from.

The durian.

To get an idea of how potent the smell of a durian is, here are some facts. Almost every quality hotel in Bangkok will stop you at the front door if security suspects you are carrying a durian. At the dodgier establishments they'll let you in with hash, heroin, or even with the occasional bar girl. But a durian? Forget it!

Nor can you carry a durian on to an aircraft. I'm told that in many East Asian countries it is against the law to take a durian onto a plane, a train or a public bus.

Few, if any, upmarket restaurants in Bangkok, Singapore or Jakarta will allow it near their dining rooms. And if you, as an unsuspecting foreigner, ask for fresh durian for dessert, they will look at you as though you are crazy.

So if it is such an ugly, disgusting-smelling fruit, then why does anybody bother with it?

The answer seems to be: the taste.

Six years ago when I toured Sri Lanka, our guide pointed to a pile of durians at a fruitseller's. 'That is the durian,' he declared. 'It smells like shit but tastes like heaven.'

And what does heaven taste like?

(Please, this is only a rhetorical question. We can do without the outraged letters to the editor complaining of blasphemy.)

Well, here are some descriptions of the taste. In 1869 Alfred Russel Wallace offered this version: 'A rich butter-like custard highly flavoured with almonds gives the best general idea, but intermingled with it come wafts of flavour that call to mind cream cheese, onion sauce, brown sherry and other incongruities.'

Confused? Wait till you read Anthony Bourdain's more recent description: 'Lobes of cheesy, gooey, spreadable material—the consistency of a ripe St Andre . . . cheesy, fruity, rich with a slight smoky background. Imagine a mix of Camembert cheese, avocado and smoked Gouda.'

If this leaves you bemused (and it should; Bourdain must have been drunk when he wrote that passage), then remember that even when Alfred Russel Wallace was raving about the almond custard flavour of the durian, there were those, like Charles Darwin (perhaps), who thought he was overdoing it. Here's a limerick about the clash of views:

*Wallace cried, 'It's delicious,'*
*Darwin replied 'I'm suspicious.'*
*For the flavour is scented*
*Like papaya fermented*
*After a fruit-eating bat has peed on it.*

As you may have gathered from my uncharacteristic excursions into poetry and historical quotations, I am hiding something.

I've never eaten a raw durian.

Believe me, I've tried. But the smell (like a dead rat decomposing in a pool of vomit on your dinner plate) has been too strong for my delicate sensibilities. So I've done the next best thing. I've eaten foods flavoured with durian. (Same principle as truffles. Truffle oil may not give you the full picture but it can act as an effective trailer.)

I've eaten durian preserves. I've tried durian pastries. And I've struggled with a cup of durian ice cream.

Believe me: it was truly, deeply, disgusting.

If this is what heaven tastes like then we should all book our berths in hell. First of all, you can't divorce the smell from the taste. Would you eat a dead rat even if you were told that the insides tasted like a gulab jamun?

My point, exactly.

Taste is, at least partly, about smell. That's the whole point of the scent of truffles. That's why we pay thousands of rupees for the bouquet of a Chateau Margaux. And that's why many of us never venture into the taste of a strong-smelling fish—the smell is enough to keep us away.

But with the durian I'll go further. Even if you were to take away much of the smell—which is what they do with durian ice cream and the like—I still don't see what the fuss is about.

Perhaps this is because I am a novice. I'm told that durian is an acquired taste, that if I give myself another chance (or two or three), I'll grow to love it. This may be true. But let's be honest. It's not going to happen. I am not a masochist.

Certainly, I never experienced the taste orgasms that Bourdain writes about: 'Remember the first time you tasted caviar? Or foie gras? Or a soft ripened cheese? There's that same sense of recognition that you are in new and exciting territory.'

Sorry Anthony, sure as hell didn't happen to me.

I admit that I can be a little, shall we say, conservative, in matters of food smell. I'm not wild about the pong of dried fish. And there was the deeply embarrassing time when I looked accusingly at the head waiter in a Michelin three-star restaurant in Rheims (Chez Boyer—I think it still has the stars), horrified that he'd dared to do something so naughty at a temple of haute cuisine. My then girlfriend had to tell me not to be so silly: it was just that the cheese trolley was passing by our table.

But that was over twenty years ago. Since then, I like to think that I've learned to love the bouquet of a Camembert, can judge a *nam pla* by its smell, and have discovered many variations on the distinctive smell of tuna fish. But a durian?

No way. I'm on Darwin's side on this one. Believe me, you'll hate the smell, and the taste simply isn't worth it.

# high on thai in mumbai

Whenever people ask me if I have a favourite restaurant, I'm always reluctant to pick just one. Different restaurants offer different experiences. If I were celebrating something in Delhi I'd go to the Orient Express; in Calcutta I would head for the cosy, wood-panelled dining room of the Chambers; and in Bombay there's really no match for the Zodiac Grill which has been, ever since it opened over a decade ago, India's finest restaurant with wonderful food and even better service.

If I wanted a more casual experience, there are Indigo and India Jones in Bombay; Diva in Delhi; Mainland China in Calcutta (though this chain now has many branches in other cities); the roomy, sunlit Raj Pavilion in Bangalore, and so many other places. And this list doesn't include the funky, so-called ethnic restaurants—Amravati in Bangalore and Madras; Trishna in Bombay; Shiraz in Calcutta (though it often makes more sense to take the food out); and Karim's in Delhi.

But yes, I do have a favourite restaurant though I'm always reluctant to name it. I like it because it is both casual and fancy; because it gets families and people who spend their own money (not just the usual expense-account lunchers) even though it is not cheap; because it features what is probably the world's second greatest cuisine (after French); because it serves the best Thai food I've ever eaten outside of Thailand; because the chef is a genius; and because, nearly a decade after it opened, I have still to eat a duff meal there, thanks to an obsession with food consistency that is rare in India.

The restaurant is the Thai Pavilion in Bombay's President Hotel, and the chef is Ananda Solomon.

If you've lived in Bombay, then you probably know about Solomon already. Along with Hemant Oberoi, the master chef behind the Taj group's luxury properties, he is the best-known chef in India's commercial capital. He features regularly in *Bombay Times*, *Upper Crust*, *Mid-Day*, the *Afternoon* and all the other publications that come out in that city, and his following has reached such proportions that diners long for the day when he comes up to their table and greets them by name.

The celebrity trap has ruined many a good chef but Solomon still manages to retain his essential shyness, his natural reticence and his passion for food. Unlike most Taj chefs who joined the chain immediately after catering college, Solomon first worked as a Continental chef at the old Supper Club (now late unlamented) at the Oberoi Sheraton (as it then used to be) in Bombay, turning out such staples of the Sheraton menu as Prawn Newburg, Lobster Thermidor and Steak Diane.

When he shifted to the Taj, he worked in Goa and other such places but made no impression till he became Executive Chef of The President. At that stage, the hotel had experimented with a Thai menu in the bar and though the initial response was good, sales collapsed within a few months. Solomon was asked to revive the restaurant. He was fortunate to have as his General Manager, Ajoy Mishra, one of the few managers in the business with a real feel for restaurants.

The duo began from scratch. Solomon went off to Thailand, worked first in a hotel kitchen and then wandered around Bangkok cooking in more modest establishments. In the process he picked up enough of the language to get by and discovered dishes that were unknown to those who stuck to five-star hotels.

When he came back to Bombay, Mishra and he planned a menu

that incorporated the results of two years of research and travel in Thailand. On 11 November, 1993 the restaurant opened and was a runaway success. It completely transformed most people's understanding of Thai food (till then this had consisted of green curry, red curry and satay) and the queues stretched long into the night.

I didn't know Solomon then but as a frequent visitor to Thailand (nearly every month in those days) I was astonished by the quality of the food. Other Thai restaurants in India—chiefly the Taj group's own experiments in Bangalore and Goa—had never even approached cooking of this calibre. My guess was that the hotel had imported a Thai chef; that the food would retain this level of excellence as long as he was there and that things would then deteriorate in a year or so after he went back.

I couldn't have been more wrong.

Because the restaurant relied on Indian chefs and because Solomon is so obsessive about the quality of his pastes and sauces, there has been no dip in standards. Instead, the Thai Pavilion has managed the impossible: with each new menu, the food gets better and more adventurous.

The latest menu, for instance, includes dishes that you won't find at any of the other Thai restaurants that have now opened all over India. The starters include a warm salad of curried clams, a tangy raw mango salad with water chestnuts, and toasted canapés of mushroom and black beans flavoured with bird's-eye chillies. And though the main courses include all my favourite Thai standards (Chicken with Cashewnuts, Prawns with Chilli, Garlic and Holy Basil etc.), there are also the restaurant's signature dishes, including Ped Noy, the Thai duck classic, which has never been off the menu and which people drive across Bombay to eat. (At Rs 750 it is also the most expensive dish on an otherwise surprisingly reasonable—by hotel standards—menu.)

And then there are adventurous leaps into Thai royal cuisine and regional specialties: steamed fish with hot celery sauce, a whole crab cooked in red chilli paste; roast chicken flavoured with raw mango and rice wine; a Thai pepper steak; and squid fried rice flavoured with hand-shredded basil leaves.

Why do I regard the Thai Pavilion as my favourite restaurant? There's so much competition within The President itself. Solomon's most commercially successful restaurant is his revamped Italian Trattoria, and his breakthrough as a chef must be the Konkan Cafe, the only Indian restaurant in the world that does not serve any kind of roti.

But I love the easy informality of the Pavilion. I love the food, of course, and the chef's spirit of adventure. And I love the relaxed but efficient service—it helps that in Shrikant Wakharkar, The President has the best Food and Beverage Manager in the country.

It is a restaurant where you can go with just a few friends, sink a bottle of wine, demolish a couple of large crabs and burn your tongue on the fiery curries. Or, you can take somebody you are entertaining, say a gourmet from abroad, and knock his socks off with Thai food of a standard that you'd have difficulty finding in London or Paris.

# the good life

# hooked on caviar

When I went to Moscow I knew I would go looking for caviar. What I didn't realize was that the trip would change my attitude to how caviar was eaten.

My first taste of Russian caviar—in Russia—was at the banquet President Putin hosted for Prime Minister A.B. Vajpayee. Russians are justly proud of their caviar so it was a fair assumption that Putin would serve it.

I wasn't prepared, however, for the manner of the service. In the West, caviar is not so much about food. It is about luxury and romance. It is nearly always served as a course or on its own. A huge song and dance is made about the trimmings. Waiters offer you a choice of thin, crisp melba toasts or fatter, darker breads. Then there are chopped shallots, wedges of lemon, mashed egg white, mashed yolks, chives, capers and God alone knows what else. Inevitably, the vodka that is the traditional Russian accompaniment is dispensed with and cold, vintage champagne is ceremonially poured into flutes.

Done properly, the romance of caviar service—mother of pearl spoons (caviar oxidizes if you use a metal spoon), silver champagne buckets, little bowls of accompaniments, plump wedges of lemon in their muslin uniforms etc.—can be wonderful. And because you know that caviar is so expensive, you enjoy the fuss that goes along with it.

Not so in Russia. Not even at a Kremlin banquet. Russians love caviar. It has graced their tables for a millennium. (The other great caviar-producing nation is, of course, Iran, but Iranians don't particularly like caviar and it has no place in their gastronomic culture.) When Batu Khan (grandson of the great Genghiz) burned Moscow to the ground, laid waste to Kiev and ravaged central Russia in AD 1240, he spared only one Orthodox Christian monastery because the monks gave him a dish of caviar. In 1280, the Russian Orthodox church, aware now of caviar's formidable powers, formally sanctioned it as a food that could be consumed during religious fasts when meat was forbidden. In 1556, Ivan the Terrible demanded that all sturgeon—and their roe—caught in the Volga and the Caspian should be sent to him in Moscow.

All this time, fashionable gourmets in Europe were either unaware of caviar or loathed what they had tasted. In 1629, Galileo discovered the wonders of caviar and sent a case to his daughter in Florence. She threw it away. In the 1730s, Louis XV was offered a spoon of caviar by the Russian ambassador. The French King loathed the taste so much that he spat the contents of his mouth on to the carpet.

It wasn't till the nineteenth century that caviar reached Europe and it didn't take off in France (where all the fancy trimmings were invented) till 1920 when the Petrossian brothers obtained the right to distribute the Soviet Union's caviar in Europe and America. The Petrossian brothers opened a shop in Paris and the great hotelier Cesar Ritz started serving caviar at Paris's Ritz Hotel.

So, as much as I respect the Western European way of serving caviar with all the trimmings, I was curious to see how the Russians themselves ate it.

The answer probably lies in the Russian word for caviar. They call it 'ikra' which simply means 'roe'. You can have salmon ikra (now increasingly popular in Moscow as caviar prices have sky-rocketed), as indeed, the ikra of any other fish.

That's all that caviar is to the Russians—the particularly tasty roe of the sturgeon. It's not a food associated with sex, romance and all the other qualities that Western caviar companies have bestowed on ikra.

The way they served it at the Kremlin was instructive. Though the Russians invented Service Russe (the serving of food in courses—the French used to put everything on the table at the same time), the most important course at a Russian meal is the first one.

Typically, Russians will have several plates of appetizers—little pies, cold slices of salted fish, marinated mushrooms, smoked lard etc.—and only when these have been consumed (usually with copious quantities of vodka) will they get on to the main course.

For Russians, ikra is just one of many appetizers that it is possible to eat during a meal.

At the Kremlin, there was already a small fish pie (pikeperch) on our plates (along with the bread) when we sat down to eat. Waiters then brought—and placed on the same plate—dollops of Beluga caviar, slices of salted salmon, many kinds of raw vegetables and a cold turkey gallantine with fruit.

Obviously, the caviar was the best thing on the plate but no special fuss was made about it. And it was served without a single trimming: no onion, no egg white, no chopped leaves of any description, and not even the otherwise ubiquitous wedges of lemon.

Most banquets in foreign countries end up being conversational disasters because of the language problem, but I was fortunate enough to sit next to an obviously prosperous and extremely well-travelled Russian publisher who talked non-stop about everything.

Nobody knew more about foreign policy than he did, especially not the experts, he said disdainfully. Heads of State came to him for advice, he continued. Moscow was the gastronomic capital of the world. Did I know anything about wine? Well, most people didn't but he, of course, knew everything. Belgian was the world's greatest cuisine. Everybody who mattered knew this. Russia had taken too long to go capitalist. He himself had been an early advocate of close ties with America. Georgian food is superior to Russian food. But of course, only he had ever eaten the best food.

Exhausted by this steady stream of increasingly audacious and mostly baseless claims, I decided to make the most of the evening. After all, if one is sitting next to the Aveek Sarkar of Moscow, one might as well try and prospect for the few nuggets of genuine information embedded in the boulders of his boastfulness.

How did Russians like to eat caviar, I asked. This was not such a good idea because he then lectured me on how only he knew where to get the best caviar. And anyway, he said unnecessarily, who said Beluga was the best? He certainly hadn't been consulted on the subject.

By the time they served the main course (duck), he finally began to answer some questions. Russians love caviar, he said, but are annoyed by the fuss made about it in the West. As for the trimmings, he said, quite perceptively, these were just a way of making the caviar go further.

According to Moscow Aveek (which is how I took to describing him), Russians like to keep it simple. Every rich Russian he knew (did he know any other kind, I wondered) would butter a piece of white bread (not brown or black, he said, it interferes with the taste of caviar) and simply spoon the caviar onto it.

Later, after a couple of days in Moscow, I decided I had cracked it. Moscow Aveek was quite right. Russians did keep it simple—but the butter was the key.

When we eat caviar the Western way, we add texture (the onions), weight (the eggs) and tang (the lemon). The weight is, as Moscow Aveek said, a way of making an expensive food go further. But both the texture and the tang are compensations for the quality of the caviar.

Good fresh caviar should have separate, distinct grains that explode on your tongue with a satisfying pop. The caviar should have the consistency of grain, not of jam. And while the intense flavour is part of the charm, this should never be overly fishy.

Unfortunately, most caviar available outside of Russia and perhaps Iran, is caviar that hasn't been properly stored. In an ideal world, caviar would always be kept at 26 °F and consumed within a year of being extracted from the sturgeon.

All this is possible in Moscow but not, alas, in the rest of the world. Many people put caviar in the freezer (especially if it is travelling a long distance). Freezing destroys the texture of caviar—the membranes that surround the eggs break and you never get the pop. Instead, you get fish jam.

Often, we come across the opposite problem: caviar that has not been kept in a cold enough environment. Like all fish products, caviar goes slightly off if it is kept too long without the right kind of refrigeration (hence the fishy smell).

The onion makes up for the absence of texture by adding some of its own. And the lemon cuts through the fishy smell.

If, however, you can get good caviar, then the way to eat it is clearly the Russian method. While they emphasize sharpness in the West (onions, lemon etc.), Russians say that caviar needs nothing more than a suitably fatty bed to lie in—hence Moscow Aveek's point about butter.

Two days after the banquet I went to the Prague restaurant, a legendary holdover from the Soviet era, full of silver service and private rooms stuffed with VIPs (it was easy to tell because their commandos were all hanging around outside—VIPs are the same everywhere in the world).

Prague does caviar the traditional Russian way. It serves blinis—buttery Russian pancakes—and encourages you to smear the blinis with good butter. Then you load each pancake with caviar and roll it up into a tube.

Next you chop off pieces from each pancake tube (I'm an Indian so I ate with my hands but this is not considered a terribly sophisticated thing to do) and drop them into your mouth.

The resulting sensation is amazing. Your mouth fills with a warm buttery feeling and then—pop! pop! pop!—the tiny eggs burst on your tongue disgorging the flavours of the Caspian.

At the Prague restaurant, they offered me the option of sour cream—popular with many Russians—but if the blinis are good, butter should be enough.

And the key, of course, is caviar so perfectly maintained that it doesn't need the crutches of lemon and onion.

But how easy is it to get such caviar?

Not very, is the honest answer.

During the days of the Soviet Union, caviar production was controlled by a simple State-owned monopoly. The State controlled the number of sturgeon extracted from the water, replenished the stock by hatching baby sturgeon and putting them back in the sea, and ensured that caviar was prepared to its exacting standards.

Caviar is an artisanal product that can only be made by an expert. You have to know when a female sturgeon (or 'cow') is full of eggs, you have to know when the eggs are at their best (experts will keep a freshly caught live sturgeon in a tank till they feel the eggs are ready). Then you have to massage the ovaries by hand to extract the caviar, quickly add a little salt (the term 'malassol' you see on every can means 'slightly salted') and keep it at 26 °F till you can get it to somebody who packs it.

In the Soviet days, all this was tightly controlled. But once the old Soviet Union broke up, the areas around the Caspian became part of five different countries. The State-run monopoly was over and Kazakhstan ended up with the largest population of the Beluga sturgeon.

The result has been poaching on a scale that is unprecedented. Every fisherman in the Caspian area tries to find a sturgeon 'cow'. Most of the poachers don't care whether the cow is ready to be taken for her caviar—they don't know how to extract the caviar properly, they misjudge the salt process, and they don't bother to keep the caviar at the right temperature.

Worse still, poached caviar cannot legally be sold or exported. At Moscow airport I saw big signs that said that nobody could take more than 250 grams of caviar out of Russia—and that only applies to the legally bought caviar; poached caviar will be seized by Customs.

So the poachers resort to smuggling. In many of the Caspian States, caviar is to their economies what heroin is to Pakistan—a source of easy money if you can get it to the West.

And of course, the smugglers don't care about how the caviar is transported, at what temperature and in what condition.

In the 1990s, when the Soviet Union broke up, there was a world glut of caviar. Americans, enjoying the bull run of the century, discovered caviar and bought it by the ton.

Hundreds of new companies sprang up. Most of them bought caviar from poachers and then repackaged it in fancy cans.

Did the quality suffer? Yes, of course it did. But here's the point: it didn't matter. Most of the caviar went to new consumers, people who had no idea what caviar should be like. For others, it was a special occasion food, the sort of thing you ate on an anniversary or in an aeroplane cabin. So as long as it was called caviar and was relatively affordable, they ate it.

The consequence of this 1990s glut is that the sturgeon is now an endangered species. Caviar yields are down to 40 per cent of the Soviet harvest. Naturally, prices have shot up again.

You can still buy caviar that is just about affordable in Moscow (I paid $ 85 for 4 oz of Beluga and $ 60 for the same quantities of Sevruga). But in the West, prices can be four times those—with no guarantee of quality because of the poaching problem.

Nor is the situation likely to improve. Russians are not great environmentalists. Moscow Aveek laughed off any threat to the sturgeon and said he bought terrific caviar from poachers.

In the long run, prices will rise as sturgeon become rarer. And the continued poaching will ensure a total drop in quality.

So if you can get hold of some caviar (and it is the price of a five-star hotel meal), do it now. Next year might be too late.

# the first class experience

A rather pampered and very rich friend of mine—let's call her the Princess—recently had to rush back to Delhi from London because of a family emergency. Time was of the essence so the Princess was unable to wait till the next morning and take the British Airways flight she normally prefers. She had to leave at once and the only option was the evening Virgin Atlantic service.

The Princess opted unhesitatingly for Virgin, but she was a little apprehensive and very curious. The reason for this was quite simple: Virgin has no First Class, just a tarted-up Club Class that it calls Upper Class.

And throughout her forty-plus years on this planet, the Princess has only flown First Class on long-haul flights.

Club Class? Never! Economy Class? Are you mad?

When she landed in Delhi she said that she had been pleasantly surprised. 'You know,' she exclaimed, in tones of wild astonishment, 'Club is not really that bad at all.'

What had she eaten, I asked. Had she made use of Virgin's much-advertised inflight massage service? Was the crew any good?

Oh, she said, she had no idea. She did what she always does on long-haul flights: popped a tranquillizer, washed it down with a glass of vintage champagne and slept all the way, waking up only when the seat belt sign came on before the plane landed in Delhi.

Did she do the same thing when she travelled British Airways First Class on this sector, I enquired. Oh yes, she said, though of course it was easier to sleep in First Class because the seats become flat beds.

It used to be said, in the 1960s and 1970s, of Harold Robbins's potboilers that they succeeded because they helped millions of Economy Class travellers learn what First Class was really like. In other words: they helped sad wannabes like you and me learn how glamorously the rich lived; how much Dom Perignon or Cristal they drank, how much Beluga they consumed, and how they were waited on hand and foot.

But the older I've got, the more convinced I've become that cunning old Harold was conning us.

The truth is that First Class is not really that much more glamorous than Economy Class: it is just a lot roomier.

Oh yes, it could be glamorous if the rich so desired. The Cristal is already in the bucket, the Beluga is on ice and the airline houris have been trained to do their stuff.

But the rich don't really care.

They don't eat much. They don't drink much. They don't want to be pampered. They get annoyed if you wait on them hand and foot.

If it is a night flight they'll sleep. And if it is a daylight flight they'll work.

On the infrequent occasions that I've flown First Class, I've watched with dismay how, half an hour after take-off, all the other passengers have changed into their sleeper suits and are ready for bed. On daylight flights they've all pulled out their laptops and are busy replying to e-mails or looking at spreadsheets.

Glamour? Forget it!

The Princess is pretty typical of her class. As far as the rich are concerned, First Class is about privacy, about leg room and about flat beds at night. It is emphatically not about the things that you and I get excited about.

Till about a decade ago, most airlines were slow to recognize this. They still served eight-course meals in First Class and kept the canapés coming. Then, they worked out that nobody—except for the odd interloper like me—really wanted this.

Within the trade, British Airways usually gets the credit for re-inventing First Class. The airline realized that Club Class (not invented in the era of *The Carpetbaggers* and *The Adventurers*) was getting better and better. Why would anybody pay extra for First?

BA's answer was to emphasize flexibility.

On BA First, you don't watch a movie when the airline wants you to. You have your own video recorder and see a film of your choice (from an inflight library) when you want to. Nor do you have to be subjected to the old eight-course dinner of old. The meal service is like a restaurant. They give you a menu and you order what you like whenever you are hungry.

Most other airlines have now followed the BA model. Some have surpassed it—on the London-Delhi sector, for instance, United had a First Class that was far superior to BA's, but then, of course, they withdrew from India and now teeter on the edge of bankruptcy. Some have added frills—Virgin offered neck massages in Club. (Air-India will now offer male masseurs in First—a great idea if your concept of fun is to have Shahnawaz Husain wring your neck.)

In the process, the concept of the First Class meal has been completely re-invented. Of the airlines flying out of India, only Air-India still does exactly the same meal service it did twenty years ago. And most times, only the mutton curry or the dal are really worth eating.

This is not Air-India's fault. The notion of gourmet food in First Class is a bit of an oxymoron. Not only do more and more travellers follow the Princess's example and steer clear of First Class food, but it is almost impossible to provide first-rate food in any class, even First Class, on an aeroplane.

All airline meals are prepared several hours before take-off. Many are then served several hours after take-off. No chef can cook food that tastes wonderful after it has been vacuum-packed for fourteen hours and then quickly reheated in a crowded aircraft galley.

Chinese (or South-East Asian) food fares the worst because, to taste right, it must go straight from the wok onto the plate. Most Italian food flops (you can't really reheat pasta). French haute cuisine is a disaster in the sky because of the time lag. Only some Indian food—dal, curry, biryani, perhaps—works because the flavours sometimes benefit from being kept overnight.

Conscious of this, most airlines have tried to work out First Class menus that get around these problems. An easy solution is to serve lots of caviar as Air-India does. I've had very good caviar on other airlines as well: Cathay, Singapore, United etc. But this is an expensive option especially if people ask for seconds.

On BA Concorde, for instance, they gave us each a small jar of caviar and nobody dared ask for more. On normal BA First Class I've rarely had caviar, but then perhaps I've flown the wrong sectors. (Some years ago when Michael Winner wrote in the London *Sunday Times* that there was no caviar on BA, the airline denied this. So obviously Winner and I have both been on the wrong flights.)

One other option is to try and do adventurous things that may not be as expensive as caviar (or foie gras, another First Class staple) but are cutesy: Baskin-Robbins ice-cream, Starbucks coffee etc. More and more airlines are also going for the freshly cooked option. The crew will toss salads, make sandwiches and even cook your breakfast eggs in the galley.

In my experience, some of this can work but you can't count on it. The best thing to do if, like me, you are the sort of chap who counts himself lucky to get into First Class, and not a jaded traveller like the Princess, is to stick to the booze.

The fact of the matter is that even those of us who are prepared to blow up large sums of money on food at expensive restaurants balk at paying mark-ups of over 200 to 300 per cent for really good wines.

The great thing about First Class is that while the food may be undependable, the wine is nearly always terrific. And it's free! (Okay, all right, you've already paid for it when you bought your ticket.)

With the notable exception of Air-India (where the First Class wines taste like urine samples collected from pregnant felines), most airlines are prepared to splash out on good wines. (They get them duty-free and at wholesale rates.) The champagne will always be vintage and the claret will come from a grand cru vineyard in a good year. The airline will also have paid some wine expert to select the best wines from unfamiliar regions so First Class is a good way to learn about new wines.

If you are lucky you'll get a crew that cares about its passengers. Last summer I flew Air France to Paris from Delhi. It was an overnight flight and as I was due to catch an early connection to Lisbon and speak at a seminar, I'd decided to impersonate the Princess and the other First Class pros and sleep the entire way.

When I got on board I found that First Class was just one row and that I was the only passenger. Oh good, I thought, that will make it easier to sleep.

But no, the hostesses wouldn't let me. How could I let the wines go waste? With their enthusiastic encouragement I drank from half a dozen bottles of excellent French wine, starting with a very good champagne and ending with a complex Sauternes.

As I was the only passenger, I was conscious that no matter how much I drank (about a glass and half from each bottle, since you ask), huge quantities of the wine that they opened would be wasted. In some strange way, that made the experience even more luxurious and special.

Of course I was a disaster at the Lisbon seminar the next day—I could barely keep my eyes open.

But who cares? Now that the professionals take First Class for granted, it is up to us amateurs to keep the glamour alive.

# a sucker for oysters

For some reason, Indians don't really like oysters. In the 1980s, when I used to be a frequent visitor to the Fisherman's Cove hotel near Madras, an underrated property with cottages right on the beach, I would ask the chef to try and find me some oysters. There would be some initial reluctance—as the chef pointed out, if I didn't eat all the oysters, nobody else would, and besides, every chef likes to think that his skills extend beyond merely opening fresh oysters and placing them on a bed of ice. But eventually, the chefs got used to me. My happiest memories of Fish Cove are of sitting on the beach, watching the sun go down, sipping white wine and polishing off dozens of plates of oysters.

It was never as easy to get oysters at other beach resorts. At the Aguada and the Holiday Village in Goa, the chefs would always offer mussels and clams. But they seemed unable to find any oysters. And Indian hotels seemed unwilling to put oysters on the menu. Sometimes you would find six imported (usually from Australia) oysters on the menu at some fancy French restaurant like Bombay's Zodiac Grill but they were always expensive. And besides, I'm not the sort of chap who can be satisfied with a mere half-dozen oysters.

Now, the relatively easy availability of Kerala oysters (packed in ice and airlifted from Cochin) makes it easier for Indian hotels to serve them. But few bother. Bill Marchetti put them on the menu at Delhi's West View but they didn't move. Now, he uses them for his buffet. At the Machan, at Delhi's Taj Mahal Hotel, Chef Tapas

Bhattacharya offers them as part of his all-you-can-eat Sunday brunch, and judging by the fact that they move so fast, perhaps Indian tastes are finally changing.

What is it about an oyster that makes it essentially different from a clam or a mussel? My guess is that it is the cooked versus raw factor: A mussel is at its best when it is cooked (Moules Mariniere or batter-fried) and the small clams we get in India go perfectly with the non-vegetarian cuisines of the West Coast. (For the best clams in India try Chef Rego at the Holiday Village in Goa. He did Oyster Masala for me too but it's not quite the same thing.)

Oysters, on the other hand, must really be eaten raw. To get the full flavour, you must take an oyster that has been freshly shucked (opened), squirt a little lemon on it, separate the meat from the shell and then shove it in your mouth. That's it.

It sounds simple but there are no words to describe the flavour of a good, fresh oyster. The American chef Anthony Bourdain says that he first discovered the pleasures of food only when he ate a fresh oyster on a trip to France. It tasted, he says, of the sea.

In England, where there is a long tradition of oyster-eating and oyster houses dot the coastline, the oyster is always associated with sex. As recently as last year, *Tipping the Velvet*, the TV dramatization of the best-selling lesbian novel, had the heroine (the daughter of oyster merchants) teaching her showgirl-lover to suck the juice out of the shell, claiming that it was the liquor (as the juice is called) that was the point of the oyster. (Yes, yes, I know it is not a very subtle image.)

But the English are funny about oysters. When I went to university there in the late 1970s, all the undergraduates acted as though oysters were the height of sophistication. Curiously, they treated the Japanese habit of eating fish raw (as in sushi or sashimi) as evidence of barbarism. I could never quite understand the distinction. Why was it okay to eat raw oysters but not okay to eat raw tuna or raw salmon?

The answer, I suspect, was that even by the 1970s, oysters had become very expensive in England. Thus, the undergraduates who spoke so knowledgeably about the sophistication of oysters hadn't actually eaten them. When they did, they usually said things like 'God, this tastes like snot!' (A wide range of gastronomic reference points, those Brits!)

It was not always so. In the nineteenth century and for the first part of the twentieth century, oysters were so plentiful that they were the poor man's food. By the second half of the twentieth century however, overfishing (the usual story) had created a situation in which oyster prices shot up remarkably. And that, I imagine, is when all the snob associations (treating oysters on a par with caviar etc.) really began.

Today, you'll find oysters nearly everywhere in London. You'll even find dedicated oyster bars like Green's or the Bibendum bar that Terence Conran runs at the old Michelin building. But because the oysters will not be cheap, they will always be a special treat.

Fortunately, this is less true of America where oysters are still relatively inexpensive. For many years, one of New York's great gastronomic experiences was the Oyster Bar at Grand Central Station (if America's greatest oyster restaurant is in a railway station then how expensive can oysters be?) and though standards have now slipped, it still remains an American institution.

But nearly everywhere you go on the east coast of the US, you'll find oysters on the menu and they won't cost much more than the other starters. I'm hopelessly confused by oyster varieties, but as far as I could tell, the Americans liked Blue Point oysters (from Long Island) in New York while I preferred the Cape Cod oysters I had in Boston and Nantucket. But then, taste is entirely subjective.

For a chef, an oyster presents a peculiar problem: what do you do with the damn thing?

A sensible chef would leave oysters alone but sensible people rarely become chefs, so there exist hundreds of ways of cooking oysters. The only one that sounds vaguely acceptable to me is to deep-fry them. The French make a production out of this— Oysters à la Normande involves poaching the oysters, dipping them in Villeroi sauce, combining them with slivers of black truffle, coating them in batter and then deep-frying them.

In my view, this constitutes a serious waste of both oyster and truffle. But you can fry them in a thin batter (as Gordon Ramsay does at the Boxwood Café in London) and then serve them as a starter with a wedge of lemon (and/or tartare sauce).

Famous oyster dishes include Oysters Rockefeller and Oysters á l'Americaine, both a complete waste of time. The Chinese and the Thais use oysters for stir-frying (and famously for oyster sauce) and though I've tried everything including the Thai oyster omelette, I'm sorry but I still don't see the point.

What you can do with oysters, should you wish to enhance the flavour, is to find ways of pairing them with interesting things. Americans serve oysters with a spicy cocktail sauce which successfully destroys all oyster flavour as does Tabasco, another popular seasoning.

But spicy flavours *can* add to oysters. I was persuaded to sprinkle a mixture of fried garlic and onions over fresh oysters in Bangkok and yes, it worked.

My preference though is for simple flavours. Last November, I had the most amazing oyster brunch at Bibendum. All that was required was some good, warm, crusty French bread and a generous dab of Normandy butter. I put the oyster on the buttered bread and washed it down with Chablis Premier Cru. (Grand Cru Chablis can be too subtle for oysters.)

The other flavour that goes well with raw oysters is sausage. A decade ago when Alastair Little was still cooking at his Soho restaurant, I had his oyster starter. This consisted of a dozen Colchester oysters, a warm home-made sausage and a raspberry vinaigrette. You took the oyster out of its shell, dipped it quickly in the vinaigrette, put it on a piece of bread and added a chunk of the sausage. Divine!

The combination of oysters, bread and sausage comes from Bordeaux but the classic recipe is Edouard de Pomiane's (from the 1950s).

Here is the whole recipe.

> Fry some chipolata sausages. Serve them very hot on a dish. On a second dish place a dozen chilled oysters.
>
> Alternate the sensations. Burn your mouth with a crackling sausage. Soothe your burns with a cool oyster. Continue until all the sausages and oysters have disappeared.
>
> Serve with white wine, of course.

Now, that's what I call a recipe. None of your 'poach oysters in a court bouillon before preparing sauce Villeroi' nonsense.

If you are eating oysters in India, they will remain a restaurant dish. This is probably just as well. Last year, my son and I, both oyster lovers, bought two dozen Whitstable oysters from the Bibendum shop and took them back to our apartment at the St James's Court Hotel in London (I know the name has changed but that's what I've always called it). Armed with an oysterman's knife (purchased from the Conran shop, also in the Michelin building) I struggled unsuccessfully with opening the oysters before shamefacedly conceding defeat. Eventually, we had to ask the butler to take them to the kitchen to have them opened. He smiled superiorly and then opened them himself with a notable lack of effort.

So, if you don't want to be humiliated by your inability to open an oyster, then my advice is to stick to hotels. Ideally, go to a buffet like the one at Machan where the Moët & Chandon champagne is included in the price of the brunch.

If you are nervous about losing your oyster virginity then start by using a spicy dressing and encasing your oyster between bits of buttered bread. As you grow more comfortable with the taste (and yes, like most good things in life, it is an acquired taste), you can abandon the trimmings one by one till you are ready to mainline.

If you like Cochin oysters then remember (and I am sorry to sound so unpatriotic but it's the truth) that, as oysters go, they are hardly first-rate. You'll get plumper and tastier oysters all over the Far East. And in Europe, you'll have a choice between the European oyster, which is round and pretty (the Whitstable, Colchester and Belon oyster) and the Portuguese oyster (preferred by the French), which is more uneven and looks like it has been scooped out of the bottom of the sea (the Fine de Claire, for instance). Sizes and flavours vary. But if you fall in love with the oyster, you fall in love with the sea. And it is a lifelong romance.

# confessions of a truffle eater

The food world is nothing if not trendy. Once a cuisine catches on then everybody is doing it: Sichuan one year, Thai the next and Mediterranean after that. It's much the same with dishes and ingredients—from foie gras to rocket.

For the last few years, truffle oil has become something of a restaurant cliché. Almost every dish is 'truffled'. You'll find a dollop of truffle oil in the centre of a cream of mushroom soup; your potatoes will be truffled; your carpaccio will come on a bed of rocket, drizzled with truffle oil; and any dish that involves mushrooms—even, say, mushrooms on toast or crostini—will have a truffle flavour.

Many critics find this obsession with the smell (rather than the taste) of truffles more than a little annoying. In America, Jeffrey Steingarten has written at length about the bogus nature of truffle oil (much of it is artificially flavoured), and about how synthetic some of the truffle smells are. It's got to the stage where you fear that at culinary exams they'll fill the paper with such questions as 'The smell of truffles is the new vanilla. Discuss.' In the UK, A.A. Gill, the critic for the *Sunday Times*, makes it a point to aim a kick on the backside of any chef who uses truffle oil.

On this one, at least, I'm not on the same side as Steingarten and Gill. I love the smell of truffles just as I love the smell of vanilla (while vanilla reminds me of my childhood, truffles remind me of pleasurable experiences that came later). Agreed, some of the synthetic truffle scents are disgusting, just as the smell of cheap, artificial vanilla can be nasty. But you don't dismiss a whole range of smells (and truffle scents can go all the way from old socks to diesel) only because somebody produces unpleasant synthetic variations.

Properly used, truffle flavours and smells can elevate any dish. At a party at the Princess's some months ago, the Maurya's Bill Marchetti truffled his mushroom crostini and elevated his porcini risotto (not made, I was glad to note, with the five-gallons-of-cream recipe he hands out to newspapers) with judicious use of salsa truffina (a sort of truffle chutney). At La Rochelle, Chef Sandeep does a killer black truffle risotto and at Diva, Ritu Dalmia has been known to truffle her mashed potatoes.

If a chef has access to the real thing—to whole truffles rather than the oil or the salsa—then the flavour of truffles can be used to enhance most great dishes. At Gordon Ramsay's London restaurant, they welcome you not with bread and butter but with slices of Melba Toast and a foie gras pâté with a hint of black truffle (a classic pairing of flavours).

But though truffles have suddenly become trendy, I still like them in the traditional way at old-fashioned restaurants. For nearly forty years, the place for truffles in London has been a wonderfully cosy, neighbourhood trattoria on Pimlico Road called La Fontana.

Each year, I wait for November when Signor Pavesi, the owner, gets his supplies of fresh white truffles from Alba. He then prepares a special truffle menu or adds around £10 to the price of any dish for a shaving of white truffles. Though his restaurant is neither fancy nor terribly trendy—Locanda Locatelli also does a white truffle menu and Giorgio Locatelli makes much more of a song and dance about them—it attracts the sort of crowd that one would describe as 'Old London': people who live in nearby Chelsea or Belgravia; people who like good food without the flash; and the kind of rich American who is booked in by the concierge at the Berkeley or the Connaught.

Signor Pavesi will make risotto from scratch over an open flame at the back of the restaurant (he takes this very seriously; one Tuesday when I told him that I was a vegetarian and the risotto would have to be stock-less, he looked at me as though I was mad). It will be brought to the table on a trolley by a waiter while Pavesi beams approvingly. Then, his stunningly exquisite daughter will bring a large jar to the table. She will pull out an object, roughly the size of a squash ball, which is wrapped in tissue paper. Once she takes off the paper you will begin to sense the mystic aura of the white truffle of Alba.

But the drama is not over yet. This beautiful woman will then produce a truffle grater and will ceremonially shave the white truffle into paper-thin slices, the polish glinting off the nails on her long, artistic fingers. By the time she is through, the smells of cheese and Arborio will have been overwhelmed by the earth-like (rather than divine) fragrance of the truffle.

Then, you sit quietly, inhale the aroma and enjoy the truffle risotto.

You can, of course, have truffles shaved over anything. They go well with carpaccio and Italians like them with rabbit. But to my relatively uneducated palate, they go with simple things: a dish of creamy scrambled eggs with shaved white truffle; a plate of flat Italian pasta (taglioni) in a butter sauce, or even fresh asparagus in warm garlic butter with shreds of truffle.

The Pavesis have been doing this for so long that they have perfected the art of serving truffles. They rarely feature in the magazines, nor are they favourites of the critics, (*Zagat* gives them 19 points out of a possible 30), but they are always full. In researching this piece, I pulled out an old copy of my friend Fay Maschler's 1986 *Guide to Eating Out in London*. La Fontana featured among Fay's favourites but even seventeen years ago she thought it 'different in style from most of London's other Italian restaurants; rather more middle-aged in decor'. What's more, that review could have been written yesterday—nothing has changed over nearly two decades.

All of this is not to say that truffles don't belong on fancy menus. Now that Bikki Oberoi is bringing Giorgio Locatelli to India (his restaurant will occupy the space where Palms now is at the Delhi Oberoi), no doubt we'll get Giorgio's takes on the truffle. And Raymond Bickson has signed up Jean-Georges Vongerichten, owner of one of the world's best restaurants (in New York) to open four restaurants at various Taj hotels in India so Jean Georges will also introduce us to new flavours.

But I like truffles, pure and simple. Fortunately, my Significant Other does too. She loved them from the time they were first shaved onto her pasta and says she can still remember the first time she smelt truffle oil.

In December last year I went to the Food Hall at Harvey Nichols in London to see what the fresh truffles were like. Sadly, the white truffle harvest last year had been low, so prices were significantly higher than in 2002. The black truffle of Périgord (a very different smell; less subtle, more comparable to diesel than mould or old socks), on the other hand, was relatively affordable (about £16 a truffle), so I bought two.

I enjoyed those truffles every way I could: shaved over pasta; in buttery mashed potatoes; on my home-made risotto (no cream, no cheese) and on eggs. Oddly enough, despite my love of truffles, this was the first time in my life that I treated them as a vegetable and not as a restaurant dish.

This has led to several surprises. First of all, it's much, much cheaper to enjoy them this way than it is in a restaurant. (And that's at Harvey Nichols's prices—I'm sure you'd get a much better deal in Perigord or Alba, if not in Paris). Secondly, you realize how far a truffle goes. The flavour is so intense that a little shaving can overwhelm a dish. Third, if you are used to white truffles, as I am, then you realize that the black truffle is quite another thing. Not only is the flavour significantly different (you can cook a black truffle, but cooking destroys the flavour of white truffles) but if you shave off a slice (and at home you can afford to shave off a thick slice), you notice that the texture is mottled and marbled, with little grey and beige dots.

Obviously I'm a truffle addict. And not everyone will like truffles. But consider this: they are not as expensive as people like to imagine. I know loads of Indians who go to London and bring back £25-bottles of malt whisky. To all those who spend money on booze, here's a suggestion: be good to your palate. Any fool can drink whisky anywhere. Why not try and broaden your horizons with something more adventurous, the next time you travel?

# some sweet truths about chocolate

When I was at school, a bar of Cadbury's Fruit and Nut cost 85 paise. For schoolboys in the pre-inflation 1960s, this was a lot of money, and a Cad (as any Cadbury's bar was called) took on the characteristics of a gold bar. Bets were denominated in terms of Cads ('I'll bet you a Cad that my house will beat yours in cricket') or, in some cases, fractions of Cads ('I'll give you half a Cad if you'll let me copy your homework').

By the time we left school, however, the Cad had gone the way of the gold standard. I was told later that this had something to do with the rising price of cocoa beans (in the 1970s a ton of beans shot up to $5,500 but prices have now declined to around $1,000 a ton), problems with making the Indian cocoa bean (as distinct from the imported version) taste palatable, and the greater profit margin in so-called 'chocolate bars' that contained very little chocolate, such as Five Star (a Mars bar rip-off), and the truly horrible Krisp which was more wheat than chocolate.

Nevertheless, a love for chocolate bars remained with me, and I was relieved to find, while studying in England in the 1970s, that the original Cads were still available there, without the disgusting new flavours imparted to Indian chocolate bars (synthetic orange, for instance). Cadbury's Dairy Milk (CDM) remained the gold standard but there was also my beloved Fruit and Nut (slogan: 'Are you a Fruit and Nut case?' Yes! Yes!) Even the reduced-chocolate bars were better than the ones we got in India. There were the delicious Marathon (mysteriously called Snickers in America), and the original Mars Bar (as distinct from Five Star).

By the 1980s I had graduated to dark chocolate (the so-called grown-up taste) but the influence of the Fruit and Nut Cad remained. I liked my chocolate in bars (no poncy truffles for me), and I liked nuts with everything.

I regarded this love for chocolate as a guilty pleasure and talked as little as I could about this secret vice till I discovered to my amazement and horror in the 1990s that eating chocolate was something to be proud of. Chocolate was the new champagne; it was the equivalent of caviar and it had a huge snob value. People now paid approximately 1,000 times what I had paid for a Cad in my schooldays for a bar of roughly the same size (*without* the fruit and nuts) and bragged about how they were so stylish for spending all this money. 'Purists' created a demand for single plantation chocolate (like Chateau-bottled wine) and the gourmet end of the business became worth hundreds of millions of dollars.

Clearly, there is no accounting for the foolishness of food snobbery.

It all began, of course, in America, and like most fads in the food business, it was the creation of giant US multinational corporations. In 1966 a small Belgian chocolate company called Godiva was bought by a US corporation, the Campbell Soup Company. In 1974 Campbell appointed Al Pechenik, a savvy marketing man, to 'turn around' the Godiva brand.

Pechenik believed that Americans could be talked into buying anything at any price if the marketing was right. 'Americans are ruled by status,' he told Joel Brenner, author of the definitive *The Emperors of Chocolate*. 'It's the Mercedes syndrome.' He threw away Godiva's old packaging, wrapped the chocolate in gold foil and silk ribbon and raised the prices.

Idiotic Americans bought the whole scam, lock, stock and chocolate.

Between 1979 and 1983 Godiva opened a staggering 1,200 outlets across America. Pechenik pushed for prices of $20 a pound but by 1985, with per capita chocolate consumption shooting up, Godiva not only declared a 400 per cent rise in profits but prices had reached $40 a pound.

Since then, the multinationals have sewn up the top end of the mass-produced chocolate market but have nearly always disguised the true ownership of fancy chocolate companies. Let's take Perugina, maker of fancy Italian chocolates. That's owned by Nestle, makers of Nescafe. What about other European brands—Côte d'Or, Van Houten, Tobler and Suchard? They are all owned by Kraft (makers of the processed cheese), which, in turn, is owned by cigarette giant Philip Morris.

The techniques employed by the snob chocolate business have hardly varied for two decades. The first is good, old-fashioned snob-value advertising. In 1979 Pechenik's first Godiva ad had four truffles arranged on a Limoges dish with the caption 'Dessert'. This kind of nonsense is still used to sell overpriced chocolate. The second technique is junketeering. Food companies will spend lavishly on inviting greedy but ignorant food writers to visit their factories, will fill them up with nonsense about the delicacy of the chocolate flavour, the perfume of cocoa etc. and will then wait for PR-filled write-ups to appear.

The third technique is the most daring: it involves the use of biology to boost chocolate's claims. To be fair, this is an old trick. As far back as 1825, Brillat-Savarin wrote that chocolate could allay 'hectic heats' and improve 'consumptive complexions'. Casanova said he used it instead of champagne for seduction, and Madame Du Barry gave it to all her suitors.

But now, chocolate manufacturers have found a scientific basis for these claims. PEA (phenylethylamine) is a chemical found in the human brain that is linked to feeling happy. Fall in love, make a windfall profit or win the lottery, and PEA levels shoot up. Chocolate, it has been demonstrated, contains PEA. So, say the chocolate companies, eat chocolate, and you feel as euphoric you do when you fall in love.

This is too good to be true—literally.

The truth is that nobody has ever been able to prove that by eating PEA you can make your PEA levels shoot up. (That only happens when the brain produces its own PEA.) Researchers at America's National Institute of Mental Health made subjects eat pounds of chocolate and found no change in PEA levels, no matter how much chocolate was consumed.

But here's the clincher: while chocolate contains about 1 milligram of PEA per standard (1.4 ounce) chocolate bar, many other foods contain more PEA. These include cheddar cheese and smoked salami.

And have you ever heard of the euphoric effects of salami?

Yes, chocolate can make you happy. But that's because it contains fat and sugar, both of which are great comfort foods. The problem is that the fancy, expensive chocolate for which these myths are advanced actually contains *less* sugar than your average Cad or Mars Bar. So, if you are taking chocolate as a mood-altering substance, stick to Snickers.

So, what chocolate *should* you have and why? My advice is to ignore all the snob rubbish and to steer clear of the outrageously priced crap (profit margin 2,000 per cent). Yes, there are probably a small number of people who can tell the difference between a very good chocolate and a great one (just as there are people who can tell the vintage of a Chateau Margaux by sniffing its bouquet).

But you and I are not among these people. These distinctions are of little use to us (and of less use to our wallets). If you love chocolate as much as I do, try and develop a taste for dark chocolate, ideally the kind that has a high cocoa content (80 per cent plus)—it is more rewarding. With the collapse of import restrictions, more and more chocolate is now available in India, so you'll probably get something like Lindt Excellence if you look hard enough.

But don't feel embarrassed about what you like. My fridge is still full of bars of basic Fruit and Nut from Tesco's (but the dark chocolate variety) which remind me of school. And if you like milk chocolate, good for you. Remember that the invention of milk chocolate came after the submarine, the electric tram, the telegraph, the camera and the machine gun. Chocolate and milk are molecular enemies and it wasn't till 1875 that Henri Nestle managed to invent a decent milk chocolate. So gorge away on Snickers (I finally discovered that Mars called it Marathon in England so that the name wouldn't be confused with knickers!), bite into a Mars Bar and crunch away at your Kit Kat.

# don't duck the goose, try some foie gras

When I started writing my food column a couple of years ago I bravely declared to the editor of the *HT* Sunday magazine that I wanted it to be different from the gaff that already appeared in other Sunday papers. There were to be no press releases masquerading as news, no plugs for chefs who had fed me large free meals, and none of that high-flown nonsense that so dominates all food writing.

Instead, I announced grandly, the column would deal with real food: who invented the first tandoori chicken; can you make good pasta in India; why has the Nizam's Roll never spread out of Calcutta; where do you get the best *bhelpuri*—stuff like that.

Which is why I am embarrassed to reveal that this piece is about foie gras.

Okay. I've taken a deep gulp. I'll explain why I'm doing it. Partly it is because—and this is come-clean time—I love the stuff. Partly it is because I find it on more and more restaurant menus in India. Partly it is because its image (on a par with caviar and truffles) suggests an extraordinarily high price, a misconception that needs to be corrected—at most restaurants, it only costs slightly more than other first courses, and at many (Delhi's Orient Express, Bombay's Zodiac Grill etc.) it is just another option on the set menu. And partly, it is because so many people have begun asking about foie gras that I thought it made sense to do a piece that demystified the stuff and rid it of all the snob appeal.

In essence, foie gras is the enlarged liver of a duck or a goose. If you don't like liver—and personally I loathe all offal and glandular meat—you'll still like foie gras because it does not have the sharp taste we associate with dark liver meat.

There's a good reason for this. Foie gras is not dark meat at all. It is fat. It has a buttery, silky, rich taste that is hard to describe to anyone who hasn't eaten it.

The biology of foie gras is as follows: each year geese and ducks migrate south in the autumn and north in the spring. This migration often involves flying 600 miles non-stop without stopping to eat. Moreover, they fly at very high altitudes and require insulation from the cold.

The solution to all these problems is fat. The liver, which is the centre of the body, becomes the storehouse of fat. This fat provides both nourishment and insulation. Before birds fly off on these migratory journeys, they fatten themselves by eating everything in sight. This food is stored in the liver which engorges to contain all the fat. Once the birds reach their destinations their livers return to normal size. A duck liver drops from two pounds to two ounces and a goose liver from four-and-a-half pounds to a mere quarter pound.

To obtain foie gras you've got to catch the bird after it has fattened its liver but just before it flies off. This is possible in theory but is an enormous hassle in practice. So nearly all foie gras is farmed. That is to say, the ducks and geese are fattened by farmers before being slaughtered.

The fattening process is the subject of a rather tiresome controversy. No matter what the farmers may say for PR purposes, the truth is that no bird likes to eat too much if it knows that this is not the migrating season. So the farmers force-feed the birds for at least two weeks. Animal activists claim that it is cruel to force-feed a bird. Farmers retort that they are only doing what nature does anyway. And neither side is convinced by the other's position.

For our purposes (assuming that you, dear reader, are not an animal activist who is going to picket my home and confiscate my feather quill pen), all that matters is that foie gras farming, once restricted to France, has now spread all over the world.

In the late 1980's two foie gras farms opened in America (one in Sonoma in California and the other at Hudson Bay in New York) and turned the US into a nation of foie gras lovers. It now appears on nearly every fine-dining menu. Over the last decade, Eastern Europe has emerged as a centre of foie gras farming. And now the Chinese are preparing to enter the market—they expect to be the world's largest producers of foie gras in five years' time.

The net result is that foie gras is now not only plentiful but it is relatively cheap. This makes it accessible to nearly everybody who wants to enjoy it. The French still claim that their stuff is better than everybody else's and the goose farmers of Strasbourg say that duck foie gras, which is cheaper than goose, is not the real thing.

The truth, of course, is that if you've been brought up on foie gras you can probably tell the difference. For the rest of us, it doesn't matter. In Delhi, the Orient Express used to serve a starter that combined a piece of duck foie gras with a piece of goose liver. Nobody I asked could tell the difference when they ate it.

Because foie gras is essentially duck or goose fat, it doesn't require much cooking. Most chefs will slice it into escalopes and then either quickly sauté or pan-sear it. A few minutes is all you need. The trick is knowing what to do with the cooked foie gras once it is done.

Most chefs have worked out that punters like their foie gras paired with something slightly sweetish. Usual accompaniments include balsamic vinegar (which finds its way into nearly every foie gras recipe), a port wine sauce, caramelized fruit, apples, berries, peach marmalade. Another trick is to play with texture. Place the buttery slice of foie gras on something crunchy (*rosti* potato for instance) and then use fruit or a sweet acidic sauce to bring out the flavours.

In the years when he ran the Longchamp restaurant in Delhi, Richard Neat made a killer foie gras starter with baby onions and baby turnips in the sauce and two crisp fried potato slices around the liver. In Bombay, Hemant Oberoi now offers India's best range of foie gras dishes at the brilliant Zodiac Grill: there's a Champion Terrine, an amazing hot soufflé, and an interesting risotto. More and more restaurants are now adding foie gras to their menus (it has always been on the cards at La Rochelle and the Orient Express in Delhi). As prices fall, I imagine we'll see some kind of foie gras explosion in India as we have in the rest of the world.

My advice to anyone who wants to try it (and everybody should) is to forget all the snob nonsense and to treat it as an unusual form of duck fat rather than a kind of glandular meat. Ideally foie gras should be eaten with a sweetish wine so refuse all the snobbish offers of dry champagne (completely unsuited to foie gras) and ask for a Barsac, a Sauternes, or even a Gewürztraminer.

Obviously, no dish that is all fat is going to help you lose weight. But remember that because it is poultry fat, foie gras is actually much healthier than the pork fat and the lamb fat non-vegetarians normally eat. Foie gras is rich in unsaturated fats and the French claim that it lowers LDL (bad cholesterol ) and raises HDL (good cholesterol). I'm not sure how accurate this is but Gascony, where the population virtually lives on foie gras, has the lowest incidence of heart disease in all of France—and France has half the incidence of heart disease of America. (The so-called French paradox.)

So don't feel guilty about the fat in foie gras, forget all the snob associations (they'll collapse anyway along with the price once the Chinese reach full capacity and flood the market) and treat yourself to some foie gras.

My guess is you'll grow to love it.

# the right smoke on the salmon

There was a time when people referred to smoked salmon in the same breath as caviar. The suggestion was that it was such an expensive and luxurious food that we were to consider ourselves lucky if we got any.

Partly it was because nobody used to legally import smoked salmon in India. Throughout the 1980s the smart set in Bombay would go off to such stores as Rustom's in Cuffe Parade where packets of salmon would be stored next to cans of caviar (both probably stolen from Air India planes and sold by the crew) in vast deep freezes. Then they would serve sides of salmon at elegant dinner parties where the guests would be too drunk/stupid/polite to remark that smoked salmon, once frozen and then defrosted, runs the risk of tasting like a slice of cold, soggy cardboard.

All that's changed now with the liberalization of the import regulations on food. You can get pre-packed smoked salmon at most upmarket grocers (though you should still beware of the frozen variety). Or better still, you can buy it at the Oberoi Charcuterie (what they now call the old pastry shops/delis in the fond hope that somebody will learn to pronounce the new name one of these days), where it is served refrigerated (but not frozen) at very reasonable prices (Rs 195 for a packet of 100g).

Of course there is a huge snob industry in the West about the different kinds of salmon but I am not convinced that it applies very much to the smoked variety. The best salmon in the world is the wild variety—the kind that a fisherman gets. For obvious reasons this is hugely expensive and demand vastly exceeds the limited supply. Consequently, most of the salmon we find in the shops is farmed.

Fans of wild salmon say that it has a meaty flavour derived from its diet—small shellfish mainly. The farmed variety, on the other hand, can be bland and taste of nothing at all. (Needless to say, all of the imported salmon served at very high prices by Indian five-star hotels is farmed.) There is a halfway point in the form of what is called organic salmon. This is still farmed salmon but the taste is richer because they feed the fish on crushed shrimp shells. (The diet for farmed salmon is soya bean and bits of chicken waste.)

I'm still not convinced that it makes a huge difference to the quality of smoked salmon—unless you have a fish food fetish—and indeed it is rare to find smoked wild salmon. The expensive variety tends to be salmon that is organically farmed.

More important is how the fish has been smoked. Cheap smoked salmon can have a nasty industrial flavour. Ideally the fish should be smoked in a brick kiln with smoke from wood (oak, for instance) chips. Fans of this sort of thing say that Scottish smoked salmon is better than the cheaper and the more plentiful Norwegian variety because of the quality of the smoking. Others argue that Irish salmon and Scottish smoking techniques make for the ideal match.

If you are willing to pay good money for the best smoked salmon (wild) then expect to pay upwards of £70 (around Rs 6,000) for a kilo direct from suppliers and up to double that amount if you buy it in the shops. Serious foodies and gourmets will want to spend that kind of money but the rest of us will probably be happy enough with the (quite acceptable) Oberoi variety.

The best way to eat smoked salmon is, in my view, entirely on its own, with a sprinkling of freshly ground black pepper and a dash of lemon. The traditional accompaniment is buttered brown bread, and some people prefer Melba toast.

Chefs enjoy doing fancy things with smoked salmon but are

stymied by the fact that very few flavours truly complement it. To serve smoked salmon with caviar is a waste of fish—the flavour of caviar will overwhelm the salmon. You can serve it with salmon roe (a sort of mother and child reunion), but it looks better than it tastes. (Nevertheless, I quite like the way salmon roe explodes in your mouth.)

Eggs go well with salmon, so smoked salmon and buttery scrambled eggs are a traditional combination. Restaurants try mixing cream with smoked salmon for fancy dishes but I'm not convinced that this improves the taste.

My suggestion for a luxurious first course is to buy the Oberoi's salmon (it is pre-sliced) and to thinly layer it on to a quarter plate so that the whole plate is covered by the fish. If you want to add a little texture, finely slice a cucumber, and marinate the slices in a good white-wine vinegar for half an hour, and then layer the cucumber slices over the fish. Serve with lemon and black pepper.

# about wine

Ancient India had its own art forms: dance, drama and the like. Modern India also has its art forms but these tend to be rather less elevated and somewhat more ephemeral in nature.

In Bombay in the 1980s I decided that the new upper middle class art form was the fashion show. This was when the designer boom was just taking off and the new breed of fashion designers chose to draw attention to their output with glossy, glamorous fashion shows.

Night after night some designer would take over a lawn, poolside venue, a hotel banquet room or even a shop floor and parade a dozen models through a crowd of hundreds of half-drunk men and overdressed women.

Around 90 per cent of those who attended the shows had no interest in the clothes; 95 per cent would never buy a single item from the collection on display. But they came anyway.

The guys came for the babe factor—on and off the ramp. The women came to be seen and to fight for front-row seats. In a city where the elite had consciously rejected culture the fashion show became the art form of the decade.

By the 1990s the fashion-show-as-art-form had spread to the rest of India. But as we entered the new century the crème de la crème of the elite had begun to tire of designers and their anorexic models. Besides, fashion shows had become so common that anybody could get a first-row seat, dahling.

Enter the first Delhi art form of the new century: wine tasting.

If you are a regular reader of *HT City* then you'll know all about the so-called wine explosion. Month after month some patient Frenchman (or Italian or Spaniard or Californian) is interviewed about the wine from his vineyard. Usually, he poses awkwardly for pictures with his importer (nine times out of ten it's Aman Dhall or Sanjay Menon). The piece ends with praise of the wine ('fruity but spicy' or 'better than Dom Perignon' etc.) and a discreet plug for the restaurant where aforementioned Frenchman (or Spaniard or Italian etc.) will be serving free bottles of his produce to a select gathering.

In certain circles the name of the game is to get into this gathering. Arguments break out over the seating. To be on the left of the winemaker is a great honour. (Even better if he doesn't speak much English. You don't have to even bother to make conversation with the fellow.) Little cliques form among the guests. Hearts get broken (but that is an old and now, very boring, story). The tastings themselves differ from fashion shows in the sense that they are a participatory art form. At fashion shows you merely check out the babes as they walk past. Here you have to actually make conversation and seem like a wine snob of long standing.

This is where the skill comes in. There are probably about two dozen people (outside of the trade and the restaurant business) who know anything about wine in all of India. As each tasting takes in about three dozen guests and the wine lovers are unwilling to turn up at every wine dinner, you usually end up with two or three people who understand wine, and a roomful of frauds.

But the confidence! They will wing their way through the main course. (Doesn't the claret go perfectly with the lamb, darling? 'Er, well . . . actually, no. It's a burgundy and that's pork you are eating.') They will drop names with shameful abandon. They will mention wine shops they have visited. They will wrap their tongues around the names of chateaus and still smile when they get them bitten off. (Don't laugh. Try saying Chateau Marquis-d'Alesme-Becker without pausing for breath.)

All of this is doubly sad because amidst the nonsense that is served up at wine tastings, there are also some gems. If you are drinking Vieux Chateau Certan or Cos d'Estournel then it probably helps if you can tell them apart from Riviera Red.

While the tastings are masterpieces of foolishness and pretension (yes, all right, I still swallow my pride and go if the wine is exceptional), they are supposed to be only the tip of the iceberg. All of us who made fun of fashion shows in the 1980s did not recognize that they were only the most visible manifestation of a new trend: the arrival of the Indian designer.

So, are the tastings the precursors of a new wine revolution? Will we all be drinking Rioja with our raans or Tafelwein with our tandoori chicken?

Frankly, despite the efforts of such enthusiasts as my knowledgeable colleague Sourish Bhattacharya and Subhash Arora's Delhi Wine Society, I have yet to be convinced that a wine revolution is imminent.

Yes, wines are more freely available thanks to such importers as Dhall and Menon. And yes, many people (women mainly) often opt for a glass of wine where once they would have drunk something stronger.

But neither is a sufficient condition for a wine revolution. When and if the revolution does come to India its arrival will not be heralded by the classed growths that are served at most wine tastings but by more ordinary and thus affordable wines. And there will be no revolution till people start drinking wine with meals. 'A glass of white wine before dinner' may sound sophisticated but it doesn't add up to the volumes that a revolution will require.

And unfortunately, Indians are not drinking wine with food. There are many reasons for this of which the most important is price. Wine is not cheap, duties make it even more expensive, and then the hotels get in on the act with mark-ups of 150 per cent or more. You would have to be crazy to order wine at a five-star Chinese restaurant when you could get the same wine (with food that is probably better) at a stand-alone restaurant like Imperial Garden. So it is with Italian food. Why pay La Piazza's mark-ups when you get better food and (cheaper) wine at Diva?

The other problem is that most of us know nothing about wine and the flurry of wine promotions has done little to remove that ignorance. To really understand wine you have to drink it every day (drinking a full bottle of good wine at a freebie wine tasting every month is not enough), and in India, that's almost impossible.

So, should you drink wine? And if so, when, and what?

There are two answers to this question. There is no doubt that wine improves the experience of certain foods beyond belief. For instance, I cannot eat a steak without a glass of red wine; foie gras without some Sauternes, or oysters without either Chablis or (if I am feeling poor) Muscadet. So if you are eating Western food, then yes, I think you are missing something if you don't order wine. If, on the other hand, you are eating dal-chawal, I'm not convinced that a bottle of vintage Chateau Margaux will do much for the taste of your meal.

The second answer is that wine can be fun to drink for its own sake and not because it goes with the food. When you drink one of the world's great wines you look for food that matches the wine, not the other way around. So if you develop a taste for wine then you should drink it anyway, no matter what you are eating.

The question of what wine to drink is more complicated. I don't buy wine from bootleggers and smugglers on principle, so that rules out Cuvee Giraud and all the other rubbish that is served on the Delhi party circuit.

If you are just getting into wine then you'll probably also be thrown by the wine industry's labelling systems. Old-world wines are named after regions (Chablis) or tradition (Chianti). New-world wines tend to be named after grape varieties (Chardonnay, Cabernet Sauvignon etc.) This is confusing because old-world wines are often made from the same grapes as their new-world counterparts

(Chablis, for instance, is made from Chardonnay), but it won't say so on the label.

My advice to anybody who is not a wine drinker and wants to start is to forget about wine and food for the time being and to ignore all the fancy imported stuff. Stick instead to Indian wine.

Wine snobs will turn up their noses but I think the Sula Sauvignon Blanc (the preferred wine of most Bombay trash but don't let that put you off) is a good white wine to start with. You can chill it so that it cools you down in a hot summer and the wine itself is so agreeable that it doesn't matter what you eat with it. And it tastes fine on its own.

Red wine is a little more complicated. I'm vastly partial to the Grover La Reserve but some wine critics keep knocking it. I find that the Chantilly Red (which is much cheaper and which the Bombay Taj offers free to guests) can often be quite acceptable, and I regularly cook with it. No doubt you'll find more variety in the marketplace because domestic producers are constantly trying new things. As for wine in restaurants, my advice is: splurge if you are eating Western food but don't bother to pay five-star mark-ups if you are eating Indian, Chinese or Thai.

But never forget the golden rule: Wine is not about snobbery, it is about fun. Most wine snobs are sad, insecure creatures, who use wine to make up for their own pathetic inadequacies.

So don't be intimidated by wine snobbery. Treat the tastings with the contempt they deserve. And just enjoy the wine.

# whisky? no thanks

Sophisticated (and here I use the word as a euphemism for 'rich') friends of mine treat me with a scarcely veiled contempt on the rare occasions that I do drink whisky. My problem is simple enough: I know diddly-squat about whisky and whether you serve me a Red Label, a Black Label, a Blue Label, a Gold Label or a Purple Label (actually, I think Purple Label is a Ralph Lauren clothing brand, which just shows you how little I know), I can't really tell the difference. I can probably tell real whisky from IMFL but this is easy to do. You don't even have to taste the damn thing. Just sniff it. Real whisky—and Scotch in particular—will yield a richness of aromas. IMFL will smell so bad that you'll probably pass out. And I can tell the taste of the more assertive single malts—a smoky Lagavulin, for instance.

But, on the whole, I drink my whisky with Coke.

I'm sorry if this sounds barbaric but it's about the only way that I can enjoy whisky. And, as you can imagine, if the whisky flavour has to shine through oceans of Coke, it doesn't really matter whether it is Red Label or Chivas Regal or Royal Salute or whatever.

I've tried hard to convince contemptuous rich friends that I find whisky snobbery incredibly tedious. 90 per cent of the Indians who say that they 'only drink Scotch' don't know what they are talking about, anyway. The vast majority of pegs of 'Scotch' poured outside of five-star hotels are mainly IMFL. Bootleggers usually mix something like one-fourth Scotch with three-fourths IMFL and flog it to snobbish but ignorant customers who take the line that if it's expensive it must be genuine.

Many years ago, in a famous experiment, the Taj group of hotels bought several bottles of Johnnie Walker Black Label from all over Bombay, including the duty-free shop at the airport. Many of the bottles were procured from the city's top bootleggers, people who used to supply Bombay's business elite.

The Taj sent all the bottles to Johnnie Walker in Scotland: What proportion were authentic?

Well, Johnnie Walker replied, that was an easy question to answer. They were all bogus.

And that included the bottles bought at the ITDC duty-free shop.

(Apparently, ITDC had an explanation. When customs authorities raided bootleggers they sent all the seized stock to ITDC to flog. And the bootleggers would rather be prosecuted than admit that their stock was bogus. It was a question of prestige for them.)

Ever since, I've been doubly suspicious of any 'Scotch' served in India. If I ever offer it to friends it is always a bottle that I've bought abroad. They say, after all, that more Johnnie Walker Black Label is consumed in India than is produced in Scotland.

But even when I can be reasonably certain that the Scotch on offer is the real thing, I prefer to drink something else. Sadly, many hosts do not provide that option, imagining that a Scotch-only party represents the height of sophistication.

In those cases I ask for a simple Scotch with three cubes of ice in a glass filled to the brim with Coca-Cola. (If I'm abroad I opt for the newly introduced Vanilla Coke, which, sadly, is not available in India as yet.)

When the sneers begin I'm ready for them. 'What a waste!' is typical of the sort of contemptuous remark I have to put up with. My response is as predictable. 'Yes,' I usually say, 'It's a real waste—of Coca-Cola.'

But it doesn't matter how much B-movie wit I employ, people will still sneer. (The response I use is stolen from one of the worst movies of all time, *The Stud*, starring Joan Collins and Oliver Tobias, and based on an even crappier book by Jackie Collins. One Collins is bad enough. But when you put the two together the result is too awful to behold.)

And even when I tell them that Scotch-and-Coke is an age-old and perfectly acceptable combination, nobody is convinced. In vain do I explain that my mother started drinking Scotch-and-Coke when she was at university in America in the 1940s. (And she enjoyed it even more when she came back to India because that way nobody could tell she was drinking alcohol.)

Nor does it cut much ice when I say that Scotch-and-Coke was the acceptable rock star drink in the 1960s. (Before they all graduated to acid and heroin and choked on their own vomit, presumably.)

At the Beatles Apple headquarters on London's Savile Row, Scotch-and-Coke was the house drink. Almost as soon as you entered they handed you a tumbler of Scotch with three fingers of Coke poured in.

So, if I don't drink Scotch at most parties because I can't be sure of its provenance and I'm the sort of chap who doesn't like it too much anyway, then what do I drink?

Well, I drink rum.

There's a reason for this. I love vodka. I'm a fan of flavoured vodkas. And I pride myself on being able to concoct wonderful vodka-based cocktails. I like gin too. It's hard to beat the juniper scent of a Tanqueray with good tonic (Schweppes), or the wonderful aromas of a martini made with Bombay Sapphire.

But sadly, even Indians who are willing to splash out on a bottle of Scotch will take the line that 'Indian gin is very good' or that 'we now get foreign vodka in India.'

This is crap.

The point of a gin is the flavour that comes from the botanicals (juniper, citrus peel, liquorice etc.) that give each brand its distinctive taste. With vodka, the flavour comes from the ingredients with which it was made. Stolichnaya is made from grain, for instance, while Wyborowa is made from rye. Others are made from potatoes.

Indian vodka and gin, unfortunately, are made from industrial alcohol which is then artificially flavoured to give it a gin or vodka taste. (This is true even of the so-called foreign brands made in India despite such claims as 'made from a recipe originated by Pierre Smirnoff in 1852' or whatever—rest assured that old Mr Smirnoff had never heard of IMFL or ever imagined that one day some vast multinational would put his name to this stuff.)

Indian rum, on the other hand, has a huge advantage over all other kinds of IMFL (gin, vodka, brandy, whisky etc.) because it's made from molasses, a sugar cane derivative. And rum is a sugar cane-based drink. So, of all the rubbish we make in India (and force down the throats of consumers while keeping import duties absurdly high so that we can protect the domestic manufacturers of this bilge), our rum comes the nearest to being authentic.

This is not to say that such staples of my misspent youth as Hercules XXX or Old Monk would win many competitions for the best rum in the world (in fact, when you read books and articles about the rums of the world nobody even bothers to mention the Indian variety), but only to say that they are quite drinkable. They go well with Coke and with 7 Up and can be used in cocktails without damaging the taste of the original recipes. (Which sadly is not true of other IMFL products.)

Why isn't our rum world-class? The short answer is that the domestic manufacturers couldn't be bothered to turn out a good product because the industry enjoys such hefty government protection. Rum is not a First World product. Most Third World sugar-growing countries turn out globally famous rums.

The most famous, of course, are Cuban rums, the best-known of which is the slightly citrussy Havana Club (you can't make an authentic mojito without it). And then there's Bacardi, Cuban in origin but now made in other countries by an anti-Castro family of Cuban exiles. (Such is the power of marketing that Bacardi has become a generic term for white rum.)

It wasn't till I went to the Caribbean in 1998 that I discovered the local rums. They were simply amazing, and I would prefer them over much more expensive malt whisky any time. In Jamaica I fell in love with the slightly fruity, golden Appleton VX, and most of the premium rums of the West Indies (light Eclipse from Barbados, dark Myers from Jamaica etc.) are richly rewarding. Even Mauritius manages a subtle Green Island white rum.

But our stuff is, at best, acceptable, and shines only in comparison to the other booze we produce.

So if you are having guests, cannot get your hands on a bottle of Scotch bought abroad, and still want to do something unusual, what should you do?

My recommendation: stick with one of the premium Indian-made rums. You can serve the rum with a variety of mixers, and something like Bacardi Reserva has enough body to enliven a glass of Sprite or Coke. Rum is also a good base for all punches; it mixes well with even the most difficult fruit juices (canned pineapple, for instance) and can add depth to a bottled mango drink (Mangola, for instance).

If you want to get ambitious you can make all the famous rum cocktails including the mai tai, the pina colada, the mojito and the daiquiri. They may not taste entirely authentic but after three drinks no one will notice.

Moreover, rum has one other great advantage. Good rum is always much cheaper than good whisky, no matter where in the world you buy it. An estate-bottled vintage rum will always be cheaper than an equivalent fancy whisky.

And once you get past the snob value attached to whisky you'll realize why global whisky consumption is going down. It is, quite simply, a drink that is past its time. And there are many better and cheaper alternatives.

## vodka goes vanilla

Just when I thought that vanilla-flavoured vodka was becoming a style cliché Absolut launched its own brand of vanilla vodka, with loads of publicity, including a product placement in the new series of *Sex and the City*, the self-consciously trendy American TV show that women seem to love but which bores the life out of me. Expect more vanilla-flavoured cocktails, more articles in style journals and more product placements.

I love flavoured vodkas and I love vanilla, so I would seem like the obvious candidate for a vanilla vodka manufacturer. But the truth is that I didn't even know that there was such a thing as vanilla vodka—you always associate vodka with such flavours as lemon, orange, pepper and blackcurrant—till one day sipping at a cocktail at the Long Bar at London's Sanderson Hotel five or six years ago I began to wonder why the drink had a vanilla flavour.

The bartender—taking a break from crushing mint for his mojitos—showed me the secret ingredient: a bottle of Stoli Vanil, Stolichnaya's brand of vanilla vodka. I was immediately entranced.

Then, nearly everywhere I went, cocktails that featured vanilla vodka (with such names as the Vanil-Berry Martini) seemed to turn up on the menu. In no time at all the craze had transferred itself to India. Rick's at the Delhi Taj began serving Stoli Vanil and though the barman never had the imagination to do very much with it, this became my drink of choice whenever I went to Rick's.

But there was still a problem. As much as I liked vanilla vodka I was unable to find it on sale anywhere—not in New York, not in London, and not at any duty-free shop at any airport. All that the booze stores had were the standard vodkas—four different kinds of blackcurrant, three brands of orange vodka, six kinds of lemon vodka and Absolut's pepper vodka (great for a Bloody Mary, by the way).

In frustration I took to asking barmen where one could buy a bottle of vanilla vodka. This was no good. Most barmen have never bought a bottle of exotic liquor in their lives. They are dependant on beverage suppliers and booze distributors who sell them liquor by the case. It never occurs to them that normal people have to go to shops to buy their liquor.

Then, two years ago, a London barman took pity on me. He'd never bought a bottle of vanilla vodka for himself, he cheerfully conceded, but he did know of a shop that had the best collection of vodkas in England. He didn't have the address but he knew it was in Soho and was called Gerry's.

An afternoon of walking around led me to Old Compton Street where, amidst the gay pubs and the shops selling tight, muscle-revealing, rubbery, gay gear (you know the kind I mean, the sort of clothes that become macho when Salman Khan wears them in Hindi movies), I found this determinedly unfancy booze shop. To go to Gerry's is to be spellbound—especially if you like vodka. Unlike most shops which only stock the stuff that large distributors sell, Gerry's prides itself on selling vodkas that nobody in England has ever heard of. Because some of the booze is so obscure each of the bottles has before it a long card on which some vodka buff has explained what it is that makes the vodka so special. It is, in a sense, a wine shop with a difference: the clients are not wine snobs but serious drinkers. Gerry's must have over 200 vodkas. Some are relatively commonplace (Stolichnaya, Smirnoff, Absolut etc.), some are premium (Belvedere), and some are well-known mainly in their countries of origin (Wyborowa, for instance). Then there are the flavoured vodkas: every flavour you can think of from caramel to bison-grass. And then, there are the gimmicks. There's a vodka with marijuana, vodka with gold dust and even a bottle that has a little scorpion inside it (though I suspect it was tequila not vodka—I wouldn't know because I queasily averted my face). As you would expect, I found my bottle of Stoli Vanil there. I also found a slightly cheaper vanilla vodka, the Smirnoff version. But on the grounds that the people who run Gerry's clearly know their stuff I asked a salesman which one he recommended. He said that he'd never liked the Smirnoff version; he thought it was too chemical, which is why no barman ever used it. You are better off with the Stoli, he said.

And of course, he was right.

Since then I've been back to Gerry's many times. I have bought a cherry vodka, a chocolate vodka (great in theory, not so good to taste) and a coffee vodka. But my favourite remains Stoli Vanil. I should be using it for all the fancy cocktails that barmen specialize in, but truth be told, if you like a long, sweet, cool drink on a hot summer's day then your best bet is to pour a generous measure of Stoli Vanil in a tall glass, add lots of ice and fill to the brim with 7 Up, Sprite or (if you like a slight tang) Indian tonic water. It won't be particularly alcoholic. That's because Stoli makes its vanilla vodka at 35 per cent alcohol while most vodka is 40 per cent. The Absolut version (which, just for the record, I've never tried), is the full 40 per cent, and Stoli fans say that the vanilla flavour loses out. Stoli has a strong vanilla taste while Absolut is said to be more caramel-tasting.

This will probably make Absolut Vanilia (the silly spelling and variations on the word 'vanilla' are so that they can trademark the name) the new favourite for bartenders who like to use vanilla vodka for sugary cocktails. *The Sex and the City* episode features something called the Hunk Martini (the tiresome premise of this tedious series is that New York city women are *really* liberated and treat men as sex objects), though frankly I wouldn't want to date any woman whose favourite cocktail was made as follows: two parts Absolut Vanilia, two parts pineapple juice, half a part lemon juice and a quarter part sugar syrup.

But there's loads and loads of things you can do with a good vanilla vodka. You can substitute it in virtually all vodka recipes (it probably won't work well in a Bloody Mary but a screwdriver or a Cosmopolitan or a martini should be fine). You can mix it with Diet Coke. (Alternatively, you can mix ordinary vodka with Vanilla Coke.) You can use it with berry-based drinks. A typical bartenders' trick is to squash strawberries or raspberries, add a little sugar syrup, two parts of vanilla vodka and then top with tonic or (and this works much better) a little sparkling wine or champagne.

You can use vanilla vodka for desserts as well. Take a good vanilla ice cream (in Indian terms, Baskin-Robbins is your best bet), add some fruit (strawberries, *chikoos* or even bananas, but no citrus fruit), then douse the whole thing with a liqueur glass full of vanilla vodka. Why does it work so well? You know the old theory: vanilla smells remind people of their youth so you can drink alcohol and still feel virtuous. It also mixes brilliantly with any sweetish flavour (including chocolate), so it is the perfect cocktail ingredient.

Whatever the reason, vanilla is the hot flavour for nearly everything these days. And that suits me fine. The coffee I drink in the office is vanilla-flavoured. So is my bath gel. So is my favourite kind of Coca-Cola. So is a new range of flavoured Bacardi rum. So if you are the sort of chap who combines my love of vanilla with a taste for alcohol (which regrettably I do not possess; I have to keep using mixers), then the way to drink vanilla vodka properly is to take a shot glass, fill it to the brim with Stoli Vanil and down it in one go. Otherwise, put a few cubes of ice in a whisky tumbler, pour in the vodka and sip slowly.

As of now, I don't know anybody who sells vanilla vodka by

the bottle in India (you can get it on the Net from drinksdispensary.com but I'm not sure how they can deliver it to you), but most good (i.e. expensive) bars will stock it. In Delhi Rick's and Agni are still the best choice, and with so many new places opening in Calcutta and Bombay, you should have no difficulty finding it. Go out and look for it. You won't regret it.

*desi* delights

# the king of kababs

Is the day of the tandoor over? More and more people of my acquaintance seem to have tired of chicken tikkas. The fancy kabab, as far as they are concerned, is not one that comes out of the tandoor. Instead, it is the charcoal-grilled, melt-in-the-mouth *kakori* kabab. When sophisticated Indians want to order a sophisticated kabab, the *kakori* is the one they go for.

I hadn't recognized how far the legend of the *kakori* had spread till I spoke to a foodie relative who was due to visit Bombay. Was it easy to get foie gras in Bombay, she asked. I assured her that it was. Well, all right, she responded, adding, 'But what I really want to eat is the *kakori* kabab.' Fine, I said, but remember that foie gras is easier to find—even in Bombay—than a genuine *kakori* kabab.

What accounts for the legend of the *kakori*? Part of it is the simple scarcity factor. It is not a kabab that you will get at many restaurants. And many of those who do put it on their menus simply tart up their *seekh* kababs and pass them off as *kakori*s. Part of it is the texture; nearly everybody who has heard of North Indian food has heard of this flavourful kabab, so delicate that it dissolves in the mouth. And much of it—or so jealous hoteliers claim—has to do with the hype engendered by ITC, the hotel chain whose signature dish the *kakori* has become.

There are many stories surrounding the origin of the *kakori*, and I'm not sure that I believe any of them. But for what it's worth, here's the most common version: the Nawab of Kakori in Uttar

Pradesh had a dental problem which made it difficult for him to chew. But the Nawab was a noted gourmet who longed for the taste of meat which, alas, he could no longer bite into. So he commanded his chefs to come up with a kabab that would melt in the mouth. And they invented the *kakori*, a kabab so delicate that even a toothless man can enjoy it.

It is a good story but I've heard so many variations of the same basic tale—often involving Wajid Ali Shah—to explain the origins of so many other dishes that I have yet to be convinced that this story bears any relation to reality.

What is true is that the kakori is a kabab which originated as a part of UP Muslim cuisine. (Very different from the tandoori kababs that Punjabi Hindu restaurateurs dished out: the chicken tikka for example.) People in Lucknow say that they've grown up with the *kakori* and that it has been a favourite dish on wedding menus for many decades now.

It came to national attention, however, only in 1977, when ITC opened the Maurya Hotel in Delhi. According to Manjit Gill, now ITC's Corporate Chef, the *kakori* kabab had first appeared on the menu at the Mughal in Agra (ITC's first hotel, which opened in 1976), and had been a runaway success. It was retained for the menu at Delhi's newly opened Mayur restaurant where, recalls Gill, it became the best-selling item.

And how did ITC, then comprised mainly of defectors from the Oberois and ITDC, hear of the *kakori*? Nobody is sure, but most people are inclined to give the credit to Ajit Haksar, ITC's legendary former Chairman and the founder of the hotel division. Haksar was a foodie and encouraged the chain to hire cooks from Lucknow. Men like Imtiaz Qureshi, who ran profitable wedding catering operations, were asked to don chef's uniforms, work in hotel kitchens and introduce their dishes to a wider audience.

One such dish was the kakori.

At that stage, most restaurant-going Indians (outside of Lucknow) knew only the standard kababs of tandoori cuisine. And so the first reference point was the *seekh*, which the *kakori* resembles. But while there were obvious points of similarity—both kababs are made from mincemeat and are the same shape—the *seekh* is a much cruder kabab, lacking both the *kakori*'s melt-in-the-mouth texture and the complex spicing that is its hallmark.

Though nobody at today's ITC is wild about accepting this, my guess is that the take-off point for the kakori came in the late 1980s when the old Mayur was closed and the new Dum Pukht opened. (In those days Gill was Executive Chef at the Maurya.) ITC asked Jiggs Kalra to help with the Dum Pukht menu and its promotion. Jiggs settled on Imtiaz, whom he sold to the media as the greatest Indian chef in history, and then also pushed a few dishes: the *dum* biryani, the *raan*, and of course, the *kakori* kabab.

The effect of Jiggs's hyping was that ITC received (well-deserved) recognition as the chain that had the best Indian food, the best chefs, and the best dishes. Though Dum Pukht never approached the financial success of Bukhara (which does over Rs 3 lakh worth of business a day versus a more modest Rs 80,000 or so for Dum Pukht), it became ITC's signature restaurant. If Bukhara was India's answer to a steak house, Dum Pukht was the Michelin three-star fine-dining equivalent.

By the end of the 1980s and the early 1990s, the *kakori* had begun to appear on menus all over India. The Taj group, in direct homage to ITC, stole a manager and two chefs from the Maurya and started Sonargaon (a North Indian restaurant with a Bengali name) at the Taj Bengal, introducing a menu that was uncannily similar to the ITC tradition. Sonargaon brought the *kakori* kabab to Calcutta, but the Taj version never quite approached the quality of the original, and on at least one occasion I found it wasn't available because the chefs they had stolen from ITC were off and nobody else in the kitchen could get the mixture to stay on the skewer. (Arvind Saraswat, then the Taj's Director of Food Production for the Northern Region, says that he doesn't think this is likely. But believe me, it did happen.)

Other hotels that tried to reproduce the *kakori* produced variations that ranged from 'edible' (sometimes) to 'plain lousy' (most times). To this day the *kakori* has remained an ITC signature dish. Everybody else may say they know how to make it but to get the real thing you have to go to an ITC hotel. (Or to Lucknow.)

What makes the *kakori so* special? The broad answer is that not everybody can get the tenderness right. In North Indian cookery, 'tender' is usually a code word for 'animal fat'. So it is with the *kakori*. Except that it can't be any old animal fat. To get the right sort of tenderness you have to take the fat from around a lamb's kidneys.

At the Maurya, where Dum Pukht is currently on a culinary high, Chef Sultan says that they mix 80 per cent minced meat with 20 per cent minced kidney fat and then mince the mixture again five times to get the perfect texture.

Next, they come to the difficult bit. They add papaya to tenderize the meat. But, according to Manjit Gill, this is harder than it sounds. The enzymes in the papaya are supposed to break down the fibres in the meat. But you need to be a kakori expert to know how much papaya to add, depending on the temperature, the time of year, and the ripeness of the papaya.

Then comes the so-called secret part. The cooks who make the *kakori* closely guard the secrets of their masala. We know that it contains garam masala, rose petals, *kewra*, cloves and the like, but the exact quantities are never revealed. All the same, given that so many people in Lucknow can now make the *kakori* mixture, the recipe can't be that much of a secret. Certainly, you can now buy a pre-prepared *kakori* masala in Lucknow.

Once the mixture is ready, you need to keep it out for an hour. Then, it is either put in the fridge or in the deep freeze. At the Maurya, Chef Sultan tells me that they find a cold mixture is easier to place on a skewer than the warmer version. The kabab is charcoal-grilled over a medium flame for three to four minutes. It is then jerked off the skewer with a delicate flick of the wrist. Use too much pressure and you will break the *kakori*. It must be taken to the table as soon as it is ready. After fifteen minutes away from the flame the *kakori* will lose the velvety texture that is its claim to fame.

A close relative of the *kakori* is the *galouti*, made famous by the Tunda kababwallah of Lucknow (who, in turn, was also made nationally famous by Jiggs). Apparently (and I claim to be no expert—the Tunda kababwallah's restaurant is so full of flies that my investigatory expedition came to an abrupt halt), they use the same basic mixture as the *kakori* but they shallow-fry it. As each lump of meat hits the pan, it takes on its own shape and is known as a poor man's version (no problems with making it keep its shape on the skewer) of the *kakori*.

So, is the *kakori* worth all the hype?

I have to say that I don't know. Many years ago, when I first went to Lucknow, I was delighted to be exposed to so much good food. At the time (perhaps he is still there), the celebrated chef Ghulam Rasool was cooking in the kitchens of the Lucknow Taj and he made the most amazing meals for me, including, of course, a killer *kakori* kabab.

Except that it turned out—quite literally—to be a killer *kakori*. After three days of a diet rich in animal fat my liver resigned its position in my body and went on a protest strike. I was so sick that I spent a whole day in bed recovering from the good food.

For several months after that I steered clear of the *kakori*. When the same foodie relative who longs for foie gras and *kakori* kababs asked me what the food in Lucknow was like, I told her, 'I will throw up if I ever see another *kakori* kabab.'

So, let's be clear about this. To eat the *kakori* on a regular basis you have to have the constitution of a nawab. Put crudely, so much animal fat is simply not good for you. Of course, that doesn't rule out the odd kabab, but you have to be aware that the dish comes with a health warning.

As for the taste—well, again I don't know. When Jiggs first took me to Dum Pukht, it was the *kakori* I fell in love with. But the older I've got the less keen I have been on it. Perhaps I am still wary of all that animal fat after being laid low in Lucknow.

Arvind Saraswat says it is sacrilege to be rude about the *kakori* but push him and he'll tell you that he thinks that the kabab is a triumph of hype over taste. He thinks that the meat is minced too fine for anyone to enjoy the taste, and reckons that all you get is an overdose of animal fat and way too much masala.

Others, such as the Maurya's Chef Sultan, regard it as the king of kababs (well, he would, wouldn't he?), and I suspect that if you were to conduct a poll among diners, it would probably emerge as the favourite kabab of those who have eaten it.

So I'm not passing any judgments. Try one for yourself and make up your own mind.

# the unsung nizam's roll

Every great city adds to India's gastronomic heritage. Bombay gave us *bhelpuri* and *paav bhaji*. Madras gave us the dosa (though it was restauranteurs from Karnataka who took it national). Delhi—or more specifically, the old Moti Mahal restaurant—gave us tandoori chicken. (Don't believe all that rubbish about the North West Frontier—it was Punjabi Hindu refugees who more or less invented the dish we know today.)

Only Calcutta seems to have lost out. The only Bengali dishes that have passed into the Indian mainstream are the sweets. And even they are not really made by Bengalis any longer. In most of the country, it is sweaty *halwais* from the cow belt who churn out the *rasagollas*. People who've lived in Calcutta say that the city has many gastronomical delights to offer: *jhaal muri* (it's rubbish—what *bhel* would be like if you left it to Bengalis); the *dal vadas* you get near Vardaan Market in Camac Street (crap); *telebhaja* (Bengali *pakoras*—better than the North Indian version but that's about it); and the famous *puchkas* (very good, but from the same family as Delhi's *golgappa* and Bombay's *pani puri*).

There is, however, one genuine classic Calcutta dish: the Nizam's Roll. The great mystery about it is why it has never travelled successfully out of Calcutta and enjoyed the national (or international) success that is its due.

You are probably familiar with the essence of a Nizam's Roll, even if it is in some distant *avatar* as the *kathi* kabab roll or even

Bombay's not terribly appetizing Frankie.

The roll gets its name from Nizam's, one of Calcutta's oldest restaurants, where it was either invented or made famous depending on who you believe. Nizam's still makes the roll and this is how the classic Roll is made.

First, pieces of boneless mutton are marinated. (It is mutton. Big signs declare 'we do not use beef' so perish that unworthy thought.) Then, they are cooked on wooden skewers over a charcoal fire. When the kababs (because that is basically what they are) have been cooked, they are taken off the flames and put aside.

Next, the cook takes out a huge, thick *tawa* that is allegedly sixty years old. On this *tawa*, he makes a *maida paratha*. The egg is broken on the *tawa* and while it is scrambling, the *paratha* is placed on top of it and turned around quickly, so you have the egg nicely tucked inside the *paratha*.

While the *paratha* is still on the *tawa*, he takes a couple of the already cooked mutton kababs and places them in the centre. Then, in a quick, almost continuous movement, he rolls the *paratha* around the kabab to create the cylindrical shape of the classic Nizam's Roll.

The end result is divine. You can eat it with chutney but you should really eat it on its own.

While Nizam's still serves the real thing, you get variations all over Calcutta. Usually, these bastardize the dish by refusing to go the extra mile of charcoal grilling the kababs first. Often, the kababs are pan fried and because they don't taste right, some roll*wallahs* add a thick gravy or a masala. This is not necessarily bad; it just isn't the real thing.

So why hasn't the roll travelled out of Calcutta? If you can eat dosas in Delhi, tandoori chicken in Bombay and *bhelpuri* in Madras, why does this classic dish remain the preserve of the Calcutta*wallah*?

It is one of those gastronomic mysteries to which there is no easy answer. If the *kathi* kabab roll (which is the same concept) can find wide acceptability, then why can't the world's greatest roll?

Sadly, to enjoy the real thing, you'll have to go to Calcutta.

## *bhelpuri*: it's all about texture

*Chaat* is, for better or for worse, a North Indian invention. Vijay Goel, the affable Minister of State in the Prime Minister's Office, was researching the history of his Chandni Chowk constituency and his staff traced the origins of many of today's popular *chaat* dishes to the Mughal period.

No doubt the *chaatwallah*s of Lucknow claim a similar provenance for their own varieties and almost everywhere in India where you find *chaat*, there will be a North Indian (possibly a UP-ite) behind the stall, mashing the potatoes with his hands and ladling in the *dahi* while simultaneously chewing *paan*.

In Calcutta, where *puchka*s (a cousin of the *golgappa*) are a civic obsession, the men who make them frequently speak no Bengali, have no idea who Rabindranath Tagore is and smile tolerantly as their customers address them as 'bhaiyya'. As proud as Calcutta is of the *phuchka*, the dish is as Bengali as N.D. Tiwari.

The same is true of Bombay where the *chaatwallah*s actually encourage you to call them 'bhaiyya' (not as in 'brother' or even 'milkman' but as in 'fat, sweaty person of possible North Indian origin'). The famous *chaat* stalls on Chowpatty beach now have the owner's name emblazoned in neon lights, but as they all say 'Sharma Bhelpuri Centre', this is not much help when it comes to telling one from the other. (The easiest way to clear the beach, I've always thought, would be to stand by the water, shout 'Sharma' and then watch as all the *chaatwallahs* drop their *puris* and rush like lemmings to the sea.)

Despite the dominance of 'bhaiyyas' (their term, not mine) on the beaches of Chowpatty and Juhu, Bombay has the distinction of having invented the one item of *chaat* that does not have a North Indian origin: *bhelpuri*.

The origins of *bhelpuri* are now the subject of some dispute but legend has it that the dish was invented not on Chowpatty beach but at a restaurant called Vithal, near the Victoria Terminus railway station. (Don't bother going there now. They have a 'vegetarian Chinese' menu and offer 'Chinese *bhelpuri*'.)

The tang in the *bhelpuri*—the onion, the garlic in the chutney and the sweet-sour *khajur-imli* tastes—has nothing to do with the pious Sharmas and their time-honoured techniques of crumbling deep-fried foods (samosas, *kachoris*, *tikkis* and God alone knows what else) on a *patta* before adding *dahi* and *chaat masala*. It was the contribution of the city's Gujaratis who recognized the potential for complex flavours in the sweaty simplicity of North Indian *chaat*.

While North Indian *chaat* usually had two or three basic ingredients (*papri+dahi+aloo*, for instance), *bhelpuri* had up to fifteen (*sev*, crumbled *puris*, onions, raw mango, potatoes, coriander, three kinds of chutney, etc.). Unusually, the final product did not depend on *dahi*, nor was it built around a single deep-fried dish (a *tikki*, a *kachori*, etc.), though some of the ingredients (*sev*, for instance) were deep-fried. The complexity was heightened by the mixture of textures.

Generally, Indian food is not too hot on texture; *chaat is* no exception. But *bhelpuri* is all about texture: soft but firm boiled potatoes, crunchy *sev*, crispy puffed rice and small pieces of onion that squish as you bite into them.

And because there were so many ingredients and each serving of *bhel* had to be made fresh (otherwise it got soggy), everything depended on the *chaatwallah*. If he had a generous hand with the onions for instance, he could throw all the flavours out of gear; less potato and the dish would lack the starchy solidness that the potatoes contributed, and so on. All food (and *chaat*) depends, to some extent, on the cook; but *bhel* was the first *chaat* dish where the individual *chaatwallah* counted for so much.

Even if Vithal did invent *bhelpuri*, the restaurant soon lost any special claims to it. Gujarati housewives began making it—at home along with more typical Gujarati snacks such as *dahi-wadi* (sometimes called *khandvi*), *patra* and *dhokla*.

Because the dish lent itself to so many variations, there were soon so many different varieties that each version became known for the nice Gujarati lady who perfected it.

Not content with *bhelpuri*, Gujarati housewives then took on the rest of the *chaatwallah*'s repertoire, revising, inventing and renaming his dishes. For instance, the *chaatwallah* made *pakodi puri* by stuffing a large *golgappa puri* with cooked *pakodi*s and then adding *dahi* and chutney. In the hands of the housewives, *pakodi puri* came to be made without any *pakodi* at all. Instead, boiled potatoes, sprouted *moong* and *channa* (gram) became the filling. To this day Gujaratis will offer you this version of *pakodi puri* though *chaatwallah*s call their version *dahi batata puri* (usually made without gram and *moong*). But Gujaratis also surrendered any claims to their *chaat* (as they have to *paav-bhaji*).

Because *bhelpuri* consists of so many different and quite varied ingredients, it soon became a metaphor for the cosmopolitan nature of Bombay itself. Nearly every community began producing its own *bhel*.

The *chaatwallah*s included it in their repertoire—but you'll always miss home-made *bhel* if you try the Chowpatty version (unusual for a *chaat* dish).

Mangalorean owners of Udipi restaurants produced their adaptation (marked by excessive use of lemon) at restaurants with such names as Shetty's. And even Sindhis produced a hit version, perfected at the Kailash Parbat Chaat House in Colaba.

Sadly, *bhelpuri* does not travel well. You can't get a decent *bhel* in Delhi: most North Indian *chaatwallah*s are foxed by the complexity of the dish. And the only halfway decent *bhel* I've ever eaten in Calcutta was at Tit-Bits which did the home-made Gujarati version, but I've not been back for ten years.

For the real thing, I go to Bombay.

# the lost art of tandoori chicken

When you consider that tandoori chicken is the most famous Indian dish in the world it is a little mystifying that we know so little about its origins and history. The mythology of tandoori chicken links it with Afghanistan or the North West Frontier where, or so we are led to believe, rough-hewn Pathans survive on a diet of family *naan, dal bukhara* and chicken tikka masala (if not tandoori chicken and *murgh makhni*).

This is an attractive image but it may owe more to hotel restaurants with such names as Kandahar (known as IC 814 to regulars) and Bukhara than to history. Yashwant Raj, *HT*'s resident Afghan expert, has travelled from Kabul to Mazhar, greeting warlords and defeated Al Qaida fighters, but has never come across a tandoor. 'They do barbecue their food,' he says, 'but they tend to do it on open fires. I've never seen any evidence of any tandoori cooking. Even the *naan* is different from ours.'

So where does tandoori cooking come from? Though thousands of trees have been felled to publish learned treatises on the origins of that celebrated British dish, Chicken Tikka Masala (made traditionally, with that most Indian of ingredients, a tin of tomato soup), relatively little attention has been paid to the origins of tandoori cooking (without which there would be no Chicken Tikka Masala to begin with).

The first time that most people in India heard of tandoori chicken was when Moti Mahal in Delhi's Daryaganj popularized the dish in the 1950s. It travelled abroad in the 1960s and became popular in London in 1966 when the first Gaylord opened on Mortimer Street. Till then the Bangladeshis, who ran 90 per cent of the UK's Indian restaurants, had never heard of it (though they were called East Pakistanis in those days and should have had some idea of what Punjabis were eating in the western part of their country). By the 1980s however, nobody could open an Indian restaurant anywhere in the world unless he put tandoori chicken on the menu.

So did Moti Mahal invent the dish? Clearly not. The ownership of Moti Mahal has changed since those days but there is broad agreement that the first tandoori chickens came from West Punjab along with refugees from Lahore.

One romantic version (of which I could find no substantiation) has the dish being invented in a Lahore restaurant in the 1930s. During Partition, the entire staff fled to India and, or so this story goes, the owner opened a restaurant in Dehra Dun while one of the waiters came to Delhi. The owner's version was forgotten while the waiter struck it big in Delhi.

If you disregard all such apocryphal stories, some things remain clear—if surprising. For instance, here's surprise number one: unlike the bulk of North Indian vegetarian cuisine, tandoori chicken has a Hindu rather than Muslim origin. Surprise number two: it was actually invented by Punjabis.

The origin of the tandoor—as in the clay oven itself—is the subject of some speculation (like everything else in the saga). One thing is certain: it is subcontinental in origin. There are ovens (including one called a *tandeel*) in West Asia, but the tandoor itself is only found in India and Pakistan. According to K.T. Achaya, author of definitive texts on the history of Indian food, early tandoors have been found in the ruins of the Indus Valley Civilization.

In his *Science and Civilization in India (3000 BC–1500 BC)*, A.K. Bag writes of small, mud-plastered ovens found in the Indus Valley site of Kalibangan, 'very strongly resembling the present-day tandoor'. We have no record of what was cooked in these early tandoors but my guess is that it wasn't chicken.

Long before the tandoor became the home of the dead chicken, Punjabis installed tandoors in the courtyards of their homes to bake rotis. The history of the tandoori roti is well documented. What is not clear is: when did some bright spark decide to put a whole chicken into the tandoor?

We do know that when Punjabi refugees had to make a living in Delhi in 1948-49, many of them opened *dhaba*s. They had very little money and could not buy utensils for their kitchens. So they served a simple menu. They placed rotis and chicken on skewers and cooked them in the tandoor. And at night, after the customers had gone home, they slow-cooked a black dal. That basic menu—roti, dal, and tandoori chicken—remains a staple of North Indian restaurants to this day, though other tandoori items (tikka, *seekh* and the like) have been added to the repertoire.

The original Hindu Punjabi refugees had economic reasons for the simplicity of their menu—you could cook a dozen chickens at a time in the tandoor—but modern-day restaurants stick to those principles for the most basic of reasons: give the public what they want.

Where India has lost out has been in the explosion of tandoori-based dishes from 1970s onwards. The Chicken Tikka Sandwich and Chicken Tikka Masala have both been popularized in Britain. Most restaurants at five-star hotels offer Tandoori Prawns but the dish has never really taken off. Contrast this with Tandoori Scallops, first invented in the 1980s in London by the Bombay Brasserie (the scallop is not native to our waters) and the forerunner of a variety of fancy tandoori fish preparations (such as the Salmon Tikka).

Sadly, we've never built on our tandoori heritage. The term itself has become a bit of a joke. (Sample 1980s joke: What is the national bird of Khalistan? Answer: Tandoori Chicken.) A new generation of hacks has destroyed the flavour of the original dish by using tasteless broiler chickens and too much ariticial food colour.

And we don't even care that it is nearly impossible to get a first-rate version of the most famous Indian dish in the world at most of our restaurants.

# hot on the idli-dosa trail

Whenever people point to the success of fast food chains in India—the queues at McDonald's, the ubiquitous Domino's pizza man trying to beat the half-hour deadline and so on—I always respond that we already have an Indian fast food that beats the hell out of the *channa* burger (or whatever it is that McDonald's sells after the demise of the goat burger) or the Pizza Margarita. It is called the dosa and along with the idli it is the fast food of choice for most Indians.

Unlike the US imports it is not wildly expensive, it does not need brand building or heavy marketing, it is always vegetarian and its cooking requires a certain modicum of skill. Best of all, it is a dish you can find all over India. Everybody orders dosas for lunch at my office in Delhi; they did the same when I worked in Calcutta and I grew up on dosas from Udipi restaurants in Bombay.

One day, when I find a TV channel with money to burn, I would love to make a documentary film on the Masala Dosa's Trail to Fame (other episodes: In Search of the First Tandoori Chicken; The Invention of Sino-Ludhiana Cuisine; The History of Indian *Chaat*; and many more). Most of us think that the dosa has always been popular as a cheap and easily available fast food but I remember it differently.

It was a canteen staple in Bombay in the1960s but as late as 1972 I remember introducing bemused Punjabi students at my North Indian boarding school to the delights of a hot, crisp dosa and a fluffy, steaming idli. They had never heard of either, growing up in North India.

I remember, also, my mother returning from a trip to Delhi in the early 1970s and marvelling that she'd eaten a masala dosa at a relatively fancy restaurant (it was the Woodlands at the old Lodhi Hotel), rather than the more modest establishments we associated it with in Bombay. And though we often stayed at the Oberoi Intercontinental Hotel (as it then was) in Delhi in the late 1960s, the breakfast menu stuck to such staples as 'eggs, sunny side up'; 'minute steak', and 'pancakes with maple syrup'. (Very nice pancakes actually, if my childhood memories are to be trusted.) I never actually saw a dosa on a five-star hotel menu till 1973 when it turned up at the Shamiana at the Bombay Taj (which also put it on the breakfast menu, serving the cross between a normal dosa and a paper dosa that has now become a five-star standard).

So when did the idli and dosa go national? When did they become a truly all-Indian (as distinct from South Indian) fast food? When did the simple set dosas of South Indian home cooking transform themselves into the crispy wonders of restaurant kitchens?

As far as I can tell, nobody seems to know. India now has a multiplicity of food writers ready to tell you how to eat foie gras or twist your pasta around a fork (I'm not knocking those subjects, having done a fair amount of that sort of thing myself), but the only time any of us bothers to write about Indian food is when a restaurant chef decides he wants to publicize his biryani or flog his kababs. The less glamorous dishes—the idli-dosas, the *channa-bhaturas*, the butter chickens—simply do not register on the truffle and foie gras scale.

So I've had to struggle to conduct a little research into the origins of the dosa and idli boom and what I've found is more than a little surprising.

First of all, the North Indian notion that dosas are a 'Madras food', is only partly correct. Yes, the dosa (or more correctly, the *dosai*) is popular in Tamil Nadu, but that's not the version that has spread all over India. The Tamil dosa is a soft, thick product, but it is the Karnataka version which is thin, crisp and large that has really travelled all over the country.

Both versions have their origins in ancient India. According to food historian K.T. Achaya, the *dosai* first appears in Tamil Sangam literature in the sixth century AD. The Malayali *appam*, a close relative of both the idli and the dosa, is mentioned in the *Perumpanuru* of the fifth century. But while the *appam* recipe has remained unchanged for sixteen centuries, the early dosas were pure rice products, without the dal that is now an integral part of the recipe.

The idli came later and the first references are in Kannada (rather than Tamil) literature. In a Kannada work of AD 920, it is referred to as one of the eighteen items offered by a lady to a young man who visits her home. The first Tamil references came only in the seventeenth century. There is some dispute as to whether the early idlis had any rice (the recipes recommend only *urad* dal), whether the batter was fermented, and how the steaming was done.

One innovative theory is that the modern idli has an Indonesian origin. The Indonesians were fond of rice, understood fermentation and used steaming techniques. They even have a steamed, fermented dish called *kedli*. So, could the Hindu cooks who accompanied the Indonesian kings on their travels have created the modern version of the dish using the techniques they had learned?

All this awaits further research but we do know that it was restaurateurs from Karnataka who took their version of the dosa to Bombay. The Udipi restaurant has long been a staple of humble eating out in Bombay and the early masala dosas found fame there. The Udipi*wallah*s also introduced us to the *medu vada* (or just '*vada*' on most menus). This dish can be traced with some certainty to the small town of Maddur, midway between Bangalore and Mysore. The *vada* first came to public attention eight decades ago and is still made the same way with *rava* and fried onion shreds.

More controversially, Achaya claims that the *bajji* originated in the same area, travelled North, reached Gujarat and became the *bhajiya* and then turned into the pakora when it reached North India. Further, he suggests, Portuguese missionaries and seamen took it to Japan where it became *tempura*.

Without wishing to make excessive claims for South Indian fast food (next we'll be claiming that pancakes descended from dosas), it seems clear that some genius took an ancient South Indian snack food, dispensed with some of the authentic touches (gunpowder with the idlis rather than *sambhar*) and turned it into a genuine Indian fast food.

There have been fancy variations since then: in the late 1970s, Delhi restaurants were trying chicken dosas and *keema* dosas, and in 1977, Paul Bocuse, on a visit to India, tried fusion prawn dosas. But such is the brilliance of the dish that you can't improve on the version we know and love.

Some day we will find the people who took the *dosai* national, and give them the credit they derserve.

# the race for indian food

People often ask me if I have ever encountered any racism at fancy London restaurants. (Answer: no, don't be ridiculous. At those prices the only people who can afford to go there are rich Arabs or foreign tourists with more money than sense.) So I was delighted to finally read about a restaurant in England that refused to serve dinner to a couple of South Asian extraction—for reasons of race. At least, now, I'll have a story to tell, I thought.

But here's the catch: it was an Indian restaurant.

Our story is set in the picturesque Lake District in the small town of Bowness-on-Windermere. A South Asian couple, Moshinali Darugar and his wife Rehmat asked the receptionist at their hotel, the Royal, if they knew of a good Indian restaurant in the vicinity.

Yes, said the receptionist, and directed them to the Emperor of India.

When the Darugars arrived at the Emperor of India, they were told that the restaurant did not have a table for them. This was odd, because, as far as they could judge, it was virtually empty.

The Darugars returned to the Royal hotel and complained to the receptionist. She was surprised enough to phone the Emperor of India anonymously and ask for a table.

Oh yes, said the restaurant, we have plenty of room.

The Royal's manager, Maria Walker, then got in on the act and asked for an explanation from The Emperor of India. She was told that it was a policy not to serve Asians 'as they caused too many problems and English people were easier to look after.'

Ms Walker was outraged. 'It was racist,' she declared. 'We will certainly not be sending any other visitors there.'

I was intrigued.

An Indian restaurant run by racists who wouldn't serve Indians?

It defied belief. Had some curry-loving fascist decided to set up a restaurant that would only serve white people like himself? After all, we know that there's a certain kind of yob who treats a hot curry as a virility test and thinks that Balti cuisine comes from India, not Birmingham.

But no. The restaurant's manager is named Fozle Rabbi, according to *The Times* (London), and as far as I can tell, the Emperor of India is—like 90 per cent of all Indian restaurants in the UK—run by Bangladeshis.

So why would Bangladeshis turn away Mr and Mrs Moshinali Darugar?

Mr Rabbi (is that really his name or has *The Times* got it wrong?—with Anglicized Bengali names, it is hard to be certain) explained why the Emperor of India did not like serving Indians.

'People from India and Pakistan complain that our dishes do not have enough hot spices. Our menu is for the English . . . so we say that we are fully booked if Asians ask.'

So, it wasn't about race at all. It was about authenticity.

Until the early nineties, when Brits began to eat sophisticated (i.e. genuine) Indian food, the cuisine at most Indian restaurants in the UK was about as authentically subcontinental as the food in Calcutta's Tangra is authentically Chinese.

The parallel is apt. Indian Chinese is a cuisine in its own right. I've been to a restaurant in Bangkok called Copper Chimney—no relation to the Bombay original—that actually serves a menu of 'Indian-Chinese' food. (Because most of our so-called Chinese chefs are Nepalis or Tibetans and even the local Chinese have never been further east than Calcutta, there is no sense of authenticity. Nor are the guests looking for the real thing. They want Sino-Ludhianvi cuisine.)

So it is with Indian food in the UK. The British have always been obsessed with Indian food. Not many people know, for instance, that Worcestershire Sauce started out as a chutney.

According to the most popular version of its origin, a retired Raj Colonel went into Lea and Perrin's establishment in Worcester, gave them a recipe for a chutney that he had brought back from India and asked them to make up a batch for him.

Lea and Perrin did so. But they also ran up a barrel's worth for themselves. This lay, unattended, for several months till somebody noticed it. By then the chutney had fermented so that it tasted nothing like the original, but Lea and Perrin loved the decomposed version so much that they promptly sold it as their own sauce.

But while the early curries were largely authentic because of the Raj connection (the first Indian restaurant outside of India was opened by Edward Palmer, a Raj hand, who called it Veeraswamy's), everything changed in the late fifties and early sixties when a flood of immigrants, nearly all from the East Pakistani district of Sylhet, arrived in the UK and entered the restaurant business.

Because Brits had no time for oily Bengali fish curries and were singularly unimpressed by the alleged magical properties of *ilish maachh*, the Sylhetis stole Punjabi dishes and bastardized a cuisine. Then, they stole the names of dishes from other parts of India: *vindaloo* from Goa, *patia* from the Parsis, *bhaji* (for what we call pakoras in North India) from Madras etc. and applied these names to crappy dishes that no self-respecting Indian would eat. In the late sixties, they discovered tandoors and managed to bastardize that cuisine as well.

The food was uniformly disgusting, but because the East Pakistanis paid themselves low wages, they were able to keep prices down. So, Indian food became the cheap option for Brits and eventually the Sylhetis even invented their signature dish—Chicken Tikka Masala, which had a recipe that called for a can of Campbell's tomato soup, not an ingredient that is normally much in demand in kitchens in Delhi or Dhaka.

Though there are many restaurants that claim to have introduced 'real' Indian food to the UK, the significant ones were probably Gaylord, which, in 1966, popularized tandoori cooking; Shezan, which in the seventies became Egon Ronay's restaurant of the year; and of course, the Taj group's Bombay Brasserie which rewrote all the rules by hiring a head waiter from Langan's Brasserie (in 1982, the trendiest restaurant in London), serving dishes nobody in England had heard of, inventing new variations (tandoori scallops for instance) and taking Indian food upmarket.

Now, there is a clear division between the classy/genuine establishments (nearly all owned by Indians) and the curry houses (all owned by Sylhetis). The Brasserie still flourishes, but two Indian restaurants, Zaika and Tamarind, have a Michelin star each; a new place, Benares (with the old Tamarind chef), has been massively hyped; and the Cinnamon Club attracts British MPs.

My problem is that because I'm loath to eat Indian in London (it's a long way to go for tandoori salmon), I can't tell you how good the upmarket places are. But I gather that Chutney Mary now has the best Indian food in London, Veeraswamy's (it still exists but has been revamped) is terrific and I heartily recommend Masala Zone where I go for *chaat* whenever I'm in London on a vegetarian Tuesday. All three are owned by my friend Namita Panjabi, the brightest, most breathtakingly elegant restaurateur I've ever met—so I must declare an interest. Similar qualifications apply to the highly-rated Chor Bizarre, owned by another friend, Rohit Khattar; and the Bombay Brasserie, whose manager Arun Harnal I've known for twenty years.

So what did the Darugars do wrong? They went—I would guess—to a Sylheti curry house where the chef had probably made two basic curries in the morning, added meat, prawns, chicken, cream or chilli to them as per the order and contented himself with serving Indian food to people who couldn't tell a chapatti from a chopstick. The last thing he wanted was for some Indian or

Pakistani to come in and ask for the real thing. Far simpler to stick to ignorant Brits.

You could blame Mr Darugar—who has lived in Britain for forty-three years—for making the mistake of going to a curry house. But I know the feeling. Two months ago, tired and low in London, I decided that I'd had it with Gordon Ramsay's Cream of Cauliflower and Nobu's Black Cod in Miso. I needed some dal therapy. And so, as the staff of the Michelin-starred Tamarind watched incredulously, I ignored the fancy menu and had plain yellow dal and chawal and washed it down with Diet Coke.

And very good it felt too.

# back to basics: *desi* food still rules

A fortnight ago, Manjit Gill, ITC's Corporate Chef, asked me to come and attend a culinary conference for chefs. I don't—if I can help it—accept speaking engagements, and so a compromise was reached. The organizers of the conference would arrange a session in which various people who ate out a lot or wrote about food would form a panel and I would play the moderator.

Did I, the organizers asked, have any ideas on who should attend? Well, I said, I knew various people in Delhi who were very knowledgeable about food, among them my friends Shankar Bajpai (the former diplomat who is an accomplished cook), Namita Kaul Bhattacharya (before she turned vegetarian), and of course, the mainstay of my food column, the Princess, who despite her vegetarianism, has managed to go to every trendy restaurant in the world (and sent back the Spaghetti Alio Olio at every Italian restaurant that serves it). None of them, alas, I warned, would want to come.

As for food writers, there were very few in Delhi I respected. There was Marryam H. Reshii, whose praises I have sung before, there was *HT City's* Sourish Bhattacharya, and there was of course, the Queen of Delhi's food writers, the formidable Sabina Sehgal Saikia herself. And that's about it.

But, I told the organizers, the final decision was theirs.

And so, when I turned up at the Intercontinental Hotel (the

one owned by Lalit Suri, not the thing in Nehru Place), to chair the two-hour session, I was curious: who had they invited?

My curiosity turned rapidly to terror. It turned out they had invited nobody. Obviously there had been some miscommunication, because they said they sensed that my unwillingness to provide any names meant that I didn't want anybody else on the dais. Apart from the arrogance that this implied on my part, there was another problem. Having arrived at the venue ready to say things like 'and how do you respond to that?' or 'let me throw that question to the whole panel', I now found that I had to wing it for two hours—sit alone on stage and try and seem knowledgeable in front of an audience of trained culinary professionals.

In the end, I did what I always do in moments of panic. I spoke for forty-five minutes (forty-five minutes? I hear you gasp. Not bad for a bullshitter, eh?), and then spent the rest of the session encouraging the chefs to talk instead.

That still left the problem of what to actually say to fill up the time. So I made three points, all three of which I'm going to cunningly recycle here.

1. There is a much greater sophistication at the top end of the food market. My thirteen-year-old son's favourite foods are (a) sushi and (b) carpaccio. You could argue that he's not exactly representative of his generation but two things are worth remembering.

First of all, he can get both foods in India. Virtually every Italian restaurant you can think of will make carpaccio (though my son's favourite remains Ananda Solomon's version at Bombay's Trattoria). Sushi is slightly more difficult to find but my son manages to find it at India Jones at the Bombay Oberoi (or the Hilton or whatever they're going to call it) and says that it is also available at some hotel in Juhu. In Delhi the Hyatt does sushi, but the only world-class sushi in India of course remains the stuff at Sakura at Delhi's Nikko Hotel (the rice is perfect and they even do toro—which is nice for those who can afford it at Rs 450 a piece).

Even five years ago all of this would have been difficult to find. Food and beverage managers would have insisted—probably accurately—that Indians don't eat raw beef. And as for raw fish, forget it!

It is, I think, possible to argue, that though there is a greater variety of cuisines available now than a decade ago, most of them are junk food versions of the real thing. TK's is a Benihana-type fun restaurant; La Piazza is a pizza and pasta place with ideas above its station; there's no real adventure in the menus at Delhi's La Rochelle or Bombay's Rotisserie, Maroush does what most people abroad would regard as takeaway Lebanese with a belly dancer thrown in; Delhi's Pan Asian is basically a South East Asian food court (though the Bombay version has the best Chinese food in India); the only thing Middle Eastern about Kafe Fontana is the shish touk; India Jones is an SOTC package tour of the Orient; and so on.

But never mind haute cuisine. At least all these places exist. What's more, most of them do well. So at the top end of the market Indians are becoming more adventurous.

2. But does this adventurousness extend to the rest of the market? I don't know. I have this terrible suspicion that it is only a tiny minority at the top that bothers with gastronomic adventure. The average punter, I suspect, hasn't changed that much.

It is a truism that when most middle to upper class Indians go out to eat they want to eat Indian food of the sort they don't get at home. Usually this means North Indian restaurant food of the kind that is never made in home kitchens (tandoori chicken, butter chicken, dairy-product black dal). In Bombay, it means so-called South Indian food: there's no shortage of people who go to Trishna and order Crab in Garlic-Butter Sauce under the misapprehension that it is a Mangalorean dish. The great success of places like Trishna (where the masalas and curries can vary wildly from day to day) is that they get people to pay large sums of money for fresh seafood.

And then, of course, people go out for Sino-Ludhiana Chinese food, i.e. food that is so heavily adapted to local tastes that it is more Indian than Chinese.

And that's about it.

To see how little Indian tastes have changed you have to look for stand-alone restaurants outside these categories. You'll find relatively few. The explosion in Thai restaurants that rocked Bombay five years ago is over. Most have closed down or are becoming more Chinese. Only Ananda Solomon continues to do the best Thai food in India at the Thai Pavilion, and that's in a five-star hotel. My guess is that something similar will happen in Delhi—certainly many of the stand-alone Thai restaurants in Delhi (with such exceptions as Ego Thai) serve overpriced rubbish.

The one exception to this trend is so-called Italian. But if you look closely, you'll find that most of these places survive on pizza and pasta and serve as canteens for rich vegetarians. And if I want pizza, I'd rather order Domino's than go to Moshe's Oliva or some such not-very-good, fly-infested place.

Very few restaurants outside hotels manage to be adventurous and get away with it. Top of the heap in Bombay is Indigo. In Delhi, Imperial Garden is often very good but when I went to its sister restaurant in Vasant Kunj, the food was disgusting. The other exception is of course Delhi's Diva, but according to owner Ritu Dalmia, she can recognize most of her guests each evening. It is a small crowd that goes again and again.

So how adventurous are Indians, really?

3. In 1996, I spoke at one of the very first Chefs' Conferences. All of us agreed that the priority was to get Indian food recognized as one of the world's great cuisines. Further, we all said, we should move away from the chicken-and-paneer formula.

Eight years later, nothing has changed. Most Indian restaurants are still serving the same menus. The breakthroughs had all taken place before the first Chefs' Conference. ITC had opened Dakshin in Madras (the Taj Group had retaliated with Southern Spice); the Taj had opened Karavalli in Bangalore (the true trendsetter for South Indian fish restaurants), and South Indian non-vegetarian food had already become established as a viable option.

There have been some attempts to do different things with Indian food in the last few years. The Konkan Cafe in Bombay is now far superior to even Karavalli. Both Masala Art (in Delhi) and Masala Craft (in Bombay) have interesting menus.

But there's been no eureka moment, comparable to the opening of Bukhara in the seventies or Dum Pukht in the eighties. Basically, all we are getting is more of the same.

Some progress has been made in London (oddly, by chefs trained by the one hotel chain that has no record when it comes to Indian food—the Oberoi) at such restaurants as Zaika and Benares. And while I've had an outstanding meal at Chutney Mary, which was genuinely innovative, I'm still to be convinced that many of the other over-hyped restaurants do much more than offer Western-style presentation to the same old dishes. (And the Michelin inspectors, it is clear, know damn-all about Indian food.)

So that's the real crisis of Indian food at restaurants: no new regional cuisines and no real, creative development either.

Does it matter? Thai is one of the world's trendiest cuisines, and despite the odd Vong-like restaurant, most chefs are content to churn out the same old stuff. Even when chefs trained in the Western tradition (such as David Thompson of the Darley Street Thai and Nahm) look at Thai food, they tend to dig up old recipes, not reinvent.

Well, perhaps.

But can anybody claim that Indian is one of the world's great cuisines when the best chefs are still content to do pretty much what they did a decade ago?

# going places

# rooms at the top

When the big hotel chains—the Hiltons, Intercontinentals, Sheratons, Hyatts—first spread their tentacles around the world, they brought with them the mantra of standardization. If you stayed in a Hilton, no matter where you were—in London or Teheran—you would get the same kind of room, eat the same kind of hamburger in the coffee shop and look up at the same portrait of Conrad Hilton.

The so-called upmarket chains which began to take over from the late 1970s onwards, broke slightly with this formula. An average Regent or Four Seasons or Mandarin Oriental property will be far more luxurious than your average Hilton or Sheraton and there will be some attempt at making each hotel seem different.

But such is the importance of standardization (now described as 'systems' in corporate-speak) that all chain properties—no matter how upmarket the image—manage somehow to seem the same. Even if the buildings and the grounds are different, there is a certain predictable similarity to the hotel rooms.

Anyone who has tired of chain hotels will feel a certain kinship with Keith Moon. Those of you who are as old as I am will remember Moon well. As the drummer with The Who, he had a propensity for outrageous behaviour (driving Rolls Royces into swimming pools etc.), but his particular passion was trashing hotel rooms.

When The Who were on tour (in the US mainly), Moon would

be angered by the sameness of each hotel room and would do his best to redecorate his surroundings. If he was very drunk or very stoned, this took the rather boring form of throwing the TV out of the window or attacking the flimsy partitions between rooms with an axe.

But if he was sober (and this was always a relative term with Moon), he would use his imagination. On one memorable occasion, he nailed every single item of furniture in his room to the ceiling so that when the maid walked in for morning service, she wondered if the world was upside down.

Led Zeppelin, contemporaries of The Who, showed less imagination when it came to trashing rooms but made up for their predictability by paying for all damage on the spot. At one American hotel, the band's manager, Peter Grant, was busy peeling off hundred dollar bills from a wad of notes for the damage when he noticed that the hotel manager was actually grinning. He asked the man why he wasn't upset about the damage.

'Oh,' said the manager. 'I understand the impulse, I've always wanted to trash these rooms myself.' Grant pulled off a few more notes and handed them to the manager.

'Go ahead,' he said. 'Trash the place. We'll pay.'

And then, to Grant's astonishment, the manager grabbed an axe and destroyed one of his own hotel rooms.

Public anger with the dullness of US hotel rooms—even the luxurious ones—led to a boon in the so-called boutique hotels. While the rich will stick to the expensive New York hotels (the Carlyle, St Regis, Pierre or even the truly dreadful Waldorf-Astoria), the trendy guest will go to places like Hudson or the Mercer.

I don't know when boutique hotels were invented, but, speaking for myself, I first discovered them in 1988 when I stayed at the Royalton on New York's 44th Street.

The hotel was owned by Steve Rubell (since deceased) and Ian Schrager, who had found fame in the 1970s as owners of the legendary disco, Studio 54. It had all gone badly wrong for them when they were arrested for tax evasion and had been forced to sell Studio 54 but they resurfaced as hotel magnates, buying and converting the Morgan's Hotel in New York.

The success of Morgan's was followed by a refit of the Royalton. In the late 1980s, when I first stayed there, the Royalton seemed like a breakthrough. For a start, it had no signage (unless you noticed that the name had been carved into the pavement) and no discernible entrance—just two formidable swing doors with small glass windows. If you didn't know what you were looking for, you could walk past 44th Street and not notice it.

Then, there was the lobby. Designed by Philippe Starck (who had yet to make his name in the US), it was like no hotel lobby I had ever seen. It was a long dark blue room with a trendy restaurant (called 44: it became the Condé Nast canteen so, on a good day, you could see Anna Wintour, Tina Brown and a host of designers pushing leaves across their plates) at the end.

The sofas were covered in a white fabric of the sort we use to protect furniture when a house is going to be unoccupied for some months, but somehow it seemed to work. Clever design and an imaginative use of recesses meant that you didn't notice the reception area till you looked deep to the right of the lobby. The bar was so cunningly disguised that you deserved a prize for finding it. The final bizarre touch came from a decor innovation: large glass bowls of Japanese fighting fish.

The staff all looked like out-of-work actors (which I imagine they were), wore designer uniforms and added to an ambience that was so fashionable that on one occasion when the fire alarm went off (by mistake) and four New York firemen entered the lobby, I worried that they might be turned away for not being trendy enough. (After all, Schrager and Rubell invented the velvet rope at Studio 54.) But I was wrong about the firemen. The staff treated them like Village People-style gay icons.

The rooms themselves were small but amazing. Starck said that he wanted to make guests feel that they were on an ocean liner (hotel-speak for 'our rooms are small') and he had designed sleek, cool rooms of the kind that I'd never seen. On later visits, I shifted to what the hotel called 'loft suites' (what you and I would call normal-sized rooms) which were even better, not only because they were larger, but because the bathrooms had huge, circular bathtubs.

I tried Schrager's next hotel—the Paramount—when it opened but abandoned it when I discovered that the rooms were even smaller than the Royalton (Adnan Sami would have to take two rooms to fit his entire body in) though it was considerably cheaper. And then, alas, as my claustrophobia got worse, I abandoned the Royalton entirely because the dimly lit corridors with portholes (the ocean liner effect) made me dizzy.

Fortunately, Schrager opened two hotels in London in the 1990s where he took care to light the corridors well so that those of my sensitive disposition could walk to the lifts without experiencing a seizure.

The more famous—and probably trendier—of his two hotels is the Sanderson on Bemers Street (off the wrong end of Oxford Street). The Sanderson is fashionable, showy, has an Alain Ducasse restaurant (Spoon+ which is only so-so), hosts pop stars and is famous for its Long Bar.

I've stayed there twice and though the rooms are of characteristic Schrager dimensions (i.e. small), the hotel itself counts as an experience. Sadly, my views were coloured by the ineptitude of the front-office staff and I began looking elsewhere.

The best alternative to an Ian Schrager hotel is another Ian Schrager hotel. And so I shifted to his older, less trendy, St Martin's Lane Hotel. Different people look for different things in hotels so I'm wary of making recommendations, but in my view, St Martin's is the perfect London hotel. There's the location to begin with—on the divide between Soho and Covent Garden and walking distance from such restaurants as The Ivy and J. Sheekey.

And then, there are the rooms. Or more specifically, one category of room (the 21 series) that I always take. These are large rooms, decorated in minimalist style. Two of the walls look out to the street and are made entirely of glass. The desk and chairs are made of thick transparent plastic to increase the sense of space. The stone bathrooms are huge and include an old-style bathtub and Philippe Starck's extraordinary fixtures.

The beds are more than comfortable. Each is bathed by an ambient light installation that allows you to change the colour of the light in your room. The sheets are made from customized Egyptian cotton (with a 300 thread count), and the comforters are filled with soft goosedown.

There is nothing in London to beat the experience of a St Martin's Lane room on a summer afternoon, with the sunlight pouring lazily through the glass walls, ambient music purring on your room's sound system, the air gently perfumed by a Diptyque candle.

Could it work here? Could we build such extraordinary hotels in India? I'm not sure. I don't think the big chains could. The Park in Bangalore (designed by Terence Conran's firm) comes closest to a modern boutique hotel, but it has never had the kind of impact or acclaim that it deserves.

I suspect that most Indian businessmen—and businesses pick up the tab for 99 per cent of the Indian guests at our hotels—are looking for something quite different: much safer and more reassuring. My heart sinks when I hear the term 'business floor' or 'club floor' in a hotel because usually it just means the same bland room with free laundry and a separate reception desk at a rate that is 30 to 40 per cent higher.

Many Indian businessmen—and let's not bother to be too polite, here—have no sense of style and no spirit of adventure. Sadly, few seem to understand luxury either.

Gone are the days when people loved the Taj Mahal Hotel in Bombay—still the finest city hotel in India—because every room was different, because the painting on your wall was likely to be an original Husain or an Ara, because the suites were filled with antiques and because the hotel changed the furniture around every six months or so to keep the rooms from looking predictable.

Even luxury is a concept that fewer and fewer Indians seem to have time for—though people are much richer today than they used to be. Bikki Oberoi, a born hotelier who understands both style and luxury, has built India's finest retreats in his Vilas properties—once you've used the bathroom at Raj Vilas in Jaipur, no other hotel will ever seem as special—but it is foreigners who appreciate the nuances more than Indians do.

Sadly, the invasion of the foreign hotel chains has increased the blandness quotient of Indian hotels. The Hyatts, Radissons, Marriotts, Sheratons, Intercontinentals etc. run smart and efficient hotels but few have any distinctive character. In most, each room is not only identical to the other, but is also exactly the same as a similar room in another hotel run by the same chain elsewhere in the world. Room factories cannot, by definition, have any charm. So far at least, the so-called luxury chains have not had much impact in India.

The Four Seasons pulled out of Goa after a disagreement with the Indian partner (you can sense what the hotel would have been like if you look at the Leela Palace in Goa). The Regent opened a Bombay property that was never up to the chain's international standards and then pulled out when it realized that the investment to upgrade the hotel was not forthcoming. Mandarin Oriental is now out of Ananda in the Himalayas.

There are signs that this might, at last, be changing. The Taj's luxury hotels are due for an upgradation with some input from George Rafael, the legendary hotelier. There are constant rumours that Bikki Oberoi will tie up with an upmarket chain (say, the Four Seasons). And Adrian Zecha (of Aman Resorts fame) plans to build a new hotel on the site of the old Lodhi hotel in Delhi.

So I expect that we'll get a taste of luxury soon enough. But as far as flair, fashion and style are concerned, the era of the Ian Schrager-style hotel still seems far, far away.

# tipsy-turvy on the pm's plane

Travelling with the Prime Minister sounds a lot more glamorous than it really is. When journos announce to civilians that they will be on the PM's plane, the intention is to suggest that they will not only be rubbing shoulders with the Prime Minister but also advising him before every key summit and then settling down in the evening for a quiet dinner with him.

The reality is very different. In the old days there used to be a caste system. The delegation sat in First Class, Air-India officials took the Club Class seats on the upper deck, and the section behind First Class was reconfigured to create a cabin for the PM.

The rest of the aircraft was all-economy and journos, security men, secretarial staff, attendants etc. all clutched their knees and huddled uncomfortably in those seats.

Under Vajpayee things changed somewhat. First, editors were promoted to the Club Class section on the Upper Deck and then, when it proved too troublesome to decide who counted as an editor or not (is a managing editor an editor—if yes, then what about a business editor, and so on), the PMO did the sensible thing and reconfigured the aircraft so that all journos, regardless of designation, got to travel Club Class.

This makes the flight more comfortable. And the service is always first rate because Air-India assigns its best crews to the aircraft. But it doesn't mean that Vajpayee settles down for chai and samosas with the press party.

Usually, the PM will make an appearance in the press section at the beginning of the trip. And then, at the end, when the aircraft is heading back to Delhi. There will be an on-board press conference where journos will crowd around and shout out sycophantic questions while Vajpayee will smile a lot but desist from revealing anything of value.

And that's about it.

Most times the press never gets to see the PM in any other context during the trip. He deplanes from the front; we rush out from the back. He gets into his motorcade; we take the bus. He stays in a really nice hotel; we stay in a more modest establishment. He boards the flight just before it takes off; we reach the airport three hours earlier.

So, yes, we are all members of the PM's party. But it's a very large party.

Of course, there are exceptions. Sometimes when Vajpayee is in a good mood or self-important editors have got very hassled, then some harassed PMO official will arrange a visit to the PM's cabin on the aircraft.

These visits follow a predictable pattern. Self-important editor arrives in cabin and makes vaguely jokey remark. Vajpayee smiles politely. Editor asks token question: 'What did you think of Bush/Blair/Putin?' Vajpayee gives non-committal answer: 'I've met him before.'

The pleasantries out of the way, the real work begins. The editor then lectures the PM on how he should handle India's foreign policy. He makes many complaints about members of the cabinet. He asks for special favours for himself or his group. And then he makes the usual doomed request for an exclusive interview.

Vajpayee is amiable, jovial even, and always friendly. But he rarely says very much. Of course, the editor doesn't notice because he's too busy doing the talking himself (Indian journalistic definition: a reporter is a man who asks questions of politicians; an editor is the man who answers them). Then, after about ten minutes or so, the encounter is terminated, the editor is frog-marched back to the media section and other journalists then seethe with resentment at the 'special treatment' being offered to senior editors.

So, if you think that all of us on the plane are going to be buddy-buddy with Vajpayee, forget it! The reality is much more mundane.

And yet, trips with the PM's party offer journalists many opportunities to see foreign policy in action. The last time I travelled with the PM, we went to Copenhagen for the India-EU summit. At the end of the summit there was a joint press conference where the Danish Prime Minister made remarks that were clearly inimical to India. As soon as that briefing ended Yashwant Sinha held another impromptu, informal, press briefing only for the Indian media only about why we disagreed with EU line. When Danish journalists tried to join our group Sinha switched to Hindi to exclude them from the briefing.

The next day the Danish PM addressed yet another press conference. He had been informed of the strong reactions on the Indian side and his tone was completely different. This time there was a noticeable pro-India tilt to his comments.

Then, there's the opportunity to interact with key government functionaries. This tends to vary, depending on the individual, but Brajesh Mishra is nearly always available to answer questions. Arun Shourie, who was on the plane to Japan, reverted to type, and spent lots of time with his former colleagues in the media. Yashwant Sinha is always one of the boys, easy-going and accessible.

All this is useful but hardly glamorous. The food, for instance (yes, I've just remembered that this book is called *Rude Food*), is rarely memorable. Vajpayee takes along some of India's best chefs (Ananda Solomon, Satish Arora and regular Hemant Oberoi), but they don't cook for the media. Most journos are not—how shall I put this?—gastronomically inclined, so meals tend to be boring. Often, press people content themselves with the vegetarian buffet that the local mission lays on.

The food on Air-India is rarely very good these days (the exception is London, otherwise Air-India's single worst-managed station, where Veeraswamy's does the catering) and the journos get the basic meal tray. This practice has remained unchanged after an uproar broke out over the revelation that everybody on Rajiv Gandhi's special flights—dubbed the Caviar Express by an ungrateful media—got First Class-style trolley service.

So, hacks tend to steer clear of the food and stick to the booze. This practice continues even after we've reached our destination. In a sense, it is not altogether surprising. Consider the fate of the hapless Indian journalist, stranded in a country where the food is unfamiliar—raw fish, rare steaks and pig liver, for instance. Obviously, he will gravitate to what little he finds familiar. And can you blame him if the only name he recognizes is Johnnie Walker?

The wine in Air-India—even in First Class these days, alas—tastes like effluent extracted from the bladders of pussy cats, so most journos who want to avoid the Scotch (and I'm sure there must be one or two of those, though I can't say I've ever come across them) stick to champagne (Dom Perignon or Veuve Clicquot at the least) which is always better.

The absence of good wine might perhaps explain why Jaswant Singh, when he was Foreign Minister and always on the move, steered dear of the PM's plane. Even when he had to go on the same trips as the PM, he came separately, presumably on an airline where he could actually stomach the wine.

My lasting memory of Jaswant is of a briefing he gave the media in Jamaica in (I think it was) 1997. We were in a so-so beachfront hotel (the PM's party, on the other hand, stayed at Half Moon Bay, location of Bond movies) whose sole redeeming feature was that it was 'all-inclusive'. In other words, the room price included *everything*.

This meant nothing to the Indian press corps till we realized that—wait for it!—all drinks were free.

So, at five-minute intervals, some hack or the other would

wander up to the bar, proffer his glass and have it topped up with pina colada or margarita or some other rum-based cocktail.

I mention all this only so that you can understand our frame of mind when it was announced that the Foreign Minister would be coming to our hotel to tell us about the visit. The MEA, entering into the spirit of Jamaica, organized the briefing on the beach in the evening. All around us people in flowery shirts, tiny shorts and swimming costumes were listening to Bob Marley, and the pina coladas were flowing like, well, pina coladas.

Into this somewhat crazed gathering stepped our impeccably tailored Foreign Minister, ready to give his briefing.

'And what will you drink, sir,' asked the MEA Joint Secretary. Jaswant Singh paused, took in the mayhem, and then ordered. 'Get me some claret.'

This caused much confusion. 'What's clarey-at, mon?' asked the Jamaican barman, more at home with tropical cocktails.

After much scrambling, a bottle of the cheapest, plonkiest, generic Bordeaux was found and poured, with great ceremony, into the great man's glass.

Jaswant Singh twirled the glass in his hands, inhaled the bouquet (given the quality of wine I'm amazed he didn't throw up) and took a delicate sip of his plonk.

'Hmm,' he finally pronounced, with the gravitas of a sommelier deciding whether a vintage Petrus had come of age, 'a bit young'.

I wish I could tell you what happened next but we all fell about laughing and then returned to our pina coladas. Still, I expect the briefing was better than the wine.

# past times: first tastes that lasted forever

I often see interviewers asking movie stars such questions as 'Which is your favourite role?' Or singers are asked 'Which is your favourite song?' God knows I've asked these silly questions often enough myself.

Usually, there's no real answer. That's when journos start getting aggressive and offering their own choices. I recall asking Sting, 'So, what's your favourite song, then?' When he hummed and hawed, I answered the question for him. '*Roxanne*,' I said. 'I don't think you'll ever write a better song.'

Out of politeness (an unfamiliar impulse with Sting when his work is being discussed), he agreed. 'Yeah, it's my favourite,' he said, resignedly. Only later did I realize how rude I had been. It's a little like telling Keith Richards, 'You'll never write a better song than *Satisfaction*.'

In both cases this translates as: 'So, you old fart, have you realized that your first hit was the best and you've spent the rest of your life trying unsuccessfully to equal that creative peak?'

(It is another matter that I was right. Sting will never write a better song than *Roxanne* and 'Keef' has spent his entire career plundering and reworking the riff from *Satisfaction*. The only comparable riff of genius in the Stones catalogue is *Jumping Jack flash* and that, Mick and Keith stole from Bill Wyman anyway.)

But enough of this gibberish.

My point is that when food writers are asked to name their favourite restaurants or their most memorable meals, the question is as difficult to answer. But there is a parallel with rock geriatrics: the best stuff always comes early in our careers.

People always expect me to say that I thought the tasting menu at Restaurant Daniel in New York was amazing (it was not) or that a twenty-two-course banquet in Hong Kong represented one of the most memorable meals of my life. But the truth is that now, when I go to a restaurant, I can no longer behave like a simple punter. Part of me is always hard at work: Is the bread any good? Why haven't they poured the wine? Hasn't the fish been slightly overcooked, and so on.

The memorable meals nearly all came when I did no food writing at all and was rarely judgemental about food. And, oddly enough many, if not most, were consumed at extremely unfancy places.

Almost every person has memories of formative taste experiences. In my case, the cuisine of my forefathers (Gujarati) did not leave much of an impression on my palate. The Gujarati food I like is peasant food (a good Kathiawari *bajra rotla* with a raw onion and a chilli or a *thepla* with *kothmir* chutney) and the great classics of Gujarati cuisine (the *kadhi,* the *tuver dal*, *khichi na papad* etc.) require a very deft hand that most cooks lack.

Commercial Gujarati food is nearly always revolting. *Dahi wadi* (now increasingly called *khandvi*) reminds me of bandages, and a *dhokla* is essentially an idli that has failed its entrance exam.

So, my earliest gastronomic memories are of non-Gujarati food. My mother had acquired a taste for bacon cooked very crisp ('like *supari*' she used to joke) from her college days in America and that's still my favourite way of eating bits of dead pig. My aunt, Sushila Subodh (author of the world's best Gujarati cookbook), was one of the few people in Ahmedabad with an oven in the early 1960s, and she taught us all to love pizza.

Otherwise, my favourite dishes came from the restaurants of Bombay. An oily but delicious mutton curry (with boiled egg) from the determinedly unfancy ('This establishment has been graded an eating house Grade III' a board proudly announced) Wilson Restaurant, behind Wilson College. A killer *keema matar* (best eaten with white bread) from—of all places!—the Kwality's at Kemp's Corner. The hot dog at Bombelli's (totally inauthentic—they even sliced a red chilli above the frankfurter—but fun, nevertheless), and *bhelpuri* from Shetty's (no good now, alas).

In Ahmedabad, at my grandfather's house, we ate home-made *dahi batata puri* (which, for reasons that were never clear, Gujaratis like to call *pakodi puri*—though *pakodi puri* is another dish entirely). And fresh fruit ice cream cranked out on a home machine. (Otherwise, it came from Havmore.)

When I think back on the meals and flavours that determined the shape of my tastebuds, it was probably these dishes rather than the creations of Michelin-starred chefs.

Even when we went abroad on holiday, I was never taken to fancy places. I remember eating my first Italian pizza when I was nine (thin crust as distinct from my aunt's American versions) at a cafe by the Fountain of Trevi in Rome. I've never been able to enjoy a fat crust pizza since.

My mother loved meat but my father always regarded my obsession with steak with an amused disdain verging on concern. Still, he indulged me. I remember being taken regularly to the Cafe de Paris in Geneva where the only dish on the menu was an entrecote steak in a delicious cream sauce served with a mountain of slender chips.

Though I recognize that a good steak should not depend on the sauce (and I usually eat my steaks without any sauce at all) I keep searching out the Cafe de Paris sauce. I found it last month in New York (at a restaurant called—believe it or not!—the Cafe de Paris), and three months ago in (of all places) a cafe on the ground floor of the Isetan department store in Bangkok.

The other formative gastronomic phase in my life was probably university. Because I never ate in college and never cooked, I spent all my time going from restaurant to restaurant. Many of my tastes date from that period.

I discovered South East Asian food in the oddest of locations: at a small cafe called Munchy Munchy run by an overseas Chinese couple (from Malaysia, I think) near the Oxford railway station. The wife did all the cooking behind an open counter and the husband served. They introduced me to *rendang*, to Malaysian curries, to the joys of satay and to noodle soup. They had no liquor licence so you took your own wine and dessert (which was always my all-time favourite, frozen Birdseye cheesecake from the supermarket next door).

There were only five tables, and many evenings my friends and I would be the only people in the restaurant (but there were a lot of us). It almost became our canteen and when it was time to leave Oxford, I gave my hosts a bottle of Bollinger and they gave me the only free meal of my entire time there. (Poor things. They ran a tight ship. And besides they *were* Chinese.)

Though my friends and I made a great show of seeming knowledgeable about restaurants, I doubt now—in retrospect, of course—that we really knew very much about food. In those days there were two great Oxford restaurants: Sorbonne, owned by a Frenchman with a very big dog, and Elizabeth which was—to undergraduate eyes at least—far grander.

Everybody tells me that Sorbonne had much better food but my friends and I much preferred Elizabeth, perhaps because we thought it was fancier. And it used a lot of garlic. I remember our usual starter of prawns with aïoli (I cringe to remember how sophisticated we thought we were dipping boiled prawns into garlic mayonnaise!) and I remember the sorbet au champagne (in retrospect, a lemon sorbet with a touch of champagne).

It is a measure of how gastronomically illiterate we were that when the young Raymond Blanc opened Les Quatre Saisons in

Summertown, we went there and pronounced the food 'not in the same league as Elizabeth, just fancified Frog rubbish'.

Within three years Blanc was being hailed as one of England's greatest chefs and Le Manoir aux Quat' Saisons, near Oxford, to which he moved once he made it big, has been incredibly influential in the culinary world.

But we were children then, pretending to be more grown-up than we really were. And sometimes when the fine wines and champagne sorbet got too much for us, we would retreat to such student hang-outs as Browns (where I had my first taste of brown bread ice cream which still lingers on the tongue).

Or we would nurse our hangovers at George's in the covered market, eating the only meal that the British really know how to make—a good fry-up of eggs, bacon, mushrooms, fried bread and baked beans. Washed down, alas, with lousy English coffee.

## bombay restaurants i grew up in

- **Bombelli's**: Billed as an Italian (or was it Swiss?) café, this had two branches in Bombay in the 1950s and 1960s. The pastries were famous and the food was basic European (fish and chips, mutton crumbed chops etc.) The stand-out was the hot dog which was delicious if completely inauthentic. Two long rolls (rather than one split down the middle) were toasted and placed on either side of a thin pork frankfurter which was itself sliced lengthwise. On top of the frank was placed an entire red chilli, also sliced lengthwise.
- **Shetty's**: *Bhelpuri* was invented by Gujaratis in Bombay who picked up on the principles of UP-style chaat. A restaurant called Vithal usually gets the credit for the invention but the UP-wallahs who came to Bombay to sell *golgappas* or *batashas* (rechristened *pani puri* by Bombay's Gujaratis) quickly made it their own and began selling from stalls on Chowpatty beach. Meanwhile, restaurateurs from Karnataka—chiefly Bunts from

Mangalore—opened so-called Udipi restaurants. Sadly they did not serve their own wonderful cuisine (though these days they all specialize in Mangalorean seafood) but made versions of Tamil-style snacks. Shetty's was unusual in that it was probably the first of these restaurants to make its reputation with *bhelpuri*.

- **The Wilson Restaurant**: Just as the Irani restaurants of Bombay have either faded away or begun serving Vegetable Manchurian, the classic cheap-but-terrific Muslim restaurants of the 1950s and 1960s have also died out, victims of the real estate boom. Places like Wilson served oily but basic Muslim curries, the dal was made with stock and boiled eggs were added to nearly everything.
- **Kwality's**: The Kwality chain, founded after Independence, by families of cousins with such names as Ghai and Lamba, was unusual in that the restaurants were not owned by the same person but by different members of the extended family. The chain was not noted for cuisine. Most of it consisted of Punjabi restaurant food, a made-up cuisine which no self-respecting Punjabi would eat at home. The Kemp's Corner branch was fairly typical with a Continental section that included things like Chicken Corn Corn. But oddly enough, the *keema* was exceptional.

# meals to live (and die) for

In the last piece, I wrote—at great and massively self-indulgent length—about all the gastronomic experiences I remembered from my childhood. I thought I'd continue the story. But try as I might, I can't seem to be able to impose order on either my tongue or my memory.

So what I'll do instead is this: list some of the most memorable meals I've had. As you'll discover, they aren't meals as much as they are experiences—eureka moments when the taste buds suddenly sit up or when the brain feels the blood rushing hungrily towards it, and you say to yourself 'Yes! This it it! This is the Life!'

Much of good cooking is about flavour. If you don't understand the power of real flavours then you can't be a good cook and—or at least, so I would argue—a good eater.

Many of my formative experiences have come when I've discovered strong, memorable flavours.

I still remember my first taste of black truffle over a decade ago. It was at lunch at Le Caprice, a restaurant in London that has managed the difficult feat of remaining trendy for two decades. The truffle was shaved over a plate of pasta and at first I thought it was just a poncey little garnish. But one bite of those thin slivers of fungus and I knew I was in love.

Since then, I've grown more accustomed to white truffles shaved over pasta, risotto or eggs (they are more expensive but there's something heady and earthy about black truffles and their scent that makes you understand why it drives pigs crazy).

So it is with real vanilla. If you've only had the synthetic version then it is hard to imagine the warm taste of the real thing. It elevates nearly every dish—from ice cream, or a cup of coffee or hot chocolate to beef or chicken, if used by a talented chef.

All of us know that bread and butter are a natural pairing. But few of us recognize how much good bread (such as the country bread made by the late French baker Lionel Poilâne but now available in most of the Continent) and a great butter (usually French) can elevate the experience. Jeffrey Steingarten, the American food writer, says that he judges restaurants by the quality of their bread. Using that test, most Indian restaurants would fail (you can't even get a good flaky croissant here).

But melted butter elevates almost anything. Pour it over a waffle and then add the honey (maple syrup is a no-no) and you'll know what I mean. Pair it with garlic (as in garlic toast) and the two flavours mingle into a naughty richness. Even seafood (prawn, lobster etc.), freshly caught and barbecued by the beach, yields its true flavour only to the union of butter and lemon. To understand the importance of flavour in simple things—in bread, in butter, in garlic or in lemon—is to look forward to years of good eating.

I've only been to Japan once but I loved it on sight. It is so totally unlike any other place in the world, a curious mixture of *Seven Samurai* and *Blade Runner,* that you can't help being entranced by the sights, sounds, smells and flavours.

I had always liked sashimi but had been less keen on sushi, not recognizing the point of taking a slice of fresh, raw fish (which is what sashimi is) and then pairing it with vinegared rice.

It was only when I got to Japan that I began to understand: the rice *was* the point. A Japanese will walk into a sushi bar and ask for the cheapest kind of nigiri sushi (say, omelette on rice) just so that he can check that the rice is perfectly cooked. If he likes the rice then he'll stay and order the real thing.

Post-Japan, I've all but given up on sashimi. The flavour that really turns me on is a good nigiri sushi (say salmon) with the vinegared rice gently soaked in a little soya sauce and the fish dabbed with wasabi and topped with a slice of pickled ginger.

You can get wonderful sushi in India. But sadly, only one place does it right: Sakura at Delhi's Nikko Hotel.

When you eat Thai food all over the world, here's what you get: curries, a few stir-fries and the odd fried starter (crab cakes etc.). All of this is amazing—Thai is, after all, by common consent, the world's second greatest cuisine—but Thai food in Thailand itself can be a more dangerous proposition.

For a start, the Thais put dried fish in everything (an ingredient they remove when they cook for foreigners). Then, in some parts of Thailand (the North mainly) they like grasshoppers, locusts and water cockroaches. The last is often mashed into curry pastes and masalas (it gives them a menthol taste).

I'm willing to be adventurous about food but I do draw the line at locusts. So I'm very suspicious when the Thais tell me that something is 'fermented'. It was for this reason that I resisted eating what they call Chiang Mai sausage, made from fermented pork—I thought the taste would be too pungent.

I was finally persuaded to be daring by a combination of too much Singha beer and loud rock music at a restaurant called Ad Makers in Bangkok.

Since then, I've become a Chiang Mai sausage addict, even bringing packets back to India. Yes, the taste is strong and takes a little getting used to. But it is so unlike anything that we eat in India or the West that the sheer unfamiliarity makes the experience exhilarating.

I love eggs and bacon for breakfast. But give me a choice, and nine times out of ten these days, I'll opt for a South Indian breakfast.

I suspect that the real reason is another association. Some years ago I was going to the Kumarakom Resort on the Kerala backwaters with some friends. I flew in first and went from the old Cochin airport (on Willingdon Island, not the horrible new one) to the nearby Malabar Hotel and waited for my friends' flight to land so we could take a speedboat to Kumarakom.

While I waited in the coffee shop, the hotel fed me breakfast. There were *vadas*, idlis, dosas, *appams*, Kerala egg masala—nearly everything you could think of. But the stars of the show were the chutneys. The Malabar had done six South Indian chutneys, with onions, with garlic, with chillis, with coconut—I've lost count.

I sat by the windows (the coffee shop is by the edge of the water) and watched dolphins gambolling in the early morning sea, smearing my idlis with the chutneys, dunking my hot, crisp *medu vadas* into bowls of onion chutney and drinking cups of South Indian coffee.

I'll never forget the dolphins or the chutneys. And I've remained loyal to South Indian breakfasts ever since.

And finally, Goan food. I love Goan food. Admittedly, it doesn't have that much variety (as they say unfairly, 'five hundred fish and one masala'), but in the hands of a good chef, Goan can be one of India's great cuisines.

I've had great Goan meals in Panjim (in 1983 at the Mandovi Hotel) and at various hotels (Chef Julia at the Taj Exotica is especially good, as was Chef Thomas Braganza, formerly at the Aguada).

But the real reason I love Goan food is just one chef and his cooking: Rego at the Taj Holiday Village. People go to Goa for the beach, the water sports etc. I go there for the food—and for Rego who introduced me to the wonders of his cuisine. The best clams I've ever eaten were Rego's, ten years ago. Likewise, the best sorpotel, the best balchao, the best *everything*. Rego's still cooking at the Village. It's one of the great gastronomic experiences still available in India.

So, go there this winter!

# the banqueting food guide

At the launch of the *HT City Guide to Eating Out in Delhi* (well, at least it was meant to be a launch but because the book had sold out by the time the party was held, we'd better just call it the Food Guide Dinner), I was surprised by the manner in which guests responded to the food.

Yes, the food was spectacularly good, in fact, the best meal that even Chef Sultan, the Maurya's talented Executive Chef, has produced, but even so, I thought that the guests were reacting—how shall I put this?—well, overmuch. Scores of otherwise seemingly well-fed individuals made so many trips to the buffet table that I began to wonder if they had starved themselves for weeks. Restaurateurs (lots of them were in attendance because it was a Food Guide Dinner) stole copies of the menu and conducted fiercely professional inspections of the table. And guest after guest went into raptures over how good the food was.

Well, it was nice that the guests enjoyed themselves so much but I couldn't help being more than a little bemused. This was a Food Guide party after all, so you'd expect the food to be good. ITC were co-sponsors of the *Guide* so they were duty-bound to do their best. And besides, if there's one thing that ITC does well—thanks to a management tradition that extends from Ajit Haksar to Habib Rehman—it is Indian food. And though Sultan is less hyped than, say, Imtiaz, he is actually one of ITC's brightest stars—and he stays sober in the kitchen.

Then it struck me: guests don't expect to eat well at a large dinner. Think about it: when was the last time you went to a dinner for more than 100 people and actually enjoyed the food? Hasn't eating become merely a ritual you go through, late in the evening, after the drinks, so that you can then make a graceful exit from the party?

It doesn't matter where you are. You could be at a Taj hotel, an Oberoi or even one of ITC's properties and no matter how much money has been spent on the party, the food will be dismal. If the party is thrown by a rich person, there will be lots of expensive seafood (big prawns, lobster, that sort of thing) but not one dish will be memorable. Regardless of how much the host has paid the hotel—and banquet prices of Rs 2,000 per head are not uncommon—the food will still be rubbish.

It is fast becoming the Golden Rule of all party catering in India that no matter who the host is, no matter who the caterer is and no matter how much has been spent on the meal, the dinner will taste like the kind of buffet airport restaurants rustle up at minimal cost to feed passengers on delayed flights.

Sadly, this applies to government entertaining as well. I'm still in denial about Abdul Kalam so I haven't been to Rashtrapati Bhavan for a while, but I can't remember a single half-decent meal I've eaten there in over a decade. Much the same used to be true of the banquets hosted by the Prime Minister at Hyderabad House.

I started being invited to them in the Narasimha Rao era. As you would expect from a PM whose idea of haute cuisine was *upma* seven times a day, nobody in his office worried too much about the quality of the food (sorry, Ramu; sorry, Deepak) and so ITDC, the official caterers for Hyderabad House, continued to produce crappy meal after crappy meal.

Matters didn't improve much under H.D. Deve Gowda. He once invited me to breakfast at 7, Race Course Road, arrived half an hour late from his residence at 3, Race Course Road, and insisted that I begin to eat.

'What about you, Prime Minister?' I asked politely.

'I have not yet taken my bath,' he announced proudly.

Presumably this meant that he couldn't eat. Certainly, it meant that I was put off my food.

Inder Gujral was too busy pulling out the knives that Sharad Yadav and Deve Gowda had stuck into his back to worry about the food at Hyderabad House. And so the usual rubbish continued to appear, i.e. one vegetarian soup made almost entirely from *maida*; one tandoori course, cooked with such expertise that if you were blindfolded you could not tell the difference between the chicken tikka and the fish kabab (or an old shoe, for that matter); the curry course consisting of one chicken curry cooked with *kaju* paste and lots of dairy products and one goat curry cooked with a total lack of interest; and the dessert course, comprising cold souffle (pineapple was a particular favourite; perhaps ITDC loved synthetic pineapple essence) and one *rabdi* type of Indian sweet.

I'm told that President Kalam has made one or two innovations to the cuisine at Rashtrapati Bhavan. Apparently, the cooks are now encouraged to supplement the Indian food with one dish from the country of the visiting Head of State. This seems eminently fair: after all, why should the Rashtrapati Bhavan cooks only destroy our own cuisine? Let them murder the cuisine of our honoured guest as well.

On the Prime Ministerial side, things have improved somewhat since A.B. Vajpayee has taken over. The Prime Minister likes his food (though there's not much call for pakoras, *kachoris* and *jalebis* at official banquets), his foster family has a hoteliering background (Ranjan Bhattacharya was the youngest-ever General Manager in the history of the Oberoi group, but his wife Namita—formerly of ITC hotels—is the true foodie of the family), and his staff are keen on checking details (his PS, Ajay Bisaria, has been known to attend food tastings before menus for important dinners are finalized).

Consequently, the food is often very good. The lunch for Pervez Musharraf before he left for Agra boasted an unusual guest list (including a chain-smoking Shah Rukh Khan) and an excellent menu by the Taj's Hemant Oberoi. (Great meal, shame about the summit.) More impressively, this PMO has also pushed ITDC into delivering better-quality food. It is still a bit hit-and-miss but I suspect the quality of the dinner depends on the importance of the guest. (Poor Thaksin Shinawatra and his delegation can go back hungry to their hotels and order Pad Thai from room service while Tony Blair gets a better Indian meal than the stuff he is used to in London.)

Sadly, corporate entertaining is not so quality driven. Nor are Delhi's professional party-givers (I'm not naming names but you know the type: a party for a new Cabinet Secretary or recently elected MP, with 2,000 guests and 3,000 photographers) who don't care very much what the food is like (though the food at Subbirami Reddy's own house is very good—oops!). Even when hotels throw parties themselves (to mark the opening of a new property etc.) the food is rarely better than mediocre.

Of course there are exceptions. The Bombay Taj managed to provide a perfectly decent sit-down dinner for 1,400 guests with individual cheese souffles (but very dodgy wine) at the party to mark its centenary. The otherwise sloppily run Taj Exotica in Goa managed the most amazing Goan food (thanks to chef Julia) at this year's World Travel and Tourism Council party. Chef Thimmayya of Bangalore's Karavali restaurant (at the Gateway) knocked the socks off delegates at a South Indian chef's competition by cooking the final dinner of the competition (served at ITC's Windsor Manor) for 500 guests. (I can't be sure but I think this was in 1997.)

But by and large, party food is abysmal. ITC will excel at special events (or when it does catering at private homes) but the average banquet meal at the Maurya will be nothing to write home about. I've never had a decent meal at a party at either the Taj Mahal on Delhi's Man Singh Road (except once in 1996, but Ajit Kerkar was the host and Richard Neat was cooking so that doesn't count) or Calcutta's Taj Bengal. The Oberoi Grand in Calcutta will only pull itself together if Arup Sarkar is the host (but then, he knows his food and more important: he knows the cooks). Wherever you go the story is much the same.

I'm not sure I know what the reason is. The same hotels will manage perfectly reasonable buffets in their own restaurants but will lose all interest when it comes to banquet functions. Partly, I suspect, it is that Indian kitchens are not good at turning out meals for large groups. Partly it is that hotels take banquet customers for granted, recognizing that most people who host hotel parties can't tell the difference between good and mediocre food.

But mainly, I suspect, it is that hotels dump the worst chefs and the worst cooks in the banquet kitchen. It can't be an accident that I remember the name of the chef at every party where the food has been good: Sultan, Hemant Oberoi, Julia, Thimmayya etc.

One reason, perhaps, why the Bombay Taj still does the best parties is because the top chefs make it a matter of pride. This is a tradition that began with Satish Arora (captured memorably on film by a British TV documentary 'The chickens are singing' etc. etc.) and continues with Oberoi, who uses banquets to experiment with new dishes and treats each party as a personal challenge.

Finally, food is not about systems and kitchen efficiency, no matter what they say in the manuals. It is about chefs, about pride, and about passion.

# a rendezvous with fine dining

In the beginning there was the Rendezvous. Sadly, it no longer exists today. But for entire generations of Bombayites, it represented the ultimate in glamour, sophistication and haute cuisine. The original Rendezvous (and yes, there were two) was situated in the corner of the old Taj (what is now called the Heritage wing and in roughly the area currently occupied by the Golden Dragon) and remained the ultimate Bombay restaurant.

The food was determinedly French, but then so was all the food in fancy hotels in those days. There were no Chinese restaurants and the Taj had no Indian kitchen to speak of. But those who remember the Rendezvous in the days of the legendary chef Masci say that, despite the paucity of the ingredients needed for classic French cuisine, the restaurant managed magnificently.

Then, in the 1970s, as the Intercontinental wing was added, the Rendezvous moved. Internationally, it was the era of the rooftop nightclub and so the Rendezvous became one (briefly it was even known as the Rooftop Rendezvous).

I have to say that I was too young to remember the original Rendezvous; most of my memories are of the rooftop avatar. But what a restaurant it was! There was an unbeaten view of the Arabian Sea, with the lights of the ships glimmering in the night, on one side. And on the other, you saw the rest of Bombay.

The service was reassuringly old-fashioned. The maitre d' hotel (called Uncle Louis by everybody from staff to regulars), made the best crêpes Suzette I've ever had, flambéing them by the side of your table. Other waiters (one or two of whom survive in today's Zodiac Grill) excelled in a speciality of that era: snake coffee. This was a hot, alcoholic, after-dinner coffee, served in a goblet with a sugar-encrusted rim. The 'snake' of the title was a length of orange peel which was doused with alcohol and then ceremonially set aflame (with the house lights dimmed to assist the effect).

The food retained the classic dishes favoured by Masci but the Taj was the first Indian hotel to discover nouvelle cuisine. Paul Bocuse came and cooked in the kitchens, so did Franz Keller, the brothers Bise and a procession of Michelin-starred chefs. A new generation of bright young Indian chefs—Arvind Saraswat, Subhash Basrur, 'Nat' Natarajan, Maria Vaz—ensured that the food never dropped below international quality.

Different people went to Rendezvous for different things. Some went for the music—played for a long time by a band named the Phantom Revival, often unkindly rechristened the Frantic Survival—and the dancing. Many went for the food. I went for the atmosphere, the service, the view and for nearly everything else. Eventually, I even found a cook at Rendezvous who made a wonderful prawn curry—not exactly the French cuisine that Rendezvous was known for—and started going for curry-rice lunches.

The death knell of the old Rendezvous was probably sounded by the new Zodiac Grill. Throughout the 1980s the Taj kept getting complaints from foreign guests who said that they wanted a grill room, a place where they could eat a steak or a rack of lamb without having to listen to a rock band. Most hotels would have built just a grill room. The great thing about the Taj was that it created India's best restaurant instead.

The credit department was moved and the space for the Zodiac (it has since swapped places with the Shamiana) was created out of nowhere. Chefs were sent to London to train with Albert Roux at Le Gavroche and Hemant Oberoi, by then the Taj's Executive Chef, made the new restaurant his personal project, scouring the world for the most perfect menu possible—of which two dishes, the Camembert Soufflé and the Kahlua Mousse, still survive.

When the Grill opened, the Taj threw another surprise. The menus had no prices. When the bill came, it was a blank sheet of paper.

'We have no prices, sir,' the waiter would explain, 'you pay what you think the meal is worth.'

It was a daring ploy. But the trust in the honesty of guests paid off. Nobody paid a mere Rs 10 and got away with having eaten caviar, foie gras and smoked salmon. On the whole, most guests paid what the restaurant expected them to.

A year later, when the restaurant was universally acknowledged as India's finest—better even than Rendezvous—the Taj finally put prices on the menu. I was ashamed to note that I had been underpaying. But then I had a lunch with a corporate fat cat who was a Zodiac regular. 'You know,' he said, 'now that they've put prices on the menus, I realize that I've been paying twice as much as I should have.'

So I suppose it balanced out: the fat cats like him and the cheapskates like myself.

The Zodiac Grill has shifted to a new location. It is now cosier, more like a gentleman's club. And the food is even better than it used to be. As for the service: no restaurant in India even comes close.

It is still the place in Bombay for any kind of celebration. If you are going out for a birthday, an anniversary or any kind of special occasion, there's simply nowhere else in the city that will do. Even if you have to save up all year, the Zodiac Grill is still remarkably special.

Where the Zodiac Grill is now located is the site of the original Shamiana. When the history of Indian restaurants and their food is written, whole chapters will be devoted to the Shamiana. It was not, as is sometimes believed, the first 24-hour coffee shop in India—the Oberoi Intercontinental in Delhi opened Café Expresso in 1966.

But it was certainly the most influential.

The new Taj building was designed by Dale Keller, an architect whose influence on Indian hotels built in the 1970s was all-pervasive. In Keller's original design, the Taj coffee shop was like the cafe at any Intercontinental hotel. He called it Canopy and thought it would serve bland, international coffee shop fare.

But the Taj turned all that around. Why bother with Canopy when you could go with the more Indian Shamiana? Wall hangings from Gujarat and Rajasthan were found, so were Indian artefacts, and the restaurant had the uniquely India-International look that was to become a Taj trademark.

I spent much of my late adolescence in Shamiana so I remember it well. I remember the ambience, the fact that it soon became the bustling hub of Bombay, the place where you saw everybody who was anybody.

And I remember the food. Five-star hotels were expected to serve club sandwiches and fish and chips in their coffee shops. And so the Taj did that. But it also introduced the kind of dishes that had never ever been on a restaurant menu. If you didn't want bacon and eggs for breakfast, you could have a hot, crisp dosa filled with tangy masala. If you were tired of the cheeseburger you could have Satish Arora's take on the burger. As the youngest Executive Chef in hotel history Arora faced a double challenge in succeeding Masci and in dragging the Taj kitchens into the 1970s. He did both magnificently, invented such coffee shop classics as the Spicy Mutton Burger and the Chicken Tikka Sandwich (now an international standard).

Two years ago when the Shamiana swapped places with the Zodiac Grill all the regulars complained. The new location is too sophisticated, we moaned. You can't see anybody!

But what do you know? Three months later we were back there. And now, not only is it my favourite Taj restaurant, it is also much more successful than the old Shamiana.

Like Shamiana, Golden Dragon has an epochal importance.

Before the Dragon opened, Chinese food in India consisted of Indianized American-Cantonese, an odd mishmash of Indian-style American Chop Suey and Masala Chow Mein.

Then, the Taj stole the manager and three chefs from a restaurant called Red Pepper in Hong Kong and charged them with opening India's first Sichuan restaurant.

From the day it opened its doors the restaurant was a revelation: Indians had never realized that authentic Chinese food could actually be spicy. There was no need to put garam masala in Cantonese food.

From then on, all Chinese food in India became Sichuan. The Cantonese style of cooking was forgotten.

Of course, the Dragon had its share of dramas. The Chinese chefs were prima donnas. Each day they would fight with all the Indian managers. Periodically, they would storm out of the kitchen.

But the Taj cooks were no slouches. When the Chinese staged their walkouts they shrugged their shoulders and took to the ranges themselves. They were such good cooks that guests couldn't tell the difference and the Hong Kong prima donnas decided to behave themselves. Most stayed on to open other Taj restaurants (the House of Ming in Delhi, Memories of China in Bangalore, Inn of Happiness in London, and Chinoiserie in Kolkata), and in the public mind, the Taj is forever associated with the best Chinese food.

In 2002, Golden Dragon went in for yet another makeover. Gone was the heavy 'Chinese restaurant' style decor of old. In its place came a new, sunny, airy room which combined sophistication with an overwhelmingly oriental ambience. Only one thing remained the same: the food was still state-of-the-art Sichuan.

Oddly enough, for the greatest hotel in India, the Taj had no tradition of Indian food. To tell the truth, nobody knew what Indian restaurant food should be like. In Bombay, you had the Muslim dhabas, the Irani cafes and the Udipi restaurants; 'upmarket' places served a bizarre kind of North Indian food that claimed to be Punjabi in origin but which no Punjabi ever ate at home.

The first Indian restaurant to break with this trend and to serve a kind of cuisine that you couldn't find at Kwality's or Volga was a Taj restaurant that nobody remembers today. In the late 1960s, the Taj finally opened an Indian restaurant in the Apollo Room (now used as a banquet room).

Because it was soon overshadowed by the opening of the Tanjore, nobody has any real recollection of it. But I remember it well. I remember how different the food was and I remember family celebrations over exquisite Indian food: we celebrated the fall of Dacca in December 1972 over a biryani.

But the Apollo Room gave way to the ornate (some would say overdecorated) Tanjore. Despite the Bharatanatyam dancer and the elaborate South Indian decor, the food was determinedly North Indian. Alas, all Indian restaurants in deluxe hotels soon become the preserve of foreigners eager for a safe sample of the local cuisine so the Tanjore never quite acquired the cult status of other Taj restaurants.

Nevertheless, I remember great meals there. I remember the young Udit Sarkhel (who later became chef at the Taj-owned Bombay Brasserie in London and now boasts a formidable reputation among British food critics) blossoming under Satish Arora's guidance and introducing Bombaywallahs to his smoky dals. I remember Hemant Oberoi's thali festivals and his experiments with *khad* cuisine.

Few people, I suspect, will remember the Tanjore in the years to come, not because there was anything wrong with the restaurant but because its successor has been such a spectacular success: it is possibly the best Indian restaurant in the world.

The origins of Masala Kraft lie in Chef Hemant Oberoi's desire to serve genuine Punjabi food (as different from the Punjabi food served in restaurants as Chop Suey is from real Chinese food). The prototype of Masala Kraft is Delhi's Masala Art which emerged out of months of travel through North India by Oberoi and a team of Taj chefs.

But Masala Kraft goes much further. Its menu contains a genuine Punjabi black dal (not the tomato purée-filled version served in Indian restaurants all over the world), home-cooked Punjabi vegetables and some of the great lost dishes of North Indian cuisine.

Among the most spectacular is the Atta Chicken. Oberoi had heard rumours that in the early part of the century Punjabis would roast a whole chicken in a casing of pastry and travel with it. Hours later, when hunger struck, they would pull out the hunk of pastry and slice through it with a knife. Inside the pastry casing would be the chicken, kept hot and steaming by its doughy container, cooked slowly in its own juices.

The problem was that very few people remembered the dish. Eventually, Oberoi asked his father, a former railway employee, if the dish actually existed. When the senior Oberoi confirmed that people took Atta Chicken onto trains with them, his son made it his mission to uncover the recipe.

Today, Masala Kraft is probably the only restaurant in the world that serves the dish.

Another innovation is the Bombay Tiffin. All over India's commercial capital, office workers get little multilayered lunch boxes (called tiffin carriers) delivered to them from their homes. When the Taj did the catering for the Indian Festival at London's Selfridges store two years ago, Oberoi sold tiffin carriers in the food department. All 3,000 disappeared in a matter of days.

At Masala Kraft, diners get a choice of three tiffins representing complete meals from three of the communities that make up Bombay's cosmopolitan population.

The newest Taj restaurant (if you take the line that Masala Kraft is the updated Tanjore) is the spectacular Souk on the roof of the new building. At lunch, the restaurant offers an unparalleled view of the Bombay harbour and the rest of the city. At dinner, three different light settings (the lighting changes as the evening wears on) and three musicians from Marrakesh, create a coolly sophisticated night-time ambience.

The cuisine emerged out of Oberoi's five-year stint as the chef at the Taj-run Royal Guest House in Oman. He spent the period travelling the Middle East and discovered that there was much more to the cuisine than the clichés of Falafel and Hummus.

Souk is not a Lebanese restaurant—though yes, you will find the clichés/classics of the cuisine: Tabbouleh, Kibbeh, Shawarma, Shish Touk etc.—but attempts to take in the entire cuisine of the Middle East.

Thus, you will find dishes that are not often seen on restaurant menus and the emphasis is on authenticity. One instance: Oberoi fell in love with the Omani lobster during his time there. He tried very hard to recreate the flavour with Kerala lobster but found the meat too sweet and not firm enough. So twice a week the Taj flies in fresh lobster from the Gulf of Oman to ensure that there is no compromise on the flavours of the dish.

That leaves just two Taj classics, both opposite each other, one deceased, one flourishing. The Ballroom is one of Bombay's greatest rooms, redolent with history, charm and grandeur. For most of my childhood—and well into my early youth—the Ballroom hosted the most magnificent buffet lunch.

It was the kind of lunch that had everything: from huge hams carved off the bone to hot bread-and-butter pudding, from a rich coq au vin to a wonderful *dhansak*. In my childhood it cost something like Rs 12 per head (but then rooms cost Rs 100 to 150, so you must see it in perspective), and even kids given pocket money for a special treat could afford it.

I remember we would go in at 12.30, start on the salads and leave at 3.30, groaning and moaning as we tried to digest the last creamy crumbs of Apple Pie á la Mode.

The buffet lunch did not last into the mid-1980s, alas—a more modest version survives in the Shamiana. But in the 1990s the Taj made a brave attempt to resurrect it as a Sunday lunch.

I remember wandering down from my room one Sunday afternoon and noticing a spurt of activity on the first floor. It was the first day of the Sunday brunch, and it mattered so much to the hotel that Chef Oberoi was carving the roast himself and Subir Bhowmick, then the hotel's General Manager, was personally showing guests to their tables.

It was the most magnificent Sunday lunch I've ever had at the Taj—the buffet table groaned under the weight of Taj classics (Prawns in Green Goddess sauce, Salad Currimbhoy) and Hemant Oberoi touches (six different kinds of olives etc.).

Sadly, this too did not survive into the new century.

Fortunately, the Sea Lounge still flourishes. It is in some ways probably the only link with the Bombay of the 1960s that has not become seedy or frayed at the edges. You can still sit at a window table, sip gently on a cup of Darjeeling tea, tenderly sample the Viennoise ice cream, munch on the *bhelpuri*, bite into a toasted sandwich and gaze down at the seaside as *madaaris* bring monkeys to perform.

If there is one experience that sums up why for me the Taj is not just a part of my growing up but also the finest hotel in India, it is the sense of peace, quiet and timelessness that the Sea Lounge epitomizes.

May it never change!

# why is airline food so bad?

Here are the three most important secrets about airline food—things that the airlines don't want you to know. One: no airline meal can ever be good. It has usually been cooked in an industrial kitchen where your portion is just one of 1000 portions being cooked simultaneously so there is no chance of the chef giving your dish anything more than cursory attention. In any case, the chef is probably a dunderhead (few talented chefs opt for flight catering). And the dish you are eating has been cooked up to twenty-four hours ago, thrown into a silver foil container and then quickly reheated by an air hostess between serving drinks and taking infant passengers to the toilet. In the circumstances, you'd be crazy to expect haute cuisine. If the food is anything more than disgusting, just be grateful.

Two: you get what your airline pays for. When you say (hypothetically) that the food on Indian Airlines is worse than the food on Sahara, do not be fooled into thinking that this reflects on either airline's culinary skills. The chances are that regardless of whether you fly Indian Airlines, Sahara or Jet, all three meals will have been cooked at the same flight kitchen. The truth is that the airline catering business in India is dominated by just two or three big players. Taj Air Caterers are the biggies, but there are also Oberoi Flight Services and the Ambassador Flight Kitchen. Plus there are a few regional players such as Kathleen in Calcutta and the moribund Chef Air subsidiary of Air-India.

The difference in cuisine is partly a consequence of menus (usually prepared by the airline concerned) but mainly a consequence of how much each airline is prepared to pay per meal. For instance, Sahara is often said to have the best food of any domestic airline. But then it also pays the most out of any domestic airline, more than either Jet or Indian Airlines.

Most domestic airlines will pay between Rs 50 to 65 per head for an economy class meal. Try and work out what you will get at a Taj or an Oberoi restaurant for that price (not much) and you'll have some idea of why the food is so bad. International airlines, on the other hand, pay far more—Rs 180 for an economy class meal, though the extra money goes on cheese, crackers etc. A top airline (United, Singapore and even Virgin) will pay up to Rs 600 for a First Class meal but many airlines will churn out First Class meals for as little as Rs 300.

This explains why flight kitchens that can turn out 'gourmet' meals for passengers on some international airlines produce such crap on many domestic flights. Basically, the price is so low that they can't be bothered to exert themselves for a Rs 50 dinner.

The third secret is the most damaging because it reflects badly on you and me: the Indian passenger. The sad truth is that the majority of Indian passengers like complaining about food quality but refuse to allow airlines to serve them anything remotely adventurous. Consider the usual problem faced by vegetarians: paneer, paneer and more paneer. You would think that by now airlines would have found some alternatives. Well, they have, but we aren't interested. Any airline that serves mushrooms to vegetarian passengers is faced with uneaten meals and hundreds of complaints. The same is true of non-vegetarians. Have you ever wondered why the basic choice consists of two options: small pieces of chicken in thick gravy with rice or a slab of rubber chicken, sometimes with revolting white sauce (the so-called Continental option)? The answer is easy enough: those are the only things we like to eat. So airlines spend their time trying to find variations on this theme. For instance, if there is a so-called Chinese option, it will follow exactly the same formula as the Indian: pieces of chicken in cornflour-thickened red sauce with allegedly fried rice.

The 'snacks' option is similarly handicapped. No matter how inventive the flight kitchens want to be, Indians want everything deep-fried. Any fool knows that anything deep-fried starts turning soggy within minutes of leaving the pan so it is hardly likely to last the minimum of eight hours (and a maximum of twenty-four hours) before it can be served. No matter. Every airline will tell you that deep-frying is the preferred option for all Indian passengers.

How does one get around these seemingly insurmountable problems? Frankly, I don't think we can. Jet Airways has tried such innovative ways of presentation as a trolley snack service but this has coincided with a sharp decline in the calibre of Jet's cabin crew so the two effects have neutralized each other.

You might want to try my solution. If I absolutely *have* to eat on a plane I pack a sandwich before I board. Or, if somebody else is paying, I get them to buy me a First Class ticket, and then I stick to the caviar.

# too exotic for good taste?

Chandrashekhar Dasgupta, who used to be our Ambassador to Beijing, told me this joke: how do we know that Adam and Eve were not Chinese? Simple. When temptation reared its delicious head, they would have thrown away the apple. They would have eaten the snake instead.

Even those Indians who regard themselves as dedicated non-vegetarians are remarkably squeamish when it comes to eating foods that are, well, exotic in nature. For most of us, the high point of gastronomic adventure is the odd meal of brain or that bizarre Punjabi delicacy, Gurda Kapoora. (No, not Shakti Kapoor's brother but lamb's testicles.)

The Chinese, on the other hand, have no such reservations. They eat animals we would never dream of eating. At many upmarket restaurants in mainland China they will direct you to a box full of squirming live snakes and ask you to pick one for your dinner.

Or, they will offer you various patently alcoholic drinks, all served from jars that contain the bodies of (dead) lizards or snakes. The rationale behind these drinks is nearly always the same: 'Make you strong, heh heh, heh.' Small wonder then that, as Anthony Bourdin recounts in his book *Cook's Tour*, many people go away with the impression that the entire East Asian region suffers from erectile problems ('strong' being a synonym for you-know-what).

When they are not eating snakes, the Chinese eat the parts of animals that most of us will not touch. Stewed Pig's Entrails is a fairly common main course at Chinese restaurants all over the world (though, of course, not in India); so are variations on the theme of cooked intestine. Fish Lips are a seafood delicacy (presumably we are dealing with the Julia Roberts or Mick Jaggers of fish here—otherwise how big can the lips be?) as are Duck's Feet nicely done with yellow bean sauce, for instance.

But why single out the Chinese? All over East Asia they delight in animals that we would attack with a canister of Flit, were we unfortunate enough to come across them. You need only to walk across Bangkok's busy Silom and Suriwong Roads after dark to see the stalls selling deep-fried insects: grasshoppers, locusts, yellow creepy-crawly bugs (I don't want to know what they are called) and yes, cockroaches.

In the Isaan region, in the north of Thailand, they mash cockroaches into their sauces so anyone who's eaten Isaan food in Thailand has probably eaten a bit of cockroach every now and then. The giveaway—or so I'm told—is a slight menthol taste, typical of the Thai cockroach. A dish made from cooked red ants is also a delicacy of North Thailand and Laos.

Lest you think that the Far East is the home of exotic eating, let me point out that a love for insects extends to other parts of the world: Africa, for instance. (In his book on their failed friendship, Paul Theroux chronicles V.S. Naipaul's brahminical revulsion at the eating habits of 'negroes', as the latter likes to call them.) Locusts are big on menus there, apparently.

All over Europe they eat the parts of animals that we throw away. The French, famously, love offal and busy themselves with cooking the linings of cow stomachs in a delicate gravy, or in sautéing the glands of sheep. In England, tripe (you don't want to know) is an everyday dish, and in Scotland, haggis, the national dish, is made in a whole sheep's stomach and consists of various entrails. With typical Scots canniness, they describe it as a 'pudding'. Some pudding!

In South America they focus on animals that we regard as domestic pests. On a visit to Guyana (the one country in the West Indies that is on the South American mainland), I got fed up of the bland 'international' food at my hotel. Didn't they have any Guyanese specialties, I kept asking. The broad answer seemed to be 'No'. The Indians ate dal-chawal and steered so clear of the blacks that they had no clue about their eating habits.

Finally, the hotel's manager called me down to the restaurant for a local delicacy whose name, I am ashamed to say, I quickly forgot. Would I like it fully cooked or a little rare, he asked. I was beginning to get excited when a sudden caution seized me. What meat are we eating, exactly? I asked.

The name meant nothing to me.

Well, is it like a sheep or like a cow?

Long pause.

Well, they finally said, it is a large rodent.

I went back to eating dal-chawal.

It is easy to make fun of people's eating habits but of course, these are matters of individual taste. When it comes to fish, for instance, I will eat most things, even if they are raw. I love sushi and sashimi and my idea of a treat is two dozen oysters with a nice bottle of Muscadet.

But when it comes to meat, I turn strongly squeamish and won't touch kidney, liver, brain or any kind of offal—a slightly contrary position for a man who adores raw fish. But then, even when it comes to fish, we have our preferences.

Take the large prawn, for instance. In most parts of India, we eat the fleshy tail and throw away the cockroach-like bit with its beady eyes and antenna.

But Bengalis regard the head (and especially the brain) as the best part of the prawn and the tail as the inferior bit. A good Bengali will first make sure that it is a fresh water prawn (the division between fresh water and sea fish is a tiresome Bengali obsession) and then greedily suck out the gelatinous juices from the prawn's brain.

But this same man will, if you say that the Chinese eat fish lips, roll his eyes with revulsion and act as though this is a barbarous habit.

Or take the meat most of us eat every day. Five-star hotel restaurants go to great lengths to suggest to foreigners that what they are eating is lamb (for instance, they call it mutton which, by definition, is lamb).

The truth, of course, is that it is goat. When foreigners find out, they are either tickled or revolted. In 1972, the Rolling Stones went off to the West Indies to record their new album. Between takes they were comforted by large quantities of alcohol with little meat patties. (They were probably also stimulated by large amounts of cocaine but that's not germane to our story.)

Only when they were well into the session, somewhere between *Angie* and *Star Star*, did they discover that the patties were made from goat's meat. They were so tickled by the idea of eating goat—which millions of Indians do every day—that they used the idea as the title for their album.

They called it *Goat's Head Soup*.

So, don't laugh at other people's food habits. They are probably already laughing at ours.

# at your service

A year or so ago, at the dinner to celebrate a century of Bombay's Taj Mahal Hotel, I went into the kitchen to say hello to the chefs. The Taj had invited chefs from all its properties all over India so there were many familiar faces.

There was one chef whom I did not recognize but who, nevertheless, came up to say hello.

'You don't know me,' he said, 'but I probably cook for you more often than any other chef at this hotel.'

I was mystified. 'You do?' I said.

'Yes,' he said. 'I'm the room service chef.'

And of course, he was absolutely right.

While I eat out at restaurants fairly often, I tend to eat in my room when I'm travelling. Partly it is that I'm usually too exhausted to phone a friend and go out for dinner. And partly it is that I enjoy the chance to relax, unwind in my own room, watch a little TV, catch up on my reading or just spend quality time with my Significant Other.

This makes me the perfect user of room service.

I've eaten room service at nearly every hotel I've ever stayed in. I've had Alain Ducasse's room service (from Spoon+) at London's The Sanderson, I've eaten yakitori in my room at Tokyo's New Otani. I've eaten som tam by the pool in my villa at Phuket's Banyan Tree. And even when the hotel has been too modest to offer full room service (a Holiday Inn in Florida, for instance), I've gone down to the deli, packed a sandwich, a Diet Coke and a bag of crisps and wolfed it all down while watching a pay movie on the TV in my room. In Copenhagen, at the once legendary SAS Royal Hotel (designed by Arne Jacobson), I found to my mortification that the room service button on my phone connected me directly to a Domino's Pizza outlet. As I have no great love of Scandinavian cuisine (roll-mop herrings and crispbread), I ordered a barbecue pork pizza and settled down to watch CNN.

Some hotels do take room service seriously. In the early 1990s, when I used to stay at Delhi's Taj Mahal Hotel, I complained bitterly to the chef about the quality of his breakfasts. I don't know what he did, but standards then shot up. I still remember a wonderful souffle French Toast, the like of which I've never eaten anywhere else (or at the Delhi Taj, for that matter; perhaps that chef has gone).

At Bangalore's Windsor Manor, currently my candidate for best-run hotel in India, the room service menu is so long that you marvel at the range of dishes on offer. The food is uniformly good—I challenge anybody to eat badly at the Windsor Manor—and the butler service is absolutely outstanding.

In the 1970s, when the Bombay Taj was transforming itself into a modern hotel, a lot of time and effort went into formulating a suitable room-service menu. An elaborate recipe for a classic Taj Club Sandwich was recorded and the hotel's Executive Chef, Satish Arora, invented the Chicken Tikka Sandwich. But because it was only for hotel guests, the Taj called it the Room Service Special Sandwich. To eat it, you had to actually stay at the Taj.

These days, alas, nobody goes to that kind of trouble. Abroad, they treat room service as a bit of a nuisance because the cost of labour is so high. Some hotels even impose a delivery surcharge on room service food. As a general rule, most modern hotels—in the West, especially—will simply offer the coffee shop menu as a room service menu.

This makes a certain amount of sense. The point of room service is that it is still available when the proper restaurants are closed. At those times, the coffee shop is the only outlet that's open, so the same kitchen services both, the room guests and diners in the cafe.

A great hotel, of course, will be more adventurous. At the Bombay Taj, for instance, there are two room service kitchens, one for the old wing and one for the new (useful at breakfast time when the orders come streaming in at a rapid rate) and two different kitchens for the two coffee shops (the Shamiana and Sea Lounge).

A guest at the Taj can order from the room service menu, from any of the restaurants when they are open (though not from the Zodiac Grill), and from the two coffee shops (this includes the *chaat* which the Sea Lounge is famous for), including the Shamiana which is a 24-hour restaurant. Since the menus are significantly different, the food and beverage service at the Taj excellent, and the old wing has the nicest hotel rooms in India, why would any guest want to venture down to the restaurants? He can simply eat room service.

Of course there are problems with room service as a concept. Some dishes simply have to be eaten straight from the kitchen. They will not survive the wait before they are picked up by the waiter from the kitchen (upto ten minutes), or carried to the room (another ten minutes), even if they are kept in hot cases.

If you are in a hotel where room service takes a while, then steer clear of steaks and the like—they'll be rubber by the time they get to you. A good hotel will advise you what to order. In suburban Bombay, for instance, I always stay at the Leela (and very good it is, too) and often my room is near the hotel's excellent top floor Italian restaurant. It was the Leela that suggested that I might want to order from the Italian menu—that kitchen was much nearer than the room service kitchen several floors below. So I now get my rack of lamb from the Italian restaurant and the butler brings it almost directly from the stove.

Because of the time factor, certain kinds of food do not always work well as room service. Burgers and elaborate sandwiches tend to get soggy. (This is especially true of burgers which often collapse in your hands.) Deep-fried food needs to be eaten quickly—a test of a good hotel's breakfast service is how crisp the dosa is when it gets to your room.

Indian food works best in such situations—curries, *sabzis* and biryanis, in particular. If I haven't eaten on the plane or am on a night flight (and I'm increasingly off airline food), I usually stagger into my hotel room and order a biryani. Some hotels do terrific biryanis (the Leela does a killer Kerala biryani as you would expect from a hotel run by a Malayali) and most kitchens will manage a reasonably edible version.

The problem with the eat-Indian-food-only approach is simple enough: vegetarians get cheated.

If I'm not feeling particularly carnivorous, then I'll order a yellow dal, rice and simple *sabzi* (*aloo*, *bhindi* or whatever, as distinct from the paneer rubbish and *navratan korma*s that hotels keep trying to shove down your throat). This is simple comfort food and for the hotels it is also low-cost food—how much *can* dal-chawal cost?

But hotels have worked out that vegetarians are the most vulnerable (because their choices are limited) and some have taken the line that vegetarian hotel guests are there to be ripped off. After all, they say, if a chap is ordering food in his room then he has no choice but to pay *whatever* you charge him.

Enter, the latest hotel rip-off, on par with the great mineral water rip-off (where hotels buy a bottle at Rs 10 and sell it for Rs 60): the great room service rip-off.

Top prize in the rip-off stakes must go to the Grand Maratha Sheraton, the new hotel that ITC has built near the Bombay airport. The Maratha offers you food from its restaurants on room service (this is a welcome ITC tradition) but doesn't bother with any designated room service menu at all. Instead, it simply recycles the coffee shop menu. You would think that a hotel with a rack rate of between Rs 12,000 to 16,000 for a room (not a suite, which costs more)—absurdly high for a tower-block airport hotel—would make a greater effort.

But it gets worse. Not only do you have to be content with the coffee shop menu but they also charge you *extra* for the same food. This might be acceptable in a country where labour costs are high (Switzerland, for instance) but makes no sense in India. Besides, what message are they sending out to the guest who has already been charged this huge room rate: We are not only charging you lots for your room, but we'll rip you off a little more if you expect us to actually provide food in that room.

Some instances. A vegetarian sandwich (say tomato and cheese) is Rs 310 at the coffee shop. Order it in your room and it will cost you Rs 375. So you get charged an extra Rs 65 (on a base price of Rs 310) only to have it delivered by a room service waiter. Likewise, the Nasi Goreng is Rs 525 at the coffee shop but it's Rs 600 for exactly the same dish (from the same kitchen) in the room. What's the extra Rs 75 for?

Vegetarians are ripped off even more. Assume you want a simple yellow dal, *sabzi* and chawal in your room. The dal will cost you Rs 350 (what's the food cost basis here? 4 per cent?) And the only *sabzis* (if you can call them that—most have paneer), are Rs 425. So, even if they throw in the rice free, and you only have a Coke (Rs 95), that simple meal will cost you Rs 870!

Surely ITC doesn't need to cheat people in this manner?

That said, the Maratha has a very nice management team, quite acceptable food (even if it's not in the Windsor Manor league), and is not a bad place to stay in if you are on that side of Bombay. But with occupancies and room rates so high in Bombay, the temptation to extract as much money as you can from your guests probably becomes irresistible.

I remember having a huge argument with Ajit Kerkar (in his last few months at the Taj) about a Rs 650 price tag for a room-service steak. Ajit's excuse was that the Bombay Taj was a luxury hotel and couldn't offer a domestic steak to its guests. If it was going to serve imported beef, then it had no choice but to charge those prices. (This was five years ago, so Rs 650 seemed even more outrageous than it does today.)

I was never convinced by Ajit's explanations. First of all, if the premise was that a luxury hotel had to serve imported steak, then why was it serving domestic cuts in the Shamiana? Was that supposed to be less luxurious than room service? And what about the Delhi Taj? Why did that serve a domestic cut? Was that not a luxury hotel?

The truth, then as now, I suspect, is that hotels are always tempted to charge whatever they think they can get away with. With restaurants, you fear that guests won't come if the prices are too high. But with room service there's no such fear.

The guest is a mere *bakra*.

# are you being served?

# rocked by bad taste

I was in Bangalore for the Rolling Stones concert in April last year and about the only thing that people in Bangalore could talk about was how elusive the Stones themselves were being. They had been expected to stay at the West End, Bangalore's oldest luxury hotel, but that plan had to be altered (even though the Taj group, which manages the West End, was the official host for the concert) when the band's management demanded four more or less identical suites for all four Stones. The West End is an old-world hotel and none of the suites are identical.

So the Stones ended up at the ritzy new Leela Palace near the airport. They checked in under pseudonyms, their management wouldn't even tell the hotel which Stone occupied which suite and security was intense in an effort to keep the rest of Bangalore out.

Perhaps, as a consequence, all kinds of stories about the Stones made the rounds. According to the most popular version, only Mick Jagger, the so-called 'educated Stone' (he went to the London School of Economics as the biographers never tire of pointing out) ventured into Bangalore or even wandered around the hotel—he was spotted in the pool the afternoon of the show (he is very healthy; his father was a PT teacher, as his biographers also remember to include).

The other three Stones—or so the story went—stayed in their suites ingesting all kinds of exotic substances. Sometimes they would ask for massages but on the whole the substances were enough for them. Apparently, they would sleep all day and then, at night, when the hotel had gone to bed, they would call up the coffee shop and demand assorted sweet drinks, milkshakes, puddings and the like. As far as they were concerned, that was all the food they needed. (This is not uncommon among users of exotic substances.)

Oh yes, rock stars and food!

On the whole, rock stars like to take their food intravenously. Those who disdain the needle puff at their meals. And as for drink, this tends to be spirits, drunk straight from the bottle. (Especially among the women: think Janis Joplin and her ubiquitous bottle of Jack Daniel's.)

When they do bother with food it is for fun. Grace Slick (of the Jefferson Airplane; also a reformed alcoholic) says that Jim Morrison squished strawberries on her body and then consumed both the strawberries and her. A false (but amazingly long-lasting) story concerns the uses that Mick Jagger and his 1960s girlfriend Marianne Faithfull (an aside: look at clean and fit Mick now and look at fat, old Marianne; perhaps rock stars shouldn't eat) used to make of Mars Bars.

Gourmets are rare in the world of rock. Elton John likes good food (and by God, doesn't it show) and his boyfriend David Furnish takes him to fancy restaurants in France. David Gilmour of Pink Floyd (he's the one with the paunch who now acts as though he wrote all their songs) likes trendy places but the group's real talent, Roger Waters (who actually wrote all the songs but was so unpleasant that he had to leave the band), is no foodie. Robert Plant (of Led Zep) likes curries (he was once married to an Anglo-Indian), David Bowie goes to fancy restaurants but doesn't eat much, and poor Paul McCartney used to eat the disgusting Western vegetarian food that his late wife Linda made. (We know this because Linda produced a range of her own packaged foods so that the world could see that, whatever her talents as a photographer, she was as crap a chef as she was a singer. Oh, all right! God rest her departed soul, etc. etc.)

Rock stars much prefer drugs on the whole. A classic rock party in the 1970s thrown by a decadent supergroup of that period featured a collection of dwarfs. Each dwarf carried a mound of cocaine on his head. As they passed guests would inhale deeply and then return to their conversations. Why dwarfs? Well, because the mounds of cocaine had to be at nostril height and this was only possible if they were placed on the heads of midgets.

But then rock people like dwarfs at their parties. An apocryphal story concerns a very rich and classy Indian of, shall we say, medium height, who once hosted Ahmet Ertegun, the legendary head and founder of Atlantic Records, on a trip around the country.

'How can I ever repay you?' Ertegun is supposed to have asked.

'When I come to New York, make me feel like I'm ten feet tall,' the Indian millionaire replied.

Sure enough, when he arrived in New York a few months later, the millionaire was invited to a party thrown in his honour by Ertegun. The time was a little early but he thought nothing of it.

Imagine his horror when he entered the party to find that all the other guests were midgets. For the first time in his life, he was the tallest man in the room. He did feel ten feet tall.

Of course, it was all a joke. The real party began later. The midgets were paid off and departed and the real guests then began to arrive.

Some years ago, I finally worked up the courage (I blame the wine) to ask aforementioned Indian millionaire if the story was actually true.

It would be overstating the case to use the word 'irate'. But certainly, he was not pleased. Yes, he knew Ertegun and they often socialized. But as for a party consisting entirely of midgets, he had no idea where I'd heard such an outrageous tale.

Shame. It's a good story anyway.

(As the story is a complete fabrication I will not name the

millionaire who is, in reality, a wonderful, elegant sort of chap. But as it appears in a book titled *Rude Food*, readers with a deductive bent of mind should have worked out who he is).

The one rock star who did enjoy food, though, was of course, the king himself, Elvis Presley. Readers who are older than I am (oh, it felt good to write those words!) will recall Elvis as this slim-hipped sex symbol who invented rock and roll. My generation, however, only dimly remembers some truly wretched films where Elvis sang execrable middle-of-the-road songs.

But at least he was slim then!

The Elvis who lingers in the public memory is the bloated fatso in a white tasselled catsuit who prowled the stage at Las Vegas regurgitating his old hits and murdering other people's songs (Barry Gibb, in particular, could have had him up for homicide, given what he did to *Words*).

This period (affectionately referred to as his Fat Bastard phase) was unique in the annals of rock because Elvis not only ate a lot he also consumed every drug known to man. A druggie rock star we can take. A greedy rock star is also acceptable. But a fat druggie? A portly junkie? That's pretty unprecedented.

Elvis got to look like a whale by eating the sort of junk food that not only made the US of A great but also made obesity its national disease. He would consume cheeseburger after cheeseburger, eat lots of fries and snack compulsively on chocolate bars. Not surprisingly, he became fat. (The drugs made him incontinent. By the end, he was appearing onstage in diapers.)

Almost all the food that Elvis ate during that period is too disgusting for normal people to even contemplate eating but by far the most bizarre was the deep-fried peanut butter and banana sandwich.

Why would you deep-fry a sandwich? Well, because Elvis liked fried food. He would even get his Mars Bars deep-fried before he touched them. (Good thing for Marianne Faithfull that she wasn't going around with him!)

But people are strange. The Las Vegas Elvis made millions (most of which his manager, Col. Tom Parker kept stealing from him) and his in-concert movies (such as *Elvis: Live in Las Vegas!* or *Elvis: That's The Way It Is*) became huge hits all over the world.

Even our very own Adnan Sami told me that he was inspired to become a singer because of Elvis. Apparently, a young Adnan (who was very thin then) went to see *Elvis: That's The Way It Is* and came back a total convert.

I was stunned when he told me this story. But that's the worst phase in Elvis's career, I protested. I was about to say 'That's his Fat Bastard Phase' when I remembered to bite my tongue in time.

But say this for Adnan: he is a true disciple. As far as I can see, he's never been thin after he became an Elvis fan. Now, that's what I call devotion.

As this is supposed to be food writing and I haven't given you much food in ths piece, I'll make up by ending with a recipe. It is Nigella Lawson's low-fat version of the famous Elvis Presley sandwich: Peanut Butter and Banana. According to Lawson, as unhealthy as this version is, the real thing was a lot worse. At least this sandwich is only shallow-fried.

Mash a ripe banana. Toast two slices of white bread and spread two tablespoons worth of peanut butter on one and the mashed banana on the other. Sandwich the two slices together.

Melt two tablespoons of butter (ordinary butter, not peanut butter) in a frying pan. Fry the sandwich in the butter, turning it so that each side is golden brown.

Slice on the diagonal. Eat.

Yes, I know it sounds disgusting. But then, that's rock 'n' roll food. It's so bad that it's good! Otherwise why would there be rock cookbooks (such as *Are You Hungry Tonight?*—a collection of Elvis recipes), restaurants run by elderly rock stars (Sticky Fingers, the seventy-year-old Bill Wyman's effort to cash in on his years with the Stones) and even rock franchises (the ubiquitous Hard Rock Cafe, home of disgusting food and loud music)?

The secret, as you've probably guessed, is that rock stars generally don't eat. They get stoned instead.

# do you want to go higher?

In the previous piece I dealt with the curious subject of rock stars and food. The trick to working out what they ate, I suggested, lay in recognizing that they weren't very keen on food at all—unless of course, they could take it intravenously.

That's why—despite the proliferation of such rock-themed restaurants as the Hard Rock Cafe and Ruby Tuesday ('She would never say where the food came from/Because yesterday don't matter when the menu's so disgusting . . .' Oh, all right, I made that up)—there's no such thing as rock and roll cuisine.

But even if rock stars are content to drug or drink themselves to death (Jim Morrison, Jimi Hendrix, Janis Joplin, John Bonham, Brian Jones . . . the list is a long one), where does that leave the rest of us? What about people who simply like the music?

My own experience suggests that while rock needs food like a fish needs a bicycle, a small (or not so small) quantity of alcohol—if not other mood-altering substances—can actually increase your enjoyment of the music. At most rock concerts, the sweet smell of cannabis hovers over the air like a fragrant cloud.

At the Stones concert in Bangalore, for instance, you could have got high just by breathing deeply in front of the stage. At the Bombay show, on the other hand, the crowd was much straighter and I couldn't smell very much. Small wonder, then, that Mick Jagger came to the expensive seats and sneered: 'Should I send you some bottles of champagne?'

The jibe wasn't off the mark. Even as he spoke, Taj waiters were ferrying trays of French wine to the fatties in the first row. You could hardly conceive of an image that was less rock 'n' roll.

The problem with drinking at rock concerts is that they don't usually let you bring alcohol to the venue. There are many reasons for this—some of them quite sensible. For a start, nobody wants drunken fans to riot during the concert. And there's always a very real danger that somebody will do real damage to the band by throwing glass bottles on to the stage.

It wasn't always so. At Woodstock *everybody* was stoned. Much of the audience was on LSD (who can forget all those shots of mad, drugged, topless hippie chicks rolling around in the slush?) and so were most of the musicians. Pete Townshend says that somebody slipped an LSD tablet into his drink before he went onstage and he tripped through his entire set.

As anybody who's seen the Woodstock movie will know, The Who performed one of their best-ever sets that night (remember *See me, feel me*?), so perhaps Pete should have stuck to the acid rather than graduating to brandy. (A dedication on one of Townshend's solo 1980s albums thanks 'the makers of Hennessy Cognac for saving my life by making their product so expensive'.)

John Sebastian (he was the buffoon in the tie-dye clothes who kept saying 'Fa-aa-ar out ma-aa-an') was so stoned at Woodstock that when they sent him out to do an acoustic set (there was a problem with the electric wiring), he sang on autopilot. He says he can't even remember going onstage. (Oh, but we can, John, we can.)

Even as late as 1973, when I attended my first grown-up rock concert (by a now forgotten hippie band called Hawkwind, best known then for their hit single *Silver machine*), half the audience (the twenty-plus crowd) was stoned while the other half (the under-twenties like me) was busy drinking as much beer as possible.

You may laugh—or seem sceptical—but try a simple experiment. Listen to your favourite album one night when you are stone-cold sober. Then, the following night, listen to it again but pour yourself several large drinks. You'll find that the nature of the entire experience will have altered. (And I guess this holds true even if your favourite album is by Daler Mehndi.)

The trick, for people like myself, is working out how to smuggle a little alcohol into rock concerts. (I suppose it is easier for you to stick to hash but I have a mental block about drugs of any kind, even the relatively harmless ones like cannabis.)

In England, where I've seen most of my shows, it is easy enough. There's a bar in the foyer, so you duck out during a boring song (when Keith Richards sings at a Stones concert, for instance) and down two large vodkas. That should keep you going for the next five or six songs. (In the old days I used to always believe that Led Zeppelin gave John Bonham that ridiculous drum solo during *Moby Dick* so that the audience could go to the loo or—judging by how long the solo went on for—consume a large meal while the fat old drunk pounded his skins.)

Sometimes it is possible to overdo this, though. Taken, in my teens, by my school to see Rudolf Nureyev in *Sleeping Beauty*, I first noted how clingy Nureyev's tights were (you could see every goose pimple on his bum) and then repaired to the bar in urgent need of liquid refreshment. When I returned at the end of the performance, the *Sleeping Beauty* had awakened but I had soon fallen asleep in my seat. My schoolteachers were not amused.

Over a decade or so later, I overindulged while watching the Moody Blues at the Wembley Arena. As you probably know, the Moody Blues have only ever written four halfway decent songs (*Question*, *For my lady*, *Tuesday afternoon* and *Legend of a mind*) apart from that early masterpiece *Nights in white satin*, so each time they played some crap number, I'd hotfoot it to the bar.

Eventually, I felt the need to go to the loo, and while I was going about my business, I idly noted that the Wembley loos were unlike any I had ever seen. There were no urinals at all, just lots of stalls and lots of middle-aged ladies (this was a Moody Blues concert after all) powdering their noses and fixing their eyeshadow.

Only when I was on my way out did I work out why the loo seemed so different—I had gone to the ladies' by mistake.

Strangely, nobody seemed to mind or even notice. Perhaps all the women had also been partaking of the liquid refreshments available in the foyer.

In Bangkok last year, I found myself at an Elton John concert. I saw Elton in London in the 1980s and while the show had its share of dodgy moments (the post-Bernie Taupin songs, mainly), he had a tight band that really rocked. But, to my intense disappointment, the Bangkok show had no band, just Elton and his piano.

Now, Elton's written some great tunes in his lifetime, but two hours of sitting in an indoor stadium watching a fat poofter in a lurid Versace suit and a silly wig is not my idea of fun. And when you are bored (show me a man who can sit through *Can you feel the love tonight* and I'll show you a fool) you begin to notice that without their rock arrangements, too many of the songs sound the same and that after thirty-five minutes or so, Elton can't really hit the top notes any longer. (Well, he *is* getting on, the poor dear.)

So, naturally, you look for liquid distraction. But the Thais who were selling Kloster beer outside the arena wouldn't let you take the bottles in (for fear that you'd aim for Elton's toupee in an effort to entertain yourself, probably). Eventually, we agreed on a compromise. Because you could take paper glasses into the show, I poured two bottles of beer into six glasses and was allowed to take them to my seat. After that, even crap like *The way you move tonight* didn't sound so bad.

But now I've learnt most of the tricks. Here are two that usually work. One: empty a litre bottle of Bisleri. Fill with 750 ml (about two-thirds of the bottle) of tonic water or any other colourless mixer (Sprite or 7 UP are perfect). Add 250 ml (one-third) of any good vodka (i.e. not IMFL). Carry into stadium/concert hall pretending that it is water. (It worked at the Stones show in Bangalore.)

Two: take along a few miniature bottles of vodka. Buy whatever drink they are selling in the foyer. Empty miniatures into aforementioned drink. Buy large packet of popcorn. Take the drink and popcorn (essential for camouflage) into show with suitably innocent air.

Of course, you shouldn't have to do this. You should be able to pair your liquor to your music without resorting to such subterfuge. In an ideal world, this is how I'd match my drink to my music, rather as some people match their wines to their food.

- High Energy Rock Band (Stones, for instance): Vodka and Red Bull.
- Old Fart (Elton John, Paul Simon): Flavoured vodka and tonic.
- Childhood Fave (Paul McCartney): Scotch and Coke.
- Eighties Superstar (Sting, Mark Knopfler): Chilled white burgundy.
- All-time Great (Bruce Springsteen): Anything you like. The music's enough.
- Rock Dinosaur (Deep Purple): Black coffee, to stay awake.
- Nineties Superstar (REM, U2): Mojitos or other rum cocktails.

Does any of this make much sense? I don't suppose it does. At the end of the day all you need to remember is this: if the music gets you high, booze will take you higher.

# rude waiters? do table your protest

Is it bad form to be rude to waiters? Yes, most definitely. Does that mean that we have to live with bad service even when we are paying through our noses for the meal? No. Absolutely not. There is always a middle path.

Let's start with the definition of bad service.

In my experience, there are three kinds of bad service.

One: Can't-help-it bad service.

This happens when a restaurant is overbooked, when the room is short-staffed and when the waiters can't cope. On such occasions, it is almost never the fault of the poor man (or woman) who is serving your table.

The chances are that he's as angry as you are—and overworked as well. In such situations, nothing is gained by shouting at him. Ask for the manager, give him a piece of your mind and, especially if you are at a hotel, write a letter of complaint addressed to the General Manager whose staff have relieved you of your money without delivering on the promised service. If you don't get a grovelling reply, boycott the restaurant and urge your friends to do likewise.

Two: Can't-be-bothered bad service.

This is usually a mark of a bad restaurant. If you haven't been asked whether you want something to drink ten minutes after you've been seated, you have a right to complain. If the menus take too long to arrive or if the waiters are busy chatting to each other (or to others guests) when they should be taking your order, then you've clearly made a huge mistake in choosing your dinner destination for the evening.

You now have three options. You can grin and bear it, in which case, more fool you. You can walk out—my preferred option—and go somewhere nicer on the grounds that usually, when the front of the house is badly run, the kitchen will be as bad. Or, if you really have nowhere to go, you can send for the manager and have a stern word with him. (This usually does the trick.)

There is another option, though I've exercised it very rarely: you order a large and expensive meal. If the restaurant has can't-be-bothered service, the meal will take a while to arrive. So wait fifteen minutes or so till you are sure that it is too late for the chef to stop. Then very ostentatiously walk out, saying something like 'I'm sorry, I've waited long enough.'

They will be angry but there's not much they can do, short of wrestling you to the ground. You'll have to find another restaurant but at least you'll have punished them by making them waste your meal. (Yes, yes, I know there are people starving and you shouldn't waste food etc. etc. but all leftover food in restaurants goes to waiters or to the homeless, so the only thing that's wasted is their money, which is the whole point of the exercise.)

Three: We-are-too-fancy-for-you bad service.

If there's any kind of bad service that really gets me angry it is when waiters think you are a fool and are either snobbishly standoffish or vainly patronizing. To be fair, this happens less and less.

In an era where five-star hotels make their money from black marketeers and corrupt politicians, waiters are careful never to look down on guests. After all, the yokel who chews his noodles with his mouth open may just be the next chief minister of UP, and the bumpkin who belches loudly as he stares at the menu will probably spend more money on his meal than anybody else in the restaurant.

Even so, you do get the odd waiter who will sneer if you mispronounce the name of a dish (even if he himself says 'let-yoose' when he means lettuce or 'peer' when he means pear). Do not be intimidated. Do not fall prey to the temptation to say something like 'If you are so smart then why am I the one sitting in the chair about to embark on a large meal while you are wearing a silly uniform holding a cheap pad and calling me "sir"?' The big mistake is to be defensive; the trick is to pretend that you don't notice.

While sneering waiters are rare, a more common subset of we-are-too-fancy-for-you service is the-guest-is-a-fool service.

This is more devious than snobbish. Generally, this consists of waiters trying to unload all the food that isn't selling. Most big restaurants have a blackboard inside the kitchen that lists all the items that are currently rotting in the fridge or which must be got rid of before they go bad.

So, if your waiter says, 'I recommend the fish. It has been flown in from Cochin', look suspicious. If he says, 'Broccoli will go well with that' when you've just ordered tandoori chicken, give him a look of total disbelief. This is not to say that waiters' recommendations are always wrong (they're just wrong most of the time), but that restaurant managements have different agendas from their customers. Our agenda is to eat well; their agenda is to make money.

A subtler variation consists of embarrass-the-punter syndrome.

Usually, it works something like this: You go to a restaurant with a guest.

'Something to drink?' asks the waiter.

Your guest says, 'I'll have whisky.'

'Right, sir,' says the waiter, 'Black Label, Chivas, Black Dog . . .?'

At this stage, you want scream, 'Don't be ridiculous! This man thinks himself lucky if he gets to down a peg of Solan No. 1.' But of course, you can't. You can't even say, 'No, he'll have a regular Scotch, not a premium whisky, thank you very much.'

Because that would be embarrassing and insulting to your guest.

The restaurant knows that. Which is why it pushes the most expensive Scotch it dare recommend (Royal Salute or Blue Label would be pushing it too far). When the bill comes you'll probably pay twice as much for your guest's drinks than you will for both your meals put together. Abroad, they get around this by using basic Scotch as a pouring brand. You order Scotch and they won't ask you for a choice of brand unless you specifically request one. In India, they steal your money instead.

Fortunately, we've seen the death of the hugely popular hotel scam from the 1970s and 1980s (invented, I think, by the Oberoi Hotel chain). This consisted of the waiter waiting till you had ordered your meal and then saying, with an eye on your date, 'And which wine would Madam like?' Not 'Will you have wine?' but 'which wine'. The honest answer would have been: 'Look pal, my babe's having a cheeseburger and I doubt very much if Chateau Mouton Rothschild goes very well with that, so why don't you just piss off and send us a Thums Up instead?' But we were too chivalrous to say what we meant (something like 'Why would I waste money on wine? Half a glass of shandy and this girl's up for it'), and so we would end up ordering bottles of hideously overpriced wine which the babe in question would waste ('It is a little sour, no?') but the restaurant owners would laugh all the way to the bank.

Why is this scam dead (or maybe it still survives and I'm just too old and tired to fall for it)? My guess is that it collapsed when differentials between wine and food prices came down.

In the 1970s, you could eat well at a five-star hotel for Rs 100, so the last thing you wanted was a Rs 400 bottle of wine tagged on to the bill. Now, the food is more expensive and so is the Scotch. If a table of three orders a bottle of wine, the hotel loses money. It would make much more if everybody had cocktails or Scotch.

How does one get around the pitfalls of bad or patronizing service?

My advice: find a restaurant where you know the service is good. Take your guests only to this kind of restaurant. Do all your experimentation on your own. And then if you don't like the service, walk out and never go back.

# who's serving the who's who

Who eats out the most in Bombay? It is a serious question. And I ask it only because, having read Rashmi Uday Singh's *Good Food Guide 2003*, I think I know the answer.

It is Amitabh Bachchan.

I kid you not. According to the prolific Ms Uday Singh, Mr Bachchan frequents the following restaurants: Bellissima, Emperor's Court, The Great Wall, Trishna, Konkan Café, Liquid Lounge, Mahesh Lunch Home (his son is a regular), Nawab Saheb, Samovar, Saffron, and Tea Centre (his wife frequents it).

Close on the tail of the Bachchans are the Ambanis.

Here's where Rashmi tells us they go: Bellissima, Copper Chimney, Cream Centre, Golden Dragon, Jewel of India, Khyber, Mocha, Saffron, Thai Pavilion and the Zodiac Grill.

(Actually, the Ambanis go to more restaurants than the Bachchans—but then there are more Ambanis than there are Bachchans.)

Within the film world (excluding the Bachchans who seem now to have become the royal family of Bombay rather than a film family), Bipasha Basu seems like she goes out a lot.

According to Rashmi's book, she can be found at Onyx, Maroush and Papa Pancho. Dino Morea, on the other hand, hangs out at Bay of Bombay, Spices, and of course Papa Pancho.

As you may have guessed, Rashmi's book lists 120 or so of Bombay's best restaurants. Two-thirds of the restaurants list two famous customers. And predictably, they all want to claim that they are frequented by the Bachchans and the Ambanis.

As Amitabh is famously a non-drinking vegetarian who is happiest eating Indian food (*ghar ka khana* ideally), and the Ambanis are also teetotalling vegetarians, you may wonder why restaurants specializing in exotic foods would want to claim them as their guests.

But the answer is simple enough. Such is the cult of celebrity that every restaurant likes to claim that it is patronized by the rich, the famous and the glamorous. Sometimes the foodie credentials of celebrities may be questionable (would *you* go to a restaurant if it is frequented by the Thackerays or the Hindujas?), and the level of celebrity name-dropping may be pathetic (I have to say that I don't know who these celebrities, listed in Rashmi's book, are: Sujata Kapoor, Subi Samuel, Vijay Kher, Ashok Bhandari, K.B. Bharat, Imtiaz Kanga, Maureen Motwani, R.J. Savio, Boman Irani, DJ Akhil and Poonam Soni—but then perhaps they are really, really famous in Bombay).

But let's face it: all of us get a secret thrill out of going to a restaurant and finding it infested with celebrities.

In London, food critics are always sniffy about San Lorenzo (though I have to say that I quite like the food), but their views make no difference because the international jet set goes there. In Los Angeles, Morton's and Spago made it because of the celebrity guests. In Washington, the Bombay Club became America's most famous Indian restaurant once the Clintons went there. And in Delhi, the tired, uncomfortable Bukhara got a new lease of life thanks to Clintonian patronage.

Do celebrities know much about food? Should their opinion really count? The answers are obvious. (Most celebrities know nothing about food.) But these answers assume that ordinary people go to restaurants only for the food.

In fact, when most of us decide to spend an evening out, food is only one of the criteria we use while deciding where to go.

Often we like to go to a place that is full and bustling. And sometimes, we like the thrill of eating dinner while Amitabh Bachchan is at the next table. I know, for instance, that though I've often eaten at London's Le Caprice, the one meal I'll always remember was a lunch way back in 1986—and that's not because the food was better than usual. It was because David Bowie was two tables away.

The problem with celebrity hang-outs is not that famous people patronize them. It is that many restaurants that are accustomed to catering to celebrities appear to have contempt for anybody who is not rich or famous. No institution is as guaranteed to turn me against a restaurant as the velvet rope: the kind that bars entry and is only removed when you've persuaded the man at the door that you deserve to get in. In its heyday, Djinns at the Delhi Hyatt would delight in keeping teenagers waiting outside in the cold while welcoming fat, rich people in an effort to remain 'exclusive'. Now, Djinns is forgotten and both of Delhi's new trendy spots—Dublin at the Maurya and Rick's at the Taj—have a far more democratic door policy.

Famous people fall into two categories. There are those who throw their weight around in restaurants, snap their fingers at the staff and will only eat dishes that are off the menu. And then there are those who only want to have a normal night out and seek to avoid attention.

Usually, the latter category has it tougher than the former. Most restaurants (particularly those at five-star hotels) love brown-nosing celebrities and delight in offering free meals to rich people (who can certainly afford to pay). Consequently famous people (at least those who like to keep a low profile) prefer restaurants that treat them like everybody else and leave them in peace. That's why so many celebrities go to San Lorenzo or Tramp in London. And that's why places like Delhi's Diva or Bombay's Konkan Cafe, which are unimpressed by celebrity guests, actually attract more celebrities than other establishments.

Whenever I've found myself in the same restaurant as Amitabh Bachchan, for instance, he has always looked as though he wished he were invisible and did not attract so much attention. Even A.B. Vajpayee, who likes a good Chinese meal (the House of Ming at the Delhi Taj is the current favourite), prefers to go to restaurants abroad only so that the waiters leave him alone.

But for you and me, there's broadly only one rule of thumb. If you go to a restaurant and have to wait for hours for service because the staff are too busy sucking up to a celebrity (even if it's only Dino Morea), then don't waste any more time at the restaurant.

Leave the staff to their celebrity guest and go somewhere else.

# the fine art of food criticism

When I was growing up in Bombay, there were only two food critics of any consequence. Both went on to become legends. The first was Jiggs (or more properly, Jay Inder Singh) Kalra, who was then the rising star of Khushwant Singh's *Illustrated Weekly* but had already begun to demonstrate a great feel for food. When Jiggs wrote about a restaurant, you trusted his judgement. The other was, of course, Busybee aka Behram Contractor.

Behram was Chief Reporter of the old *Evening News of India* (now defunct), and was regarded by everybody in the trade as the finest reporter in Bombay. To the average reader, however, he was better known as the author of the funny 'Round and About' column on the back page which he signed 'Busybee'. It was in this latter guise that he wrote his restaurant reviews and many readers did not—at least not till many years later—work out that Chief Reporter Behram and funny, food-loving Busybee were the same man.

Both Behram and Jiggs were regular journalists who treated food writing as a labour of love. They flourished in an era where there were few five-star hotel restaurants, no fancy stand-alones and little in the way of non-Indian cuisine. Consequently, they specialized in discovering restaurants, in providing tips and introducing readers to regional cuisines. There was no point in writing bad reviews or commenting on restaurant ambience—India had not yet reached that stage.

When a restaurant culture did develop, both found success doing different things. Jiggs is today one of India's foremost culinary impresarios and rarely writes about restaurants. Behram left the *Evening News* to start *Mid-Day*, left that to start the *Afternoon* and still remains, a few years after his death, Bombay's most famous byline. His wife Farzana has kept the foodie tradition alive as founder-editor of the excellent *Upper Crust* magazine.

No restaurant critic has, in the years that passed, ever managed to write with the authority of Jiggs. Nor has anybody managed to write about food with the love and affection that Behram brought to his reviews. Both have remained in a class of their own.

On the other hand, following the hotel and restaurant explosion of the 1980s and the 1990s, we now have a new breed of restaurant critic who is knowledgeable about food and paid to be critical: to tell readers where they should spend their money and what to avoid. Curiously, Bombay has yet to throw up a good restaurant critic. The biggest name is Rashmi Uday Singh who is a food writer in the Busybee mould, more interested in making the food come alive than in running down restaurants. But in Delhi, the formidable Sabina Sehgal Saikia can make or break a restaurant's business with her acerbic judgments; Sourish Bhattacharya can turn a little-known restaurant into a huge celebrity haunt; and I'm always guided by the fair and accurate reviews that Marryam Reshii writes for *HT City*.

But food critics face problems of their own.

In the late 1970s, I started writing critical restaurant reviews for the magazine I then edited. I was in my early twenties, entirely unknown and therefore undeserving of any special attention at the restaurants I visited. But within eight months of the start of my reviewing career a funny thing happened.

Each time I would go to a restaurant the manager would rush to my side and lead me to my table, while simultaneously tugging at his forelock. The chef would then emerge from the kitchen and begin genuflecting. He would contemptuously toss the menu aside and promise to cook me a special meal which was based on fresh ingredients, newly flown in from every comer of the world—'entirely off-the-menu, sir'. After each course, five waiters would appear to ask if I'd liked the food. And so on.

Obviously, my restaurant experience bore no relation to what the average guest was going to get.

In 1982, when I resumed writing restaurant reviews for another publication, I used a pseudonym and my editor agreed to zealously guard my identity. This worked much better (the chef never emerged from the kitchen and hotel PR people looked through me) but by late 1983, my cover was blown, at least among the big hotels, and the genuflecting began afresh.

I wondered then about food critics and whether they could ever claim to judge a restaurant fairly. There are, broadly, two approaches to the subject. The first is the traditional French approach in which the food critic sees himself on a par with an art critic or a film critic. When he judges a meal, he is judging a work of art and must treat it as such. Most of the great French food critics have been celebrities and have revelled in being famous.

The official position, as explained by the authors of the Gault-Millau guide is 'it is always possible to get a bad meal in a good restaurant. In fact, it happens all the time. But it is never possible to get a good meal at a bad restaurant.' In other words, even if the chef recognizes you, he can't cook a good meal if he's a bad chef. This, I suppose, was also the position implicitly adopted by Jiggs, Busybee and all the other famous Indian food critics.

But there is a second view. The red *Michelin Guide* lists restaurants it recommends (but without any description other than a list of specialities). Some get stars (three stars is tops). These ratings are devised on the basis of several visits by anonymous inspectors who go several times before deciding to award a star. Michelin reckons that this is a more reliable way of judging a restaurant because it more closely approximates what a paying (non-famous) customer is likely to experience.

In recent years, some American critics have agreed. At the *New*

*York Times*, Mimi Sheraton (who, like Sabina or Marryam, could make or break a restaurant) was so paranoid about being recognized that she refused ever to be photographed. In London, the positions tend to vary. Famous food critics (Jonathan Meades, Adrian Gill, etc.) appear on TV so often that they are instantly recognized. On the other hand, the one British critic I always take seriously, Fay Maschler, gets around this problem nicely by printing a picture with her column—the trick is that the photo looks nothing like her. I always thought it was vanity (the photo must have been taken during her childhood) but Fay claims it is a desire for anonymity that motivates her. (That's what they all say.)

My own view is that there is room for both, the anonymous reviewer and the well-known expert. In London and New York I use the *Zagat Surveys* which are based on readers' responses, so each restaurant has probably been visited at least a hundred times before the reviews are written. In Delhi I go by Marryam Reshii's reviews, not only because she is so good, but because she is largely anonymous.

On the other hand, how would I judge a truly great chef? Would I go by the views of anonymous reviewers alone or would I also be influenced by the praise of an expert like Sabina?

The answer, I suspect, is that there's no one rule for food critics. If you want to know a good place for an average evening out, stick with the anonymous reviewers. But if you want an expert opinion, then don't worry about how famous the critic is. In that sense, Gault-Millau are right: a bad chef can't produce a good meal and to judge a great meal you probably have to read the opinion of the successors to Behram Contractor and Jiggs Kalra.

In other words, if it's ambience and the total experience you want, trust the anonymous or less famous reviewers. (But always ignore the hype-laden praise of five-star hotels from freebie journos.) Food is an art, and to judge the top end, you do need to read the views of a top critic.

# saluting the chef

My favourite Paul Bocuse story concerns the great chef's response to critics who complain about his travels. (And as the most publicized Michelin three-star chef in the world Bocuse is often on the road, launching some book or cooking at some festival.) Whenever Bocuse is asked, 'Who cooks at your restaurant when you are out of town?', he always retorts, 'The same people who cook when I am in town.'

For people outside the restaurant trade, the concept of a chef is difficult to understand. In the old days, the chef was merely the chief cook ('chef' means 'chief in French) who accepted the orders as they came in from the restaurant, assigned the dishes to various underlings and then checked them before they left the kitchen.

Many famous chefs (among them the currently super trendy British chef Gordon Ramsay) still operate on this principle, but whenever you judge a chef's skill, you accept that his role as conductor of the kitchen is only one manifestation of a complex set of duties. Generally, we judge chefs on two grounds. One: the quality of all the food that emerges from the kitchen. And two: the originality of the dishes on the menu.

In most serious French restaurants—Bocuse's establishment for instance—this means that the kitchen-conductor aspect of the job is the least of the chef's responsibilities. We rate Bocuse as one of the world's greatest chefs because of the skill with which he combines ingredients and juggles cooking techniques to produce original and imaginative dishes. His restaurant gets three stars because the food is uniformly good—and rarely, if ever these days, does Bocuse actually get behind the stove himself—but his reputation as a chef is based not just on the food at his establishment but on the manner in which he created dishes and more or less re-invented the basic principles of French cuisine in the early days of what used to be called nouvelle cuisine.

The balance between turning out good food at your own restaurant and inventing new dishes is a difficult one. Alain Ducasse ran two Michelin three-star restaurants (he was therefore described as the world's only six-star chef), opened a vastly expensive place in New York and launched the Spoon+ chain of eateries (a sort of bridge line). It worked briefly and Ducasse claimed, like Bocuse, that regardless of where he was, the food was always excellent at all his restaurants. Sadly, the Michelin inspectors disagreed and he lost one of his stars.

Not everyone is as good as Bocuse at maintaining standards. Nobu, of the eponymous Japanese-Peruvian restaurants, seems to manage though I doubt if a single branch of Nobu could ever be regarded on par with any of Ducasse's or Bocuse's establishments. Gordon Ramsay is trying to expand with a second eponymous restaurant in Claridges and a new one is coming up at the Connaught. Marco Pierre White, the trendiest British chef of the early 1990s expanded so fast that he had to take refuge in his self-proclaimed genius as an inventor of dishes. On his menu, each dish would have a date next to it marking the year in which the great man invented it. It didn't work and Marco's given up cooking altogether in favour of restauranting.

In India, the situation is more complicated. For a start, we still have to learn to respect the chef. Most gifted chefs gravitate to the side of the hotel business where the fancy salaries are, and long for nothing more than to be made managers and treated as executives. Rare is the chef who is content to be a chef—and rarer still is the hotel chain that will give him that opportunity.

The Oberois have often criminally neglected their own kitchen geniuses, preferring to dip into the vast pool of Euro kitchen trash that flows from the Meridien in Phuket (or wherever) to the Sofitel in Manila (or wherever)—though there have been some honourable exceptions, among them Bruno Cerdan. ITC did a grand job of promoting Imtiaz Qureshi as the mascot of the Dum Pukht restaurants though there remains some dispute over how much input he actually had when it came to the menus and concepts.

Nevertheless, Welcomgoup's record on chefs—a legacy perhaps of founding father Ajit Haksar's love of food—remains good. Even when expert chefs have been hired, they've been of the calibre of Bill Marchetti, a restaurant chef who loves his craft.

At the Taj group, the record has been mixed. There have been brilliant chefs like Satish Arora (in his time, the world's youngest executive chef), who continue to work with their hands and create new dishes. And there's been the cerebral Arvind Saraswat, intellectually India's finest chef, a storehouse of information, ideas and practices who single-handedly changed the way we eat in North India with the success of the restaurants at Delhi's Taj Mahal, and transformed eating in Calcutta (with the Taj Bengal).

The next generation has, sadly, been bogged down by paperwork and administrative tasks but stars have, nevertheless, emerged. Hemant Oberoi runs India's most sophisticated restaurant, Bombay's Zodiac Grill, and it is virtually impossible to get a bad meal—or even a mediocre room service snack—at the Bombay Taj whose kitchens he has run for fifteen years.

But it is the youngest of the Taj group's star chefs—Ananda Solomon of Bombay's President Hotel—whose record demonstrates how a chef can make a difference. For nearly twenty years now, restaurateurs have twigged that it costs next to nothing to fly in two cooks from Bangkok and open a Thai restaurant. Yet, almost without exception, Thai cooks have failed to replicate their culinary magic in Indian kitchens. They need a good chef to plan their menu and to ensure the quality of their cuisine.

When The President opened the Thai Pavilion (after an earlier avatar had failed), it first made Solomon spend several months in Thailand (he even learned the language). Consequently, his kitchen has consistently turned out the best Thai food in India, of a standard and calibre that never varies.

A few years ago, Solomon looked at the boom in South Indian seafood restaurants and quickly worked out that even the better kitchens had no consistency because there were no chefs: everything depended on cooks. And once a cook left, his successor could make the same dish in a completely different style.

When The President opened the Konkan Cafe, it applied Solomon's skills in sourcing and reinventing dishes along with the chef's ability to ensure that the kitchen turned out food of an even standard, no matter who the cook was. The result is Bombay's finest South Indian restaurant.

Outside of hotels, few restaurants have bothered with chefs, relying instead on cooks. Those that have—usually the kind where the chef is also owner—have benefited enormously. Thus, the best non-hotel restaurant in Bombay is Indigo, where owner Rahul Akerkar is chef. In Delhi the best Italian food can be found at Diva where chef Ritu Dalmia is also the owner.

Because smaller places can't afford loads of understudies to the chef, the food suffers if the chef is off. Senso, in Delhi's Priya cinema complex is a beautiful, sophisticated restaurant. But the one time I've been, I was disappointed to find the food stunningly mediocre (and therefore overpriced). The reason was simple enough: the Italian chef had fallen ill. Similarly, there was a time when you could always tell whether Ritu Dalmia was in town by the wobbles in food quality at Diva. It is a tribute to her Bocuse-like ability to ensure quality that this is no longer the case: the food is uniformly good.

But if you need to know why a chef is important you only need to compare a chefless restaurant with one where the chef actually runs the kitchen. Take the example of the TGIF chain. An

American franchise operation, its expansion is predicated on the assumption that any moron who has read the chef's manual once can cook the entire menu. Contrast TGIF's soulless (and frequently disgusting) food with another Delhi restaurant with a similar menu: the American Diner at the Habitat Centre. The difference is that the Diner has an actual chef rather than an untrained cretin in the kitchen. Consequently it produces food that is about one million times better than TGIF at half the price. (And the service is far superior too.)

There's now an encouraging trend to treat chefs as the stars they undoubtedly are. In Bombay, Hemant Oberoi appears on Page Three more often than Parmeshwar Godrej. And in Delhi, Bill Marchetti is a bigger Page Three star than Neha Dhupia (though both are roughly the same size these days). Sometime ago *Outlook* treated chefs to a critical appreciation and other magazines are following suit.

Restaurant food in India will never improve till we learn to respect the chef—and all publicity that helps advance that process is welcome.

# seeing through mineral water

A restaurant in America has appointed a water sommelier. A sommelier, as you know, is the waiter with a silly chain around his neck (in classic establishments) who hands you the wine list and looks pityingly at you as you try and pretend you know something about wine. (Do not be fazed. In most Indian restaurants the sommelier also knows nothing about wine and the selection on the list is overpriced crap, anyway.)

A water sommelier tries to do the same thing with water. He offers you a choice of, say, twenty different bottled waters, enlightens you on the flavours and (presumably) says things like 'The Evian would go nicely with the fish' or 'The bouquet of the Margaux might overwhelm the flavour of the Perrier' or 'As you are only having the hamburger, stick to tap water; it's cheaper and a lot better'. (Well, perhaps not the last.)

You can't fault the logic but you can knock the pretension and so, for the last several months, the media have had a fine old time, making fun of the concept. All of which probably works to the advantage of the restaurant which few people had heard of to begin with and is now internationally renowned thanks to the fuss over its water sommelier. (Oh no, *I'm* not falling into the trap of naming the restaurant. So there!)

We are a long way from appointing water sommeliers in this county but bottled/mineral water is a big business anyway. Over the last decade it has been the fastest growing segment in the non-alcoholic drinks market and a huge profit generator for hotels and restaurants.

The principle behind mineral water is simple enough. All over Europe (and presumably other parts of the world) there are springs where the water is supposed to have naturally occurring minerals (which are beneficial to health), an unusual taste or natural fizz.

For decades, many people drank this water because a) they liked it, b) it was good for them and c) in many European countries the tap water was foul. It remained a relatively medium-sized, largely European industry till Americans discovered mineral water.

As anybody in international marketing will tell you, once a product takes off in America it quickly becomes a global craze. And though Americans like drinking tap water (a concept which we Indians, who treat anything that comes out of a tap with suspicion, regard as bizarre), they began to believe, in the 1970s-80s, that bottled water was trendy.

Perrier led the charge, describing its (allegedly) natural sparkling water as a zero-calorie drink or mixer (as all water is zero calorie by definition, this was a description that could fool only credulous Americans), and soon all the European mineral water companies rushed into the market. Over the last few years, even the American soft drink majors have launched their own brands.

In the process, some distinctions have been blurred. First of all, much of what passes for mineral water these days is not mineral at all. It is ordinary water that is purified and bottled. Secondly, even the so-called 'natural' fizzy waters have been shown to be artificially carbonated and Americans have been particularly sensitive to the distinction after a scare about benzene gas torpedoed Perrier's sales.

In India, the market has grown out of all proportion, not because Indians believe that bottled water has any beneficial minerals (even Bisleri is no longer 'aqua minerale' and newer entrants like Pepsi's Aquafina just call themselves 'packaged drinking water'), but because we long for water that is safe to drink.

This desire for clean water is a boon to soft drink companies.

All beverage manufacturers have to purify water before they add it to their concentrates to make Coke, Pepsi, Limca or whatever. But such is the nature of the bottled water market that they've found that they can actually charge *more* for the unflavoured water than they can for the soft drink.

So they are laughing all the way to the bank.

And why does water have to be so expensive? It doesn't. We are just willing to pay those prices. And such is our conditioning that if anybody offers cheaper water (cheaper than Kinley or Aquafina or Bisleri), our first, subconscious reaction is to believe that it must be cheaper only because it is less pure.

The water manufacturers can hardly believe their good fortune!

But the real beneficiaries of the water boom are hotels and restaurants. A litre bottle of water usually costs Rs 12 in the shops. This means that hotels buy it for under Rs 10 a bottle. But by the time it reaches your table the cost has shot up six times, so that the hotels charge you Rs 60. In other words, they make a profit of Rs 50 on an investment of Rs 10.

Boy! Are they delighted!

But wait, it gets worse. At nearly all deluxe hotels the drinking water is perfectly safe. At most even the tap water is fit to drink. After all, they've spent lakhs on water purification systems. Despite this, at nearly every restaurant you go to, they will ask 'mineral water?' and expect you to say 'of course'. They do this because they like relieving us of the extra Rs 50 that we poor suckers like parting with.

Some don't even bother to ask. Many hotels will serve bottled water as a matter of course, without asking your permission. Then, they will charge you for it.

If they are really unscrupulous, they will open a bottle of Evian or some such overpriced 'mineral' water and charge you upwards of Rs 150. At many, many so-called fancy restaurants they do this, unasked for, as a mater of policy.

It's called screwing the guest.

What should you do?

I suggest you follow my example. At a five-star hotel, I rarely order bottled water. If a hotel can't even purify its own water, then it should shut down its kitchen. Think about it: if the water is not safe, then can the food be safe?

If water is provided unasked for, I *always* drink it. In fact, if it is Evian or some fancy brand, then I drink it with greater relish.

I then wait till they bring my bill.

'Did I order the water?' I ask.

'Er, no, sir,' they usually mumble in reply.

'Well, then,' I say, 'I shan't pay for it,' and scratch out the charge and deduct it from the total.

You'd be surprised at how little they complain. You see, they know that they've pulled a scam. And when a victim complains about being conned a sensible conman usually knows when to retreat.

When he's making a 600 per cent profit on his other victims he can afford to be gracious with the few who actually see through him.

# we are what we eat

# a guide to fad diets

Why is there no Lajpat Nagar Diet? What about a Jabalpur Diet? Why is no diet named after an Indian? Why can't we have Dr Muthuswami's Diet Revolution? Or Sardar Santa Singh's Weight Reduction Da Jaadu?

These are serious questions.

Look at it this way. Diets are the big urban growth industry these days. Most Indian women seem to be on diets of some description. Going to the gym has come to occupy the same sort of importance in the lives of many young women that hosting a kitty party did in the lives of their mothers. And diet gurus are the new stars. Shikha Sharma is a household name in most middle-class Delhi households. When Anjali Mukherjee's clinic was raided by the authorities in Bombay, the story made headlines all over the country.

Why then are we so dependant on American reference points? Why can't we have Indian names for our diets? Take the currently trendy South Beach Diet, featured at interminable length in newspapers, on news channels and on the menus of restaurants. Why should we be so obsessed with a diet named after an American city? Why were we so crazy about the Beverly Hills Diet in the 1980s?

And why do we follow diets named after American doctors? Why should we care about Dr Pritkin? Who gives a damn about Dr Atkins? And as for the French, who can even pronounce Montignac?

Why do we go for anything with a foreign name? In the 1990s, everybody I knew was on the General Motors Diet. But why General Motors? Why not Maruti? What's wrong with the Telco Diet or the Hero Honda Weight Loss Programme?

The truth is that most Western diets simply don't suit the Indian lifestyle. If you are a vegetarian, you can forget about Atkins, Pritkin or Montignac. South Beach is rubbish, anyway. (Would you buy a used diet from Bill Clinton?) The only Indian I ever heard of who was on the Beverly Hills diet was Parveen Babi. And we know what happened to her.

At some level, I suspect, we recognize that these diets are not really for Indians. Which is why we go to dieticians and ask them to make sense of all of it for us.

The dieticians take bits of each diet and then put it together in an Indian-friendly form. Sometimes, their diets make sense. Often they just pretend to be innovative while trying the oldest trick in the book: restricting your calories.

Even so, we now have a new generation of diet stars. At present, the trendiest of the lot is Shikha Sharma. She's a medical doctor who gave up hospital medicine to work at Personal Point before branching out on her own. Today her client list (unusually for a doctor she doesn't like using the term 'patient') comprises the who's who of Delhi, and I always suspect that she could be more successful if she tried but is curiously laid-back and unpushy for somebody in her profession.

I've been to her so I can tell you that her diets work. Moreover, they even work for women—who find it much more difficult to lose weight. The friend who put me on to her lost kilos with no apparent effort and has kept them off. My TV producer, who went to her after I did, has lost so much weight that she looks a decade younger.

Does Shikha follow Atkins, Fit For Life, South Beach or any of the trendy diets? It is hard to say. I've seen her operate at close quarters over eight weeks and I have to say that if there was a secret formula, I didn't find it. This means that if clients put on weight again (as I have) then they have to go back to her. Only she understands the method.

Anjali Mukherjee was a craze in Bombay when Shikha was still in medical school. She may not have Shikha's girlish good looks but she has seniority on her side plus the added advantage of having cut the Miss India contestants down to size for many years. She taught the Bombay elite to eat brown rice and wholewheat bread and her operation is far more focussed and thrusting than Shikha's laid-back style.

I've been to Anjali too. (When it comes to losing weight I identify with Mark Twain's famous quote about cigarette smoking: 'it is the easiest thing in the world, I do it all the time'.) And yes, I did lose weight though not as effortlessly as I did with Shikha.

I am on her side, though, in the controversy over the ayurvedic pills she hands out. All Ayurvedic preparations are open to question and if the authorities are really serious about cracking down then there are hundreds of 'doctors', *vaids* and *hakims* they should raid first before harassing Anjali.

Personal Point is another matter entirely. It lacks the Shikha-Anjali glamour. It has probably expanded too fast. Its dieticians are not as glamorous—some can be distinctly downmarket. Plus it uses some very curious machines. On the other hand I do know people who have lost weight there.

The other biggie in the business is of course Vandana Luthra, but she seems to belong to a different category. Because she includes beauty among her activities, she is probably set to become the Shahnaz Hussain of her generation rather than a hard-core dietician.

Could any of these people invent their own diets and become India's answer to Atkins? Could Anjali create a Pali Hill diet to compete with South Beach or Beverly Hills?

As of now, I doubt it. The point about all the best-selling American diets is that they are High Concept. You can sum up Fit For Lift in one sentence: don't combine protein and complex carbohydrates. Similarly, the central message of Atkins is as simple: eat less carbohydrates. Montignac's credo is: eat more protein and do not combine your foods. The Beverly Hills Diet is: eat more fruit. The Blood Group Diet says: eat only the foods that suit your blood type.

No Indian dietician adopts an approach that is quite so simplistic. If you read the diet book that Shikha has put together (along with Neeru Gupta) it seems reasonable enough but there's no High Concept, no one Big Idea. And if Personal Point was to do a diet manual, what would its message be? Come to our clinic and use our machines?

Critics of the famous foreign diets argue that the diets are based on oversimplifications. Atkins and Montignac are said to make too much of insulin production. Fit For Life is dedicated to the proposition that foods can be classed as proteins or carbohydrates. In fact, say nutritionists, many foods are combinations of various categories so it is hard to find pure protein or pure carbohydrate.

Judged on that basis, the Indian dieticians are far more sophisticated. There's nothing simplistic about their approaches. But ironically, this is a field where Simple Is Better, especially if you want to send your message out to the mass market.

So, as good as our local dieticians may be, their theories are too complex to sweep the nation.

Which is why you won't get Shikha Sharma's Vasant Vihar Diet or Personal Point's Defence Colony Da Diet. If you want to know how they work, you'll have to go to their clinics. A single paperback will not do the trick.

As a business strategy it may make sense but it also ensures that none of them is immortal. Who remembers such passé diet gurus as Makhija and Kakkar? They were probably just as good as this lot. But once the fad fades, the dieticians are forgotten.

# why atkins rules

In January this year, Michael Bloomberg, New York's feisty Mayor, had to apologize to Veronica Atkins, wife of the late Robert Atkins, for a joke he made about her husband and his diet. Though the apology made news all over the world, most papers were too discreet to actually repeat the offending joke. From what I can gather though, what Bloomberg said went something like this: Atkins followed his own eponymous diet and so became a fatso and had a heart attack and died.

No, it wasn't very funny (nothing that Bloomberg says or does is ever funny, but that's another story), and even Bloomberg's clumsy attempt to make up to Mrs Atkins was neither genuinely apologetic nor at all amusing: he invited her to share a steak with him. Ho, ho, ho.

The significance of the incident lies in the manner in which the Atkins diet has now permeated the consciousness of nearly everybody in the West. McDonald's is offering an Atkins hamburger: without the bun or the fries (all you'll get is the cardboard, then). And restaurants are complaining that carbohydrate-rich dishes are going to waste. In London, the celebrated three-star Chef Gordon Ramsay has railed against Atkins-influenced diners who send all the bread back. Bakeries say that sales have declined. Grocery shops and supermarkets offer Atkins-style ready meals. The Atkins organization itself now runs a flourishing catering service sending over Atkins-style meals to institutions and offices.

If all this has left you somewhat mystified, here's a little background. The traditional approach to food loss is what I call accountancy dieting. Basically, you draw up a ledger. In one column you list all the calories you have consumed. And in another you list all those you have expended. When expenses exceed intake then you are said to be in weight-loss mode.

Of course it works. Any idiot can see that if you starve yourself you'll become thinner. But there are three problems with this approach. One: it is short-term. The first 10 lb you lose (usually in the first week of the diet itself, when you'll prance around singing 'It works, it works!') will be water loss. As soon as you give up the diet, the body will restore its water balance and the weight will come back on. Also, research has shown that the human body reacts to low-calorie diets by slowing down its metabolism. So you'll expend less calories and it will become harder and harder to lose weight.

The second problem is that a low-calorie diet goes against all common sense. We all know that the human body is not a calculator and that *bania* accounting is too simplistic an approach. We all know people who eat virtually nothing and put on lots of weight. And we know people who eat like pigs and stay thin. If it's all to do with a profit and loss approach to calories, then how is this possible?

And the third problem is the most crucial: nobody likes starving. Therefore, low-calorie diets always fail unless you have amazing will power.

Over the last thirty years or so, a number of diet gurus have made their fortunes by offering alternative approaches to weight loss. One school of thought (now increasingly discredited) held that it did not matter what you ate as long as you exercised each day for between half an hour to an hour. It wasn't the calories you expended that counted but the duration of the exercise itself. After half an hour, your body's metabolic rate would rise and you would burn off calories faster.

The problem with this approach is evident to anybody who visits a park and sees the regular walkers. Even if they've been walking (or running) everyday for twenty years, they will all still have paunches. No matter how much they walk they'll stay fat. (For the exercise-only approach to work you need to be a proper sportsman or a marathon man like Anil Ambani.) The same is true of golf which, or so we are told, keeps you healthy by making you walk. Go to any golf club on a Saturday and you'll think you've blundered into a weekend retreat for Weight Watchers Anonymous (Punjabi Middle-Aged Men's Chapter).

Another approach is the 'combining diet'. In essence this diet (exemplified by the eat-grass Fit For Life programme) says that you can't mix proteins with complex carbohydrates (wheat, rice, potatoes). So you can't have mutton curry and rice, or dal and roti, or a good biryani, or a proper sandwich. In fact, as the Fit For Life authors recommend, you should become a Western-style vegetarian (nut cutlets etc.). Obviously, nobody is going to waste much time on this nonsense. (But it can work. A decade ago, Shabana Azmi lost kilos on this diet and began looking years younger.)

The Atkins Diet rests on a rather simplistic theory: insulin controls the rate at which we store foods as fat. It also determines how fast we burn up the fat stored in our bodies. Certain foods—sugar and carbohydrates mainly—promote the production of insulin. Once this happens, whatever you eat is converted into fat. But if there's less insulin, then you'll burn body fat.

The bottom line is that if we eat lots of protein, then the body will not store it as fat. Instead, it will burn its own store of fat. Better still, this will happen even if you eat fat itself: butter, lard, cheese and God alone knows what else. And best of all, there are no calorific limits: eat three steaks at one meal if you like or a whole side of bacon.

In the 1970s, Dr Atkins first popularized a high-protein diet. It met with some success but most people found it boring, and in that decade the medical profession woke up to the dangers of red meat. And so, Atkins fell from favour.

But it took a Frenchman to realize what Atkins had missed: if you were into Western food, then a high-protein diet was actually the foodie diet. Dietician Michel Montignac published his own high-protein diet and took France by storm. Being French, he popularized the diet by taking the menus of three-star Paris restaurants and pointing out that people on his diet could eat half the menu without any difficulty. Americans never took to Montignac because they were sold on the medical orthodoxy of the time which said that grain is good and meat is bad.

But throughout the 1990s, as doctors said grains were healthy, America became the world's most obese country. Research studies were commissioned into the causes of this expansion of the national girth.

The broad consensus was that Americans ate too many carbohydrates. This suited Dr Atkins just fine. But he faced another problem. Even if it could be shown that his low-carbohydrate diet made people thinner, the medical establishment still claimed that it gave them heart attacks and killed them (the basis for Mayor Bloomberg's 'joke').

Then, a couple of years ago, the results of a long and exhaustive survey into the Atkins Diet were published. The survey proved that people on the Atkins diet a) lost weight and b) were not any more prone to heart attacks than people who were not on the diet.

The survey made the front page of the all-powerful *New York Times* magazine and suddenly, America went berserk. The Atkins Diet allowed you to eat to your heart's content: you could knock back the steaks and you didn't have to go easy on the butter. No wonder Americans threw their pizzas out of their windows and went looking for sirloin.

Since then, Atkins has taken over the English-speaking world. It helps that it works better and faster than any other kind of diet. Go on Atkins for two weeks and you will almost certainly lose weight. The medical establishment, of course, is furious. It can't warn people of an outbreak of heart disease (heart disease rates actually went up even as doctors were urging Americans to eat carbohydrates). So now it talks about liver disease, gallstones, kidney failure etc.

Of course, the doctors are right but only up to a point—if you eat only meat and saturated fat, it can't be good for you. Nor should you do it for too long. But it is hard, if not impossible, to demonstrate that two or three weeks of the Atkins Diet does you any medical damage. In fact, because you lose weight, your health actually improves.

For us in India, however, Atkins poses specific problems. It is a difficult diet for vegetarians to follow. Even if you are a non-vegetarian, it is hard to think of Indian food without rice or rotis.

I asked dietician Shikha Sharma what she thought. Her verdict is cautious approval. 'You'll lose weight for a fortnight,' she said. 'But unless you like non-vegetarian Western food, you'll have a problem.' Because she is a trained doctor, she is also sceptical of the long-term consequences of Atkins on health. And she has another concern: 'It is a diet that helps you lose weight. But it doesn't teach you how to keep it off. If you go back on a normal diet, you'll put on all the weight again.'

She's probably right. But my own experience suggests that there is some merit in following the principles of Atkins—more protein, less carbs—without getting too carried away. And don't worry too much about the doctors. They were wrong about calories—their advice has made America obese—and they are probably misguided about fat and protein too. Thinks about it: how many really slim Indian doctors do you know?

## the diets and how they work

**Low calorie:** Basically, you starve yourself. Because no calories are coming in, the body is forced to burn up all the fat it has stored away for a rainy day.

Problems: nobody likes to starve; you can become anorexic and fall ill; your metabolic rate reduces so it becomes more difficult to lose weight after the first week; and anyway, all the weight you lose in the first week is water loss.

Still, the diet is recommended by doctors and nutritionists who stop reading books after they get their degrees.

**Combining:** No doctor says this makes sense but it is the basis behind such diets as Fit For Life. The basic principle is that you can't combine starch with protein. And you can't eat fruit unless you eat it on its own. The Fit For Life guys also recommend that you become a vegetarian.

The science behind this is hazy; something about the digestive juices produced by the body. But people do lose weight on the diet. Doctors say that this is because the diet so restricts your choices that you end up eating fewer calories.

**High protein:** All doctors admit that certain foods increase the production of insulin in the body. But high-protein diet gurus (Dr Atkins, Michel Montignac) go further. They say that insulin is the magic hormone that determines whether the food we eat is expended or stored as fat. Therefore, if you eat foods that do not increase the production of insulin (meat, fish, chicken but also oil and butter) then you are okay because these foods will not be stored as fat. In fact, because the body has so little insulin, it will actually burn up stored fats and ensure that you lose weight.

Doctors say that this is dubious. Besides, they warn that too much meat and too much fat can have disastrous health consequences. Recent studies, however, suggest that Atkins is broadly correct and doctors are broadly wrong. That's certainly food for thought.

# deconstructing diet mythology

Doctors love to run down dieticians on the grounds that their theories and practices have no scientific basis. To some extent, this is not unjustified. The favourite target of most doctors abroad is the so-called food-combining diet, best represented in India by Fit for Life.

The essence of food combining is that the stomach produces different gastric juices to digest different categories of food. If you mix food categories then you mix your juices—with unhappy consequences. Scientists respond that a) this business about different juices has no scientific validity and b) the notion of food combining is based on the presupposition that each food falls into a particular category i.e. a carbohydrate or a protein. In fact, say nutritionists, many foods are a combination of many categories. So how then can simplistic food combining work?

Despite the scientific validity of these objections, the problem is that doctors themselves have only a limited understanding of the factors that make us put on weight. At one level their prescriptions are commonsensical: eat less, cut down on sugar, exercise more, etc. But at a more complex level—which foods are stored as fat and how this is achieved—modern medicine shifts its ground with a frightening rapidity.

Till the late 1970s the US nutritional establishment took the line that protein was a good thing and that a diet that was rich in protein and relatively low in carbohydrates was healthy. Then, as rates of heart disease began to climb, the conventional wisdom was hastily rewritten.

Red meat was identified as a villain, and its protein-rich character became the subject of ridicule. Red meat contained horrible animal fats, we were told, and these clogged up your arteries. Give up on steak, forget about that pork chop and forgo that lamb casserole. Stick instead to a diet that is rich in grain, vegetables and fruit.

Under the new food orthodoxy Americans were told to eat rice and pasta, they were encouraged to eat vegetables and were urged to consume more fruit.

At an intuitive level, any Indian should have found this suspicious. We are a nation of carbohydrate and vegetable eaters. Most of our meals consist of roti or rice with sabzi. Some of us eat a little dal (a second-grade protein), and even when the non-vegetarians among us do eat meat, rarely do we eat it at every meal—instead it is sometimes consumed as one dish in a combination meal that usually includes dal, sabzi and rice or roti.

Why then are Indians not the leanest people on the planet? If fish is so good for us then why are most Bengalis overweight?

Then there is the confusing business of the so-called French paradox. The French eat lots of meat. They are not a nation of joggers. They love cooking things in animal fat—and yet they have the lowest rate of heart disease in the developed world. And the average Frenchman is half the size of the average American.

Faced with this contradiction doctors found new virtues in olive oil and red wine. The reason the French were so healthy, we were told, was because they drank lots of red wine (which contained cholesterol-moving flavenoids) and cooked everything in olive oil.

Nice try. But it doesn't wash.

First of all, the French don't cook everything in olive oil. It is true that in the Mediterranean part of France, a lot of olive oil is consumed, but heart disease rates are actually lower in the northern part of France where everything is cooked in lard or goose fat.

And besides, if you are so convinced that red wine, olive oil and pasta are the key to good heath then surely you should be looking at Italy—home of pasta—rather than at France? And guess what? France has *lower* rates of heart disease and obesity than Italy!

It has taken some time but the US nutritional establishment is now finally re-examining the diet orthodoxy of the last decade. Part of the reason is that ever since the eat-more-carbohydrate-and-less-meat prescription filtered down, Americans have actually got *fatter*.

American nutritionists say that this is because people are eating more junk food. Well, maybe. But can you really claim that Americans did not eat junk food in the 1980s when obesity levels were much lower?

And besides, what *is* junk food anyway? The basic principle is to turn it out cheaply. In real terms that translates as: low meat content.

So junk food is mainly low protein, high carbohydrate. Think about your average McDonald's meal. How much protein does that actually contain? It's mainly wheat and potatoes. What about your average pizza? That's nearly all wheat, except perhaps for a few thin slices of ham or salami on top.

If carbohydrates are so much better for you than protein then how come carbohydrate-rich junk food is now identified as the principal source of obesity?

Over the last two months the American nutritional establishment has been caught up in a major controversy about the efficacy of its recommendations. A recent study suggests that proteins may not be so bad, that fat is actually not fattening, and that carbohydrates (in the sense of grain: wheat, rice etc.) are the real culprits.

At the heart of the controversy is the still mysterious role of insulin. Many dieticians (among them French protein-lover Michel Montignac) have long believed that insulin holds the key to weight gain. According to them, an excess of insulin causes the body to convert food to fat. Their theories have, therefore, concentrated on avoiding foods that stimulate insulin release (white bread, white rice, white sugar, all processed and packaged foods etc.) and sticking to foods that have little effect on insulin release (meat, for instance).

For years, the scientific establishment has pooh-poohed this overemphasis on the role of insulin, but the dieticians have one advantage over the nutritionists: their theories can explain the French paradox and the US outbreak of obesity. The French avoid packaged food and eat a lot of meat while the American diet now consists largely of pizza, bread, potatoes and processed food.

So scientists are finally beginning to take the role of insulin in nutrition far more seriously than before. This is good news for Montignac and Dr Atkins (the original high-protein guy).

But my guess is that even this new nutritional orthodoxy will soon collapse. I'm waiting for the American nutritional establishment to embrace these theories wholeheartedly before I formulate my own objection.

It's called the Thai paradox.

If white rice is so bad for you, if you should avoid deep-fried foods (most of which stimulate insulin release), then can somebody please explain to me why the Thais are so thin? (You can fit three full Thais into the waistband of an average American's trousers.)

Much of their food is deep-fried and they eat white rice all the time. In fact, the phrase for 'let's eat' in Thai ('*khun kha*') translates as 'eat rice'.

According to Montignac, they should be blimps. But each of them is much thinner than Dr Atkins.

Hence the Thai paradox.

So what does all this prove? Not much. Except, don't waste time on nutritional theories. By the time you've understood them they'll rewrite the rules all over again, anyway.

# the milky way: is it good for you?

Whenever I tell people that it has been fifteen years or so since I last drank milk, they look at me as though I am crazy. Some attempt to bridge the silence that inevitably follows, with a line or two of explanation: 'Yeah, sure, I don't drink milk either. Maybe a little in my tea or coffee, but that's it.'

But even this explanation collapses when I point out that I don't add milk to my tea and drink my coffee black. I don't drink milk in any form, if I can help it.

'Why do you not drink milk?' somebody will then ask, tentatively. I used to tell them that the reasons were biological: 'I am lactose intolerant,' I would say.

But over the last four years I've found that even that explanation does not fit the facts as I now know them. Nearly four years ago, I went to see a fancy doctor on New York's Park Avenue. I have been plagued by a strange stomach ailment for over a decade now and doctors have usually declared—after a battery of tests has failed to provide any evidence, let alone proof, of any disease—that I suffer from a 'condition'.

And what, I then ask, is this condition?

Well, they say, you can call it Spastic Colon. Or perhaps you suffer from food allergies.

None of this was even vaguely satisfying so I pinned my hopes on the Park Avenue specialist. Surely he would be able to tell what was wrong with me.

The doctor listened carefully as I described my symptoms before informing me that my problem was that I was lactose intolerant.

I probably am, I told him, but it doesn't matter because I haven't drunk milk for years and years.

He was not interested in my explanation. Almost as if on autopilot, he gave me what was probably his usual lactose-intolerance speech.

The problem, he said, was that many of us were intolerant of milk but did not realize it. In the Far East, he pointed out, the vast majority of the population can't digest milk. Think about it, he said, can you think of a Chinese dish that involves the use of cream? A Thai dessert made from milk? A Japanese ice cream? Milk is almost completely absent from the diet of most Orientals because they are born with lactose intolerance.

In the West, most people are not born with lactose intolerance but by the time they reach the age of fourteen or so their bodies lose the ability to digest milk. But such is our culture that it makes no allowances for this intolerance. People are put into situations where they have to drink milk—thanks to coffee machines that don't offer a black coffee option, for instance, or because many people offer their guests mugs of ready-made tea or coffee (to which milk has already been added). Because they cannot digest the milk, many people suffer unfortunate health consequences: upset stomachs, gas, bloating, bad breath, sore throats etc.

He wasn't sure about Indians, the doctor said, or about how we reacted to milk but his guess was that we were closer to Orientals than to Westerners. But even if were like Americans, the chances were that many of us were no longer able to digest milk—only we did not recognize it.

My symptoms, he continued, suggested a clear case of lactose intolerance. As for my claim that I did not drink milk, that did not really matter because I could be consuming milk products without realizing it. Take one instance: many medicinal tablets contain lactose and yet we take them quite happily, not recognizing that we are consuming a dairy product. Or, to take another instance, many restaurant dishes contain cream or milk, but the chefs never bother to inform diners.

I listened closely and told him that he was probably right. But even so, how did this help me?

Did he mean to say that if I was more careful about avoiding milk products, my symptoms would disappear?

He had no answer. Instead, he insisted that I undergo a lactose intolerance test. I retorted that this was a waste of time because I took my lactose intolerant status as a given. Nevertheless, when he persisted I agreed to undergo the test.

The test was as follows: in the morning his nurse made me drink a large dose of some lactose-rich milk product. Then, every hour I would blow into an empty injection syringe before sealing it. After eight hours I would return the eight syringes to his lab, where they would be tested to see if I was lactose intolerant.

I was not impressed with the test because it only seemed to be an expensive way of confirming the obvious. But I did some reading about lactose intolerance. I had given up milk around 1989-90 because I felt uncomfortable after I had drunk it. I had never bothered too much about the medical arguments against milk, but I was surprised to see that the anti-milk lobby had built up a huge and impressive case.

Milk was blamed for a host of sins. The stomach disorders of the kind that my Park Avenue doctor had identified were only a part of the story. Some studies even suggested that milk fat contributed significantly to heart disease. One view was that the famous French paradox—why do the French have such a low rate of heart disease when they eat so much animal fat?—could be explained by the nature of the French cow. Apparently, Anglo-Saxon cows were a different breed and their milk was richer in a certain kind of fat. This accounted for the high rate of heart disease in America while the French cows and their healthier milk were the key to the French paradox.

I thought back to my travels in the Far East. Ice cream parlours of the Swenson's variety have now opened all over Asia but yes, the traditional cuisines do not contain any milk products. And even now, most supermarkets in East Asia will sell you a variety of what are called 'non-dairy creamers', that is, powders you add to coffee to simulate the taste of milk. In many cases the creamers (the non-dairy Coffee Mate, for instance) taste far better than milk, and generally it would be hard for anyone not in the know to be able to tell the difference.

So perhaps the Park Avenue doctor did have a point.

Two days later, I phoned him (cheaper than a full-fledged appointment) to ask if there were any medicines for lactose intolerance. In health food stores across New York, many 'milk-enzymes' were routinely displayed. According to the packaging, if you took an enzyme tablet every time you had milk you would be fine.

Should I take the enzymes? I asked the doctor.

'I have good news,' he boomed across the line. 'You are absolutely fine. Congratulations!'

Fine? What did he mean?

'I mean the tests came out negative. You are not lactose intolerant. You can go ahead and have a milkshake!'

I was dumbfounded. But surely his entire diagnosis had hinged on the near certainty of my lactose intolerant status? And in any case, if I wasn't lactose intolerant, then what the hell was wrong with me?

He seemed temporarily put out. Then, a lifetime of handing out high-priced advice took over. 'Gee, I don't know,' he said. 'What did they tell you in India?'

'Spastic Colon.'

'Yeah, that's right. We call it IBS. Look, you have a good trip back to India, okay?' He hung up.

I wasn't ready to give up that easily. A year later I went to a clinic on London's Harley Street where a doctor who specialized in complementary treatment took samples of my blood and said that he would test for food intolerances. However, he said, judging by my symptoms, not only was I lactose intolerant, but my system probably couldn't handle a variety of other foods as well. He then went on to charge me a huge amount for various intolerance tests.

A week after I returned to India, he couriered me the test results.

Nope. I wasn't lactose intolerant after all. Actually, I wasn't intolerant to any of the sixty or so foods he had tested my blood against. There was only a borderline intolerance to grapefruit and perhaps a little resistance to egg-white. Other than that, I was fine.

I won't bore you with the details of my own condition. Two years ago I finally found a good doctor who explained to me what IBS was and warned against getting carried away with all this talk of food allergies and intolerances.

But I still don't drink milk. I don't care what the tests say. It still doesn't feel right. However, I am less rigid about this than I used to be. I had given up on ice cream which I genuinely love. Now I'm back to eating ice cream when the urge strikes. I no longer worry about cream in sauces or even in Indian food (which means that I can eat the Bukhara dal with a clear conscience).

Does that mean that I no longer support the anti-milk lobby?

Frankly, I don't know. There is a growing adherence to the milk-is-poison school of nutrition. More and more 'alternative health' specialists are advising us to give it up, for much the same sort of reasons advanced by my Park Avenue doctor.

On the other hand, I know loads of people who drink gallons of milk and thrive on it. And if East Asians are all lactose intolerant then how do you explain the growing popularity of ice cream parlours all over the Far East?

So I'll remain an agnostic. I don't drink milk myself (you'll get black coffee at my house) and I do think you should read up on lactose intolerance. But, at the end of the day, it is your own decision to make.

# hygienic, not healthy

It is a little funny—and I think a little sad—how, every time a Western phenomenon catches on in India, it is actually running out of steam in the West.

An example of this trend is the McDonald's phenomenon. In December 2002 I went to the McDonald's outlet in Mathura. Perhaps because it was lunch time, the restaurant (and here I use the word in its loosest sense) was jam-packed. There were no queues, just a cheerfully disorganized hustle-bustle as the good citizens of Mathura enjoyed their big outing of the week by shoving and pushing and shouting out their orders.

Whatever one's views on the food—more on that later—there was no doubt that the outlet was doing well. The story is much the same in other cities. My thirteen-year-old son is a Domino's pizza fan but when he does go out to a fast food outlet (Domino's only does home delivery), he picks McDonald's. And he's become quite the little expert on the relative merits of various McDonald's products around the globe. Two years ago he wasted his chocolate shake at the McDonald's in London's Marble Arch because he thought that the one he'd had at the branch in Delhi's Priya cinema complex was far superior.

Sadly, this boom is restricted to India and some other Third World markets. In America—whose way of life McDonald's celebrates—the chain is in deep trouble. It hasn't launched a blockbuster new product since Chicken McNuggets in 1983. It has just announced the first quarterly ($344 million) loss in its fifty-year history. Its revenues are down by a billion dollars. Its share price dropped to a seven-year low. It has announced plans to sack 600 executives. At least 1,000 outlets have been earmarked for demolition. It is pulling out of three Latin American markets. And the pace of expansion has slowed dramatically. In 1995 McDonald's opened 1,100 new stores. Last year that figure was down to 300.

It is fashionable for food critics to sneer at McDonald's but I have to say that I've never subscribed to the anti-McDonald's snobbery. I concede that some of the foodie criticisms are well-founded. If you like the taste of good hamburger made from prime steak and cooked so that it is a little rare and juicy in the centre then you are certain to find fault with the Big Mac with its array of toppings (cheese, sauce etc.) and its slender slice of processed meat.

But if you accept that McDonald's has never claimed to be a gourmet restaurant or to serve prime steak and you recognize that the McDonald's hamburger is an entirely different dish from the classic hamburger, then you begin to enjoy the convenience—if not the cuisine.

How many of us, on a visit to a strange country where we don't speak the language, have been reassured by the sight of the golden arches? It's a good feeling to know that you can always order a quarter-pounder, large fries and a medium Coke—phrases that have now passed from language to language.

Nevertheless, outside India and the Far East, McDonald's gives the impression of being a brand that is past its prime. That accounts for the problem in the US market: the formula is out of tune with the times.

McDonald's folklore has it that Ray Kroc, who sold machines for mixing milkshakes, was surprised to discover that a hamburger joint owned by the McDonald brothers was ordering so many machines. According to legend, Kroc visited the restaurant and discovered that the milkshakes sold well only because people drank them with the excellent burgers. He bought out the brothers and launched the chain, though by then the original McDonald brothers had nothing to do with it.

The trouble with this version of the myth is that it ignores the real reason for the success of the original McDonald's—the brothers took care to serve good food. Kroc's contribution was to treat the food as just one small component of the total package.

He reformatted McDonald's menus so that it was possible for people who had never previously boiled an egg to become hamburger chefs. Marketing—the invention of Ronald McDonald—and innovative meal combos (the so-called Happy Meals where you get a burger, fries and shake at a bargain price) contributed to the success. So did the emphasis on convenience and standardization. The system was designed to work so smoothly that you could get your entire meal within minutes of walking into a restaurant. And no matter which outlet you went to your burger would always taste the same.

Kroc knew nothing about food. An enduring part of the McDonald's legend is that every product he suggested was a miserable failure. He understood systems, consistency, and brand-building.

But he left his heirs with two areas of weakness. The first was that as consumers began to grow in sophistication, they demanded better food and greater variety. In the UK, McDonald's grew massively in the 1980s. But by the 1990s it was under pressure from newer chains like Pret A Manger which boasted of freshly-made gourmet sandwiches. (McDonald's solution: it bought 33 per cent of Pret A Manger.) In the US, Subway (a sandwich chain that has recently arrived in India) now has 13,100 outlets—which makes it bigger than McDonald's.

The second weakness in the Kroc formula was that he based the empire on food that was essentially unhealthy. Even before Eric Schlosser published his hard-hitting *Fast Food Nation*, McDonald's had become a synonym for a fatty, unhealthy diet.

For instance, McDonald's is not allowed to call its shakes 'milkshakes' in the US because by law, a milkshake cannot exceed 25g of fat. The McDonald's shake has 36g. Chicken McNuggets, McDonald's big 1980s success (and an alleged step away from red meat) were found to have a 'fatty acid profile' closer to beef than chicken. This may have changed now that McDonald's is using vegetable oil for frying but a McNugget contains twice as much fat per ounce than a hamburger.

Ever wondered why the McDonald's apple pie tastes so different? Simple. They deep-fry the damn thing. And of course the fries are deep-fried. So are the McNuggets, and so on.

Two years ago, when my colleague Sourish Bhattacharya wrote a searing article about the nutritional negativity of the fast food industry in the *HT* Sunday magazine, McDonald's responded that many of the foods Sourish had singled out—McNuggets for instance—were not available in India. Further, it said that the Indian shakes did not conform to the fatty American standards.

Perhaps. But you only have to walk into a McDonald's in a place like Mathura to recognize that while its menu bears only the slightest resemblance to the international McDonald's formula, it is no healthier. For a start there are no grilled meat hamburgers—even the goat version has been withdrawn.

And then, so much of the food is fried or deep-fried. The aloo-tikki burger (their biggest seller) is fried. So is the deeply disgusting Chinese burger they've just introduced. So, I suspect, are many of the other dishes. The basic formula appears to be to take low-cost foods, encase them in breadcrumbs or batter and then deep-fry the life out of them.

Finally, you begin to feel that the Indian brand ambassador should not be Ronald McDonald but Ronald McPakora.

To be fair, there are also some salsa wraps which I haven't tried but which Sourish praises and which he says are not deep-fried. But despite these aberrations the Indian formula is clear: when in doubt, add masala and deep-fry.

Can McDonald's continue to succeed in India? Or will the chain face the same problems here that it is now facing in more mature markets?

It is hard to say. My guess is that an Indian McDonald's has one huge advantage over local competition: hygiene.

Even though I'm not wild about letting my son eat fatty food, I'm still more secure about sending him to a McDonald's than I am when he eats kababs or chaat from the streets. With McDonald's you have an unspoken guarantee that the food will be hygienically prepared and that the restaurant will be clean and well-maintained.

In the West this may not count for much. But in India it matters more than people are often willing to admit.

Nevertheless, there are problems. Outside of Mathura and other so-called emerging markets I don't know of too many adults who go to McDonald's on a regular basis. In relatively more sophisticated circles in Delhi, Mumbai or Poona, McDonald's is regarded as a kiddies' restaurant. This surely is not a positioning that McDonald's can be happy with—in the long run.

Secondly, once McDonald's stops doing McDonald's-type food and becomes a McPakora restaurant, it becomes like anybody else and is easy to imitate. In the US, McDonald's has been hit by Wendy's' aggressive pricing. There's no reason why an enterprising Indian chain can't start doing its own pakora burger and fries at a much lower cost.

And finally, there's the health factor. Chefs at five-star hotels claim that guests are getting more and more health conscious. They avoid red meat, they demand wholewheat bread and ask for their food to be cooked in olive oil. The five-star world is far removed from the McDonald's market but in some ways the gap seems to be shrinking by the day.

If the average upper middle class Indian—the sort of chap who takes his kids to McDonald's—works out that chaat is probably much healthier and somebody manages to provide golgappas and paapri chaat in hygienic surroundings, then McDonald's could be in serious trouble. (Or if, for instance, Rohit Khattar turned his Eatopia into a chain.) After all, when you try to Indianize the menu you have to keep in mind that genuine Indian food can actually be healthier—and much, much tastier.

# the *maida* mystique

Bengali food is one of India's great cuisines, though perhaps it is not necessarily the healthiest. (All that mustard oil is not terribly good for the heart.) But there is one gastronomic eccentricity peculiar to all Bengalis that I could not fathom through years of living in Calcutta: they think that eating *maida* (refined flour) represents the height of sophistication.

In Bengal, they make their *puris* (*luchis*) from *maida*. Not only do they also make their *parathas* from *maida* but they have a deep and abiding contempt for those who use humble *atta*.

This snobbery is curious at the best of times, but even more extraordinary during an era when the world is turning its back on refined flour (*maida*) and rediscovering the virtues of wholewheat flour (*atta*).

The advantages of wholewheat over *maida* are well-established. Not only does it contain many of the nutrients that are lost in the refining process but it also has a mysterious effect on the insulin flow. Most diet theories that nave been evolved over the last ten years advocate cutting down on the three whites: white flour (*maida*), white rice (use brown rice) and white sugar (use a sweetener instead).

All three whites stimulate the release of insulin, which in turn plays havoc with the body's glucose levels. Dieticians differ on just how damaging this can be, but most are now coming around to the central thesis advanced by Michel Montignac in the mid to late 1980s: white flour makes you fat. You feel hungry a few hours after a white flour meal whereas wholewheat will keep you full for much longer.

All over the world wholewheat has now become the subject of a process of rediscovery. More and more people will eat brown bread (made from wholewheat) rather than white; wholewheat cakes have flooded the market and there is an increased demand for wholewheat pasta (though you still need durum—*suji*—to make most pasta taste right, unless you stick to fusili or spaghetti).

Sadly, we've gone the other way in India. Fortunately, we still consume more wholewheat than our counterparts in the West but this is because we make *atta* chapattis at home. (A former Bengali employer of mine considered it a matter of pride that he never allowed *atta* into his house. 'What about rotis?' I asked. 'What is a roti,' he harrumphed in reply.)

Unfortunately, commercial wheat products are still nearly all *maida*-based. Among the best-selling biscuits in the UK are Digestives (and their chocolate-coated cousins) which are made from wholewheat, but Americans like the disgusting *maida*-based Oreo and we've followed their example. It is next to impossible to find a good wholewheat biscuit on the shelves at your neighbourhood grocery shop.

The same is true of other baked products: cakes, pastries, patties and nearly everything else. Even good wholewheat bread is hard to find and if you are not careful, you can easily get conned.

Take the example of what many hotels describe as 'brown bread'. For years I assumed that this must be made from wholewheat as it is in the West. But as I grew older I began to wonder how the bakers managed to give it that spongy texture peculiar to white bread. (Wholewheat bread tends to squish when you squeeze it and does not bounce back into shape.)

The answer was simple enough: it *was* white bread.

Because the chefs and bakers couldn't be bothered to make real brown bread, they would use *maida* and then artificially colour it with caramel. If you complained they would say 'We never said it was wholewheat. We only said it was brown.' And yes, it did look brown.

Fortunately, this scam is slowly on its way out. I've heard chefs claim in their defence that you can't make good bread with Indian *atta*. Not only is the consistency wrong (something to do with the gluten content), but it doesn't look brown at the end of it.

The braver bakery companies are now experimenting with calling it *'atta* bread', calculating that customers won't mind even if the loaves don't look brown. And the top five-star hotels are taking the easy way out and importing their wholewheat flour.

Even so, always be suspicious when you buy your bread. Most Indian commercially produced sliced bread is downright revolting spongy nonsense. Steer clear.

Try and look for a smaller bakery company than one of the giants, or pick a brand that has some sense of quality. At a hotel, always ask if the bread is 100 per cent wholewheat. Even so-called wholewheat bread can have up to 30 per cent to 40 per cent *maida* added to the flour.

Remember also, to be very careful at restaurants. There is no earthly reason why a tandoori roti should be made of *maida*. (A *naan*, on the other hand, is always made of *maida*.) For a long time, restaurants would make their *rotis* from a mixed flour which was half *maida* and half *atta*. Sadly, they've tended to opt for 100 per cent *maida* these days. So always ask what you are eating. Every once in a while you'll find a restaurateur who is willing to make *atta* rotis.

At a five-star hotel you have the right to insist on wholewheat *rotis* (at those prices, you have a right to insist on pretty much anything you want), so always make it a point to make it clear that you won't have *maida*. Sadly, not all hotels are as quality conscious as Delhi's Taj Palace. At the new Masala Art restaurant, they make fresh *atta phulkas* for guests. When they couldn't get the *phulkas* soft enough, they worked out that the flour was to blame, and decided to make their own. So each day, they grind fresh *atta* in the Masala Art kitchen to get the *phulkas* right.

If you like Western food you'll find it difficult to avoid *maida*. All pizzas are made of *maida* (but then if you eat a lot of pizza you are probably not very health conscious anyway) as are most bakery products (quiches, pies, tarts etc.). Nearly all pasta is made from durum though I've seen Karen Anand's wholewheat pasta at some health food shops.

But if, like me, you make a deliberate decision to avoid *maida*, you won't just feel healthier, you'll find that your taste buds will become much more sensitized. I now feel like throwing up when I see a fried white *luchi* (though curiously, I'm more partial to a nice *bhatura*, particularly if there's tangy *channa* as an accompaniment), and there is no sight more revolting than a sandwich made from spongy, commercial white bread. On the other hand, if I see good white bread—*maida* bread, that is—I appreciate it more, because I know that it is a special treat. Sadly, it is getting more and more difficult to get memorable, high-quality, commercial white bread. So stick to brown/*atta* bread—when you can find it.

# what's cooking?

# there's something about vanilla

I once took a (very) famous movie star to an ice cream festival at the Shamiana at Bombay's Taj Mahal Hotel. Famous Movie Star (FMS) was not much of a foodie but he did like ice cream.

His arrival at the restaurant caused huge excitement; heads turned, women felt faint and the waiting staff all queued up to serve our table. I told the beaming manager that FMS was an ice cream fan so could he tell us what the special ice creams were?

The manager was beside himself with excitement.

'Sir, we have black currant, we have cookies and cream, we have chocolate ribbon . . .' And on and on he went, till he had run through thirty flavours of astounding inventiveness.

I looked at FMS. 'Well, which one would you like?'

FMS stared into the distance for a few seconds. Then he turned to the manager: 'Can I have vanilla ice cream with chocolate sauce, please?' he intoned in that famous baritone.

Collapse of eager manager with thirty astonishing flavours.

FMS is largely a creature of habit so I suspect his unwillingness to experiment with bubblegum-flavoured ice cream was due to a certain lack of the spirit of gastronomic inquiry. But, funnily enough, he made absolutely the right decision, choosing the one flavour we rarely get in India: vanilla.

Yup, you read that right.

In the US, any ice cream called 'vanilla' has to be made from vanilla beans (*Vanilla planifolia*). In India, no such stipulations apply. So, unless you buy your ice cream at a fancy ice cream festival (like the one I took FMS to), an upscale foreign manufacturer, or at a restaurant where the chef makes his or her own, the chances are that your so-called vanilla ice cream will be made from synthetic vanilla essence, a by-product of the wood pulp industry.

In fact, it is almost impossible to buy anything made from real vanilla in this country. If your mother baked biscuits and you remember her adding a few drops of a dark liquid from a small bottle, then you caught her in the act of adding nasty, synthetic chemicals to the cookies. All Indian manufacturers (to the best of my knowledge) who use vanilla flavour in their bakery products use synthetic vanilla. As does nearly everyone who claims to use 'vanilla'.

So if you've had a vanilla cookie, a vanilla cake, a vanilla milkshake or a vanilla ice cream, you've had the bogus flavour. If you've asked them to add a drop of vanilla syrup to your Caffè Latte at your overpriced coffee bar, then you've almost certainly been served synthetic vanilla. If you've ordered a caramel custard at a restaurant, it has been artificially flavoured with chemical vanilla.

This is a pity. Though the phrase 'plain vanilla' suggests 'simple' or 'ordinary', real vanilla is one of the world's great flavours and aromas. We may prefer the synthetic flavour in India, but over the last decade, the rest of the world has rediscovered the magic of vanilla. It is one of the best-selling aromas in the perfume and toiletries business, and candles infused with real vanilla are a huge hit. No self-respecting chef would be caught dead using anything other than real vanilla. And my favourite vodka these days is flavoured with vanilla.

The popularity—and snob value—of real vanilla has (let's be honest) at least something to do with its price. The real thing is three to four times the price of the synthetic substitute. It is still not readily available (try buying a vanilla bean in Delhi or Calcutta and see). And it is incredibly difficult to cultivate the vanilla orchid.

The vanilla plant is a creeper that is native to Mexico. Around

1,000 years ago, the local Indians discovered that if you took the (odourless and flavourless) fruit of the plant, sweated it in the sun for three weeks and then dried it for several months, something magical would happen: a chemical reaction in the dried pod would produce a natural substance called vanillin which contained the taste and aroma we associate with vanilla.

Cortez and his Spaniards were fed vanilla when they conquered the New World and they took the taste back to Europe where it was a huge success. Attempts were made to cultivate the orchid elsewhere but they always failed. And so, till 1874, the Mexicans maintained a monopoly and vanilla remained rare, expensive and much desired.

Then, in 1874, German scientists artificially synthesized vanillin from wood pulp. This process revolutionized the food industry and made vanilla the second most preferred dessert flavour (after chocolate) in the world. Artificial vanillin has a sharper, more unpleasant taste than the real thing, but it is still recognizably vanilla.

Throughout the nineteenth century the French kept trying to plant vanilla in their colonies but these attempts did not succeed largely because nobody could pollinate the vanilla orchid which opens only for a day and a half. Eventually the French cracked it by importing Mexican bees which pollinated the orchid (and by using hand pollination). They planted vanilla in Reunion, Madagascar and other colonies and came to dominate the world market. (This is why in France they tend to use real vanilla in preference to synthetic vanillin.)

In recent years, vanilla orchids have been cultivated in Asia, including in Sri Lanka, but attempts to get the trade going in Kerala's spice coast have only just become successful—one reason why we still use synthetic vanilla in India.

If you want to experience the true taste of vanilla, your best bet is a five-star hotel where the chef makes his own ice cream. Indian catering colleges are still champions of synthetic vanilla but expatriate chefs have introduced the vanilla bean to Indian kitchens.

A classy chef will chop vanilla seeds into his milk mixture, so a good ice cream will have little black flecks testifying to the authenticity of the vanilla. I'm guessing but I reckon that an American chain like Baskin-Robbins will also use real vanilla on the grounds that it would be obliged, by law, to eschew synthetic vanilla in the US. (In America you have to call vanilla ice cream made with artificial essence 'vanilla-flavoured ice cream'.)

Sadly though, you'll still have to go abroad to discover the true flavour of vanilla. Fragrances and toiletries using vanilla can cost the earth but there are some good mid-market ranges (Body Shop and Yves Rocher use the real thing) that are available all around the world. Most supermarkets in Europe and the US will sell vanilla beans. If you like cooking, buy some the next time you go abroad. You'll never use synthetic vanilla again.

And there's a bonus with the beans. You store the pod by putting it inside a jar of sugar. After two weeks, all of the sugar will miraculously take on a vanilla flavour which will stay even after you've taken out the bean. Add the sugar to coffee or to a dessert and you'll get a subtle vanilla flavour.

Or do what I do. Store your beans in a bottle of good vodka. Even after you've used the beans for something else, they'll have left their flavour behind, giving you an amazing vanilla-flavoured vodka.

# mushrooming flavours

I have a slightly complex—and more than a little troubled—relationship with dried mushrooms. In theory—or at least according to the cook books—dried mushrooms are as good as, if not better than, the real thing. Nearly every Italian recipe book will include recipes (pasta, risotto etc.) that involve the use of dried porcini mushrooms (called ceps in France and sometimes described by their scientific name, *Boletus edulis*).

Most Chinese restaurant chefs have never seen a fresh shiitake mushroom in their lives and will happily rehydrate a new batch of dried black mushrooms each day. And most menus will include such exotic sounding dishes as 'medley of wild mushrooms' without bothering to mention that the mushrooms may have been wild when they were picked many months ago (though even this is doubtful), but that they have spent weeks being domesticated in a plastic bag in the kitchen closet.

I have two problems with dried mushrooms. The first is the flavour and the second is the texture. It is a truism in the food business that a dried ingredient has a more concentrated flavour than the fresh equivalent (this is as true of herbs, tomatoes, chillies or whatever). Many chefs argue that this makes dried mushrooms a preferable alternative. Nico Ladenis writes that he actually prefers to use dried mushrooms over fresh.

Well, up to a point, Nico, up to a point.

It is certainly true that some powerfully flavoured mushrooms taste very different when they are fresh. I love the flavour of fresh shiitake, but yes, the dried version is more concentrated. So it is with porcini. Make a risotto with fresh porcini and you'll get a wonderful delicate flavour. Use the dried version and the flavour will hit you over the head but will have lost all its delicacy.

This means that any delicately flavoured mushroom is destroyed when it is dried. If you've ever tried rehydrating chanterelles or girolles, you'll know that the end result tastes of nothing as much as sawdust.

The second problem is texture. I don't care what Nico Ladenis with his three Michelin stars thinks—a rehydrated mushroom has no complexity of texture. Most times the mushrooms are chewy and feel like bits of rubber when you bite into them. This is as true of dried shiitake as it is of porcini. Only a fool would bother to sauté rehydrated mushrooms or to use them as anything other than a flavouring agent.

So, what does one do? It is all very well to hold forth about the virtues of fresh mushrooms if you can get them. But the point is most of us can't. This is more than a little odd. My *sabziwallah* in Defence Colony has all kinds of fresh vegetables flown in from Thailand (including galangal for which surely there can't be much call in Defence Colony or Lajpat Nagar), but stubbornly refuses to order any of the fresh mushrooms which are so cheap in Thai markets: shiitake, abalone, paddy-straw, enoki etc. (The last time he tried to push his dried shiitake, I asked if he had fresh ones. 'Fresh *bhi milta hain, kya*?' he asked in bemusement. 'Sardar*ji*, if they are dried, then they must have been fresh at some stage,' I explained patiently. He was not convinced.)

Whatever the reason, we'll have to accept that Indian *sabziwallahs* who fly in asparagus from Holland and fresh fruit from Bangkok couldn't be bothered to import any mushrooms from either the East (shiitake, for instance) or the West (porcini).

My solution to the mushroom conundrum has been to use dried mushrooms but to combine them with fresh mushrooms. That way you get both flavour and texture. This is cheating, I know, but it usually works.

Here's a simple recipe that'll show you how easy it is to pull this off. I call it my Cheeseless Mushroom Risotto.

### cheeseless mushroom risotto

Ideally, you should use short-grain Italian rice like Arborio or Carnaroli (both are available in the fancy markets). If you are making risotto for four people, use four fistfuls of rice and then add an extra fistful to be sure. (You should never wash risotto rice.)

The mushrooms: the classic version of this recipe uses porcini but if you can't find any use the biggest dried black shiitakes that you can find in the market. Rehydrate a fistful of mushrooms in warm water for around two hours. Also: take one plastic packet of white mushrooms and slice the mushrooms very thinly lengthwise.

When the mushrooms have been rehydrated, take them out of the water, remove the stalks and cut them into fat little pieces.

Then, take the water in which they've been rehydrated and put it in a huge pot. Add enough extra water to make sure that you've got around two litres' worth (equal to two bottles of Bisleri). I usually add a cube of stock—either a good veg. stock cube (also available at the fancy markets), or, if you are desperate, a chicken cube—once the water is boiling.

In a large pan (or a wok) fry two finely chopped large onions and lots of chopped garlic (to taste) in a good olive oil. I usually add dried herbs at this stage—just use one of those ready-made bottled combinations called Garlic Italian Seasoning or whatever.

When the onion is translucent, add the rice and cook over low to medium heat for four to five minutes. Then add enough white wine to cover the rice (Riviera or suchlike will do). When the rice has absorbed the wine, start ladling in the stock.

With risotto, the basic principle is that the creaminess comes from the rice starch, not the cheese. So you must cook it by the batch method. You add enough stock to cover the rice, keep stirring in a circular motion (to break down the starch), wait till the rice absorbs the stock and then add another ladleful of boiling stock. And so on till the rice is cooked. How long it will take depends on the age of the rice, but as rice carries no birth certificates, you'll just have to wait till it is ready.

While this is going on melt a little butter in a pan. Over a moderate heat sauté the pieces of dried mushroom so that they soak up the butter better. When they seem done, add the fresh mushroom and cook through for two minutes.

Around halfway through the risotto process (when the stock is half-finished, for instance), add the mushrooms to the rice and keep stirring.

When the risotto looks nearly ready, it is time to correct the seasoning. Taste the rice and add salt, more herbs, or whatever you need (some people put a dab of Tabasco).

Then, the final two bits of cheating. When the risotto is done, I add a knob of butter to make up for the absence of cheese or cream. I also add a few drops of truffle oil for the unmatched aroma (olive oil infused with porcini will also do). I hesitate to recommend this step because truffle oil is hardly a staple at most markets but if you can get it—go for it!

The final risotto will, if you've followed the instructions properly, be slightly dark but creamy. You will smell and taste flavourful mushrooms, and when you bite into the white mushrooms, you'll be fooled into thinking that you are tasting a wild mushroom.

# the secret of cooking risotto

If you've seen a risotto at an Italian restaurant and turned your back on it because it looks too creamy for the health-conscious, here's the good news: you can eat as much as you like.

If the risotto is correctly cooked then the creaminess comes not from fattening butter or cheese (though you can add both to a risotto) but from the rice itself. The secret of risotto cooking is that it is a technique that causes rice to release its *own* starch and produce its *own* creaminess.

Sadly, armies of incompetent and lazy chefs have forgotten this secret—at least in India. Hence the tendency of some chefs to spoon in the cream, ladle in the butter and grate the cheese. As the Maurya's Bill Marchetti says, it all only makes sense when you see risotto less as a dish and more as a method of cooking rice.

This method does not come naturally to us Indians (and that includes Indian chefs) because it runs counter to everything we know about cooking rice. Even in the Mediterranean, where two schools of rice cooking flourish, chefs who are used to the pilaf style of cooking rice consider risotto an abomination.

To make a good risotto, you must forget everything you have ever learned about cooking a pulao. In a pulao the rice must be long-grained and aromatic. Each individual grain of rice should stand proudly separate and the starch should have been washed away. In a risotto the exact opposite is true. The rice should be short and fat (Arborio rather than basmati), the fragrance is of no consequence, the rice should hold together and the starch, far from being washed away, is the key to success.

The first thing that throws many Indians, used as we are to rice dishes which use rice that has already been cooked, is that in a risotto not only should raw rice be gently cooked in olive oil and butter but that this rice should be poured from the packet without *ever* being rinsed or washed.

In a classic risotto recipe you first make the soffritto: onions gently fried in half olive oil and half butter along with the flavouring (mushrooms, asparagus, chicken, fish, bone marrow or whatever).

Once the soffritto seems done you add the raw rice and sauté it for a few minutes. Next you add enough white wine to cover the contents of the pan and wait till the rice has absorbed it all.

While all this is going on, you boil up a huge quantity of stock along with whatever herbs you want to infuse the risotto with. Pay attention to this stock because it will ultimately be the key to the taste of your risotto.

Once the wine has been absorbed, you ladle in enough stock to cover the rice and wait till this is absorbed. As the rice-soffritto mixture begins looking dry, add more stock. As soon this is absorbed, you add another ladle's worth. And so on until the rice is soft. (Some Italians like it *al dente*—firm when bitten—but you can cook it as you like it.)

By this time you will have forced the rice to give up all its starch so it must—if you've done it right—already look wet and creamy. Only then can you add a little butter and grate some Parmesan on top of the finished risotto.

That, in a nutshell, is how you make the perfect risotto. The first time I tried it I was so intimidated by the challenge of producing the creaminess that I wondered whether to cheat and spoon in cream. To my surprise, the dish was so perfect that I finally went without the butter and the Parmesan. (I am not a big fan of dairy products. Nor, for that matter, am I much of a cook, so if I can do it, anyone can.)

I'm aware that I'm making it sound too easy. There are problems, of course. To make the perfect risotto you need Italian rice. Bill Marchetti says that if you can't get Arborio (which you can but in the fancier Delhi markets), you shouldn't bother. Of course he's right but I've made risotto with the ordinary rice I use at home (Thai Jasmine) and got acceptable results. I imagine that if you were to use a short, fat Indian rice (ration *ka chawal*), you could probably manage. It wouldn't be restaurant-quality risotto but you could eat it.

As for the wine, I've used Grover's white wine which has proved to be perfectly adequate though I imagine that a fancy Italian white would produce a better risotto. Extra virgin olive oil is freely available in the shops as are grated Parmesan and most of the things you would use for the soffritto.

The big problem is the stock. A Maggi cube will do but the results will be far better if the stock is of better quality. I always hesitate to advise, in the manner of great chefs, that you make your own stock, because I don't know a single person who does. So here are some tentative suggestions: buy expensive imported stock cubes, use canned consommé or persuade a hotel chef to give you some stock (they have gallons of the damn thing). Which, of course, leads to the second big problem. What is the point of making a vegetarian risotto if you've got to use chicken stock?

Good point. Most hotels cheat, no matter what they tell you, and use non-vegetarian stock for their so-called vegetarian risotto. (But then, they cheat with the soups as well. How many vegetarians know that French Onion Soup is basically Beef Consommé?) Some restaurants (like Marchetti's place at the Maurya) give you the option of vegetarian and non-vegetarian stock even with vegetarian (i.e. mushroom) risottos.

My suggestion is: use a vegetable stock if you have to, but be prepared then for a risotto that lacks the body that only a good meat or poultry stock can give.

But then, you can't be pious *and* vegetarian *and* have everything!

# understanding the mushroom

When I was growing up in Bombay in the 1960s, the mushroom was a delicacy, rarely encountered fresh, and regarded (like the asparagus which also came canned in those days) as an 'English vegetable'. You came across it in 'Continental' restaurants where it was used in sauces and salads and it was almost always disgusting. There was a reason for this: everybody used mushrooms canned in brine which not only destroyed the colour (it became a muddy yellow), but killed the taste and replaced it with as unpleasant saltiness.

Even when fresh mushrooms began to be sold in the shops, many five-star hotel chefs refused to touch them, apparently on the grounds that they had been told in catering college that fresh mushrooms were likely to be poisonous and that the canned variety was safer! This logic must also have reached the city's Marwari and Gujarati housewives who would always offer, at every 'sophisticated' lunch party, a 'baked dish' consisting in the main of canned mushrooms baked with white sauce and Amul cheese. (The dish still survives but they now use corn, which makes it even more revolting.)

The rest of India has had a healthier relationship with mushrooms. They are cultivated in Himachal and have always been freely available in Delhi (though sadly, the wonderful mushroom pickle they used to bottle in Himachal has disappeared from our shops). When I moved to Calcutta in the mid-eighties, I was delighted to find baskets of huge, flat mushrooms (rather than the little buttons we buy in plastic bags at the grocer's) on sale in New Market.

Calcutta, in fact, had a greater familiarity with mushrooms than any other city. Apart from the flat mushroom of New Market, there were oyster mushrooms (both fresh and dried) at the grocer's and there was a flourishing trade in dried shiitake. Nepalis, North-Easterners and many others incorporated the oyster mushroom into their own cuisine.

These days, fresh mushrooms are available all over India but I have yet to come across a single restaurant that uses them wisely. Nor do most people understand just how many different kinds there are. The most common mushroom ('white mushroom') is the Champignon de Paris (*Agaricus bisporus*) or cultivated mushroom. This has the least flavour of any mushroom but is at its best when it is allowed to grow big—as in the flat mushrooms on sale in New Market. The most expensive Indian mushroom is the morel (*Morchella vulgaris*), which we call *guchhi* and associate with Kashmir. It is not very nice fresh which is why we buy them dried. Indian chefs put them in pulaos and cook them with peas, but personally I loathe them and think of them as overpriced rubbish.

Two other mushrooms are widely available in India. The shiitake is sold fresh all over Asia but most Calcutta Chinese are only familiar with the dried version which has to be reconstituted with warm water (some restaurants steam it for hours) though fresh is always to be preferred if you can get it. The oyster is one of my less favourite mushrooms. It gives off lots of water and has little flavour, which is why we chop it and fry it with masala and onions in Indian cooking.

Then, there are the so-called wild mushrooms: porcini (ceps), girolles (also called chanterelles and my personal favourite), shaggy cap, horn of plenty, etc. And there are the mushrooms of Far Eastern cuisine: mouse-ear, paddy-straw, matsutake, enoki. Most are not available in India except in the dried or canned version and of them I would recommend only dried porcini and canned paddy-straw.

The king of the mushroom world is of course the truffle, but this loses its flavour when canned and even the bottled black truffle is a poor substitute for the fresh variety.

Sadly, there is a general ignorance about mushroom recipes which works to the advantage of chefs. Each year, La Piazza at the Delhi Hyatt Regency does a truffle festival. I only went once but it was a huge con—the prices were high but nothing smelt or tasted of truffles. Far cheaper is the use of truffle oil (olive oil infused with truffle scent and flavour). Chef Bruno at Delhi's La Rochelle uses it to boost his pumpkin soup but the most imaginative use is the Wild Mushroom Risotto at Chamber's in Calcutta's Taj Bengal where Chef Rambo uses dried porcini and truffle oil to devastating effect.

If you are a vegetarian and want to experiment with mushrooms, here are some things you can do. At a Chinese restaurant ask the chef to quickly stir-fry chopped mushrooms (all the mushrooms he has in his kitchen—white and black) with onions and light soya sauce. (If you are a non-vegetarian, ask him to sauté whole black mushrooms with oyster sauce.)

At Italian restaurants, remember that reconstituted mushrooms work best with risotto or pasta. But even fresh musrooms will add texture to any dish: a simple fettuccine with pesto will be elevated by the addition of sliced mushrooms, and they also make a good pizza topping. At French restaurants, ask for the mushroom on toast as a first course. And if you are on a diet, then skip the french fries or the potato side dish and ask the chef to sauté fresh mushrooms in olive oil with garlic, parsley and a little basil.

If you want to cook at home, then make simple *ghar ka khana* but substitute white mushrooms in recipes. For instance, *aloo-matar* is boring, but if you replace the potatoes with mushrooms, the dish acquires a certain cachet. Instead of making a boring vegetable biryani (itself a bit of an oxymoron) make it to the recipe for a meat biryani but substitute mushrooms for meat.

And if you want to show off, here's my recipe for the easy, (but luxurious) Sunday brunch dish: scrambled eggs with smoked salmon. The salmon can now be bought from any Oberoi deli so all you need to make are the eggs.

## scrambled eggs with salmon

To serve two people, slice a packet of white mushrooms and reconstitute in water a handful of dried mushrooms (ceps are best but anything will do). Cook the mushrooms over high heat in half olive oil and half butter. Meanwhile, beat four eggs with two tablespoons of cream (now available in tetrapaks everywhere). When the mushrooms seem done, add a knob of butter, lower the flame to the lowest mark and add the egg mixture. Stir gently till scrambled. Just before serving drizzle some truffle oil for the scent (this is optional).

Put the salmon on a plate ( a garnish of salmon roe is great if you have it). Spoon the eggs on the same plate and serve with sea salt and freshly ground black pepper.

The original recipe was invented by La Varenne in 1651 but I've taken considerable liberties with it—and so should you. If you're a vegetarian, dispense with the salmon and serve the eggs with toasted wholewheat bread. La Varenne may not have approved, but then, he's dead.

# earning your bread and butter

Ask people to name their favourite dessert and most will think of something sophisticated: a dark chocolate mousse perhaps, or a warm Tarte Tatin. My problem is that while I don't have much of a sweet tooth—give me a choice between a dessert and another starter at the end of the meal and eight times out of ten I'll pick the starter again—I do like my desserts to be hot: a Grand Marnier souffle fresh from the oven, Crêpes Suzette flambéd at the table (frankly I don't really like Crêpes Suzette, but I love the romance and tradition associated with their preparation), a warm, velvety Crème Brûlée, or an oozing, melting chocolate cake (for many seasons, possibly the only thing on the menu at the Hyatt's La Piazza that you could order without a second thought).

But my favourite dessert is one that you can—and should—serve hot but one which I'm willing to raid the fridge for and wolf down even when it is ice-cold. Psychologists describe people like me who long for simple puddings as underdeveloped, emotional cripples, who long for the comfort of the nursery and the lost security of childhood.

There is something to this view. After all, which self-respecting foodie, asked to name his favourite dessert, would go for something as basic, as downmarket, and as unadventurous as bread-and-butter pudding?

Bread-and-butter pudding?

Yes. I'm afraid so.

And all that stuff about longing for the security of the nursery probably fits too. I love the smell of vanilla—as in aromatic candles, body sprays, room fragrances etc.—which, apparently, is also a sign of emotional underdevelopment. My idea of a great cheesecake is not some fancy baked version concocted by some poncy chef but the supermarket kind: Birdseye is best but Sara Lee will do. And my favourite Beach Boys song is not *I get around* or *God only knows* or any of Brian Wilson's complex harmonic sounds, but Bruce Johnston's wistful *Disney girls* ('Reality/It's not for me/It makes me laugh').

So, say it loud: I'm underdeveloped and proud.

Except of course, that this neat bit of instant analysis doesn't really fit anybody who grew up in India. Where did any of us get cheesecake or bread-and-butter pudding in nursery school? Why should *Disney girls*, with its idealized American references, ('Summertime/On old Cape Cod') mean anything to anyone born in India? And as for vanilla, no, that was never the smell I grew up with in Bombay. (Actually, the real smell of Bombay is much, much nastier, but as this is supposed to be food writing, I won't spoil your appetite.)

So perhaps I don't really long for my childhood.

I just have very basic tastes.

Certainly the association between bread-and-butter pudding and my schooldays does exist, but not in the way that amateur psychologists would suggest.

As long as I can remember I've loved bread-and-butter pudding. But because hardly anybody had an oven at home in Bombay when I was growing up and because restaurants were too busy making jam tarts and Black Forest pastries, I never got enough of it.

So, in my last years at boarding school, after I had been appointed Secretary of the Mess Committee (a stab at schoolboy democracy in the dining hall), I lobbied and agitated till they put Bread Pudding (there wasn't too much butter and cream in that version) on the menu.

Most of the other boys, who were used to eating Banana Custard (you slice a banana and float it in a custard made from a packet), were too stunned to protest. And it was certainly an improvement in the high spot of the school's pudding menu: Block Custard (you make thick custard from a packet, wait till it congeals and then cut it into cubes).

So how did I come to love bread-and-butter pudding? Where did I first learn to like it?

I have no idea.

But I treated my love of bread-and-butter pudding as my guilty secret, and when I went to boarding school in England, after I was finished with my Indian school, I was surprised to find that even British institutional catering frowned on bread-and-butter pudding. It was too stodgy, too passé.

Then, in the early eighties, incredibly enough, bread-and-butter pudding suddenly became fashionable!

It began with Anton Mosimann, the Swiss chef of London's Dorchester Hotel in the eighties (he now owns a rather naff club in Belgravia). Determined to reinvent classic British cuisine (in itself a bit of an oxymoron), Mosimann settled on bread-and-butter pudding—then seen as the epitome of nursery fare—as his signature dish.

I'll come to Anton's recipe in a bit, but what you really need to know is this: there is only one basic recipe.

> You take some bread, spread butter on it and put it at the bottom of a pan. Then you make a custard with milk, eggs and sugar. You pour the custard over the bread and put the whole thing in the oven (ideally at around 350 °F or Gas Mark 4). After half an hour, the custard has set and the bread has risen to the top. When you serve it, you include a bit of the bread and lots of the custard.

Much is made of Anton's reinvention of the dish—and I had his version in 1985 when my friend, the British food writer Paul Levy took me to lunch with Anton at the Chef's Table at the Dorchester—but all Anton really did was ponce up the recipe a little bit.

First of all, Anton dispensed with the sliced white bread and used fancy bread rolls which he sliced thinly and then buttered. Then, he increased the fat content of the custard. Instead of only milk, he used milk (250 ml) and double cream (also 250 ml). Next, he added even more butter to the top of the custard after he'd poured it over the bread. And then, in a truly chef-like touch, he dispensed with the oven and poached it in a bain-marie (a hot water bath) for 40 minutes.

The final version was very rich, and very smooth, but still—as far as I could see—the same damn thing with lots of dairy fat and hype added.

Mosimann's 'reinvention' of the bread-and-butter pudding became the standard for all other versions in the eighties at London restaurants. At the Connaught, Michel Bourdin (whose wonderful food has now been replaced by Angela Hartnett's Italian rubbish), had always done an extra-cream version, but because he didn't have friends like Paul Levy, he never got much publicity for it. At Green's, the chef, Beth Coventry, simply repeated the Mosimann recipe.

Younger chefs went back to the old recipe (ovens rather than a bain-marie) but had to find little variations of their own. Simon Hopkinson (then at Hillaire, later of Bibendum) offered a variation with tea cakes, a little rum and slightly less cream (150 ml to Anton's 250 ml). Others turned it into an Italian dish by using panettone, or created a French variation with brioche.

In America, they had their own variations. In the mid-eighties, Nora Ephron popularized one version (described as 'caramelized mush') in her hilarious, best-selling novel *Heartburn*, and Julie Russo and Sheila Lukins used a classic recipe from New Orleans in their influential *Silver Palate Cookbook*. As far as I could tell, the basic difference between the American and British versions was that the Americans used more sugar and less cream and served it with an alcoholic (usually whiskey-based) sauce.

Now the heyday of the bread-and-butter pudding revival is over. You don't find it on many menus. Nigella Lawson writes that it 'has gone from stodgy disparagement to fashionable rehabilitation and back to not-that-again clichédom'. Nevertheless, even Lawson featured a recipe in her hit TV series, though in keeping with her 'fat-is-great' philosophy, used more cream than any chef I know of.

If you've seen pictures of Nigella you will know that she is a large, handsome woman who likes old-fashioned foods (the term blancmange might usefully be applied—suitably doubled—to what she carries on her chest) and lots of dairy products. Her recipe is distinguished by getting us to not just butter the bread but to also smear it with ginger marmalade. Plus, like Hopkinson, she uses dark rum. And while everybody else uses 250 ml milk and between 150 to 250 ml cream, Nigella wants 200 ml 'full fat' milk plus another 500 ml double cream. Otherwise, the recipe is much the same as all the others.

If you want to make bread-and-butter pudding at home (and I recommend that you do: it is easy and it always impresses people to know that you've baked a hot dessert), then here's Marguerite Patten's basic recipe.

Take four slices of good bread (i.e. not your cheapest white bread) and butter them generously with a lightly salted butter (Amul is fine). Cut the bread slices into four or six pieces each. Place them in a baking dish. Sprinkle with raisins.

Take three or four eggs (three is okay but four may be better) and mix with 600 ml milk and 50 gm sugar. Heat gently till the eggs, sugar and milk are mixed.

Pour over the bread. Let it stand for 10 to 20 minutes.

Put the dish in the centre of a cool oven. Cook at 300 °F or so for an hour and a half.

That's the basic recipe. To tart it up, you can do the following:

- Use scones, tea cakes, slices of fruit cake, panettone etc. instead of the bread.
- Put something on the bread: marmalade, fruit conserves etc.
- Pour rum or the alcohol of your choice (if you are using marmalade, then use Grand Marnier) over the bread before you add the custard. You can also add chocolate or cinnamon to the milk.
- Substitute part of the milk with cream. Half and half is good, but you can go the full Nigella and use 500 ml cream and 200 ml milk.
- Play around with oven temperatures and cooking times. Here are some guides: Russo and Lukins first preheat the oven to 325 °F and cook for an hour and 10 minutes. Nigella says Gas Mark 4 (about 325° to 350 °F) and a 45-minute cooking time. Simon Hopkinson says an oven preheated to 350 °F and 40 minutes. Mosimann uses a bain-marie and takes 35-40 minutes.
- There are many regional variations. In India, the Parsis make their own bread pudding (Bhicoo Manekshaw and Cyrus Todiwala both have good recipes), and sometime ago, Camellia and Namita Panjabi offered their own variation with garam masala. The real Indian bread pudding, of course, is the *Shahi Tukra*—but that uses a different method.
- There is no need for a sauce if you use a cream-heavy version. My own view is that even the basic milk-only version needs no sauce if hot. If it is served cold, then vanilla ice cream makes a perfect accompaniment.
- I'm sure it is possible—and much easier—to do a microwave version of this dish. Sadly, I'm the sort of fool who treats a microwave as though it is an incredibly advanced space station. But if you understand microwave cooking times then you'll know what the high-tech version of Gas Mark 4 is.

And if you do learn to make a killer bread-and-butter pudding, then will you be a sad, nursery-longing, underdeveloped emotional cripple like me?

Probably.

But look at the brighter side. Once you master the dish you'll be turning out variations—chocolate pudding, the full-cream version, an orange and Grand Marnier variation, or Cabinet Pudding (with lots of dried and candied fruit)—in no time at all.

And because we don't subscribe to British characterizations of pudding lovers, your guests will have no idea of the sneery dismissiveness with which Brits treat nursery pudding fans like you and me.

Instead, they'll think you are a brilliant cook. And once you drop a few names (Anton Mosimann, Simon Hopkinson, Nigella Lawson etc.), they'll be ready to treat you like a Michelin-starred chef.

Trust me. I know.

It has worked for me.

Why shouldn't it work for you?

# nursery desserts for adults

Ask people about schoolboy or nursery desserts—at least of the sort that we can make at home in India—and you'll nearly always get the same answers: custard and jelly. Or, if they're being really clever: jelly with custard.

In my view, both get a bum rap, largely because of the laziness of Indian cooks.

Let's take custard first. You probably think of it as something that comes out of a powder, which you then add to warm milk. Well, all right, that is custard—after a fashion. But no, it's not real custard.

Contrary to what we are usually told in India, custard is not a dish you make by mixing cornflour with milk. Purists would probably describe the cornflour version as not being a true custard at all.

A real custard is what the French call a crème anglaise (you may see the term on fancy menus) and comprises an emulsion (a term we associate with paint but I'll explain what it means later) of egg yolks and milk.

The bogus custard—of the sort we come across in India—is a fraud anglaise; it was invented in the last century by a chemist called Bird who was allergic to eggs and wanted to make an eggless version (had he been around in India in this century he would probably have been *Panchjanya's* poster boy for his contribution to eggless cooking but that's another story . . .). The version we are used to in India lacks Bird's brand name (synonymous with custard in England)

and is more likely to be associated with Brown and Polson, purveyors of cornflour to armies of chefs in Chinese restaurants.

I'm not hysterically opposed to the bogus cornflour custard. After all, like most of us, I grew up on it. At school, dessert usually consisted of five banana slices in bogus custard or that great Mayo College invention (mentioned before), the Block Custard, which was no more than a thicker version of the Bogus Custard, congealed through cooling and then cut into small cubes for the enjoyment of credulous schoolboys.

And if you are making a custard at home—there's nothing quite as energy providing and life-affirming as a custard when you are sick—then I suppose it's okay to make a custard from a packet.

But why, I wonder, do professional chefs never bother to make the real thing? In England, any chef (outside of institutional catering) who made packaged custard would be sacked. In France he would probably be shot.

There are broadly three answers to that question. One, they are not all that hot on real custard at catering colleges so many of our chefs don't know any better. Two, most of *us* don't know better so the chefs can get away with it. And three: they couldn't be bothered.

But if you want to, you can make a real custard at home quite easily. You must remember that it is, at base, an emulsion—a scientific name for a combination of two liquids that do not, in fact, actually mix. According to Heston Blumenthal, chef at The Fat Duck in Bray (England) who takes a scientific approach to his cooking, what really happens is this: 'One of the liquids forms small droplets and becomes dispersed in the other. The other liquid surrounds these droplets.'

In cooking terms, emulsions usually involve egg yolks which have the ability to combine with other liquids in a stable manner: think mayonnaise or Béarnaise sauce. (If this makes no sense to you, do not worry. I'm also an Arts student. Just forget the science and enjoy the bloody thing.)

A custard is pretty much your classic emulsion, comprising a union of milk and egg yolks.

> According to Blumenthal's recipe, you should mix six egg yolks with seeds from six vanilla pods (synthetic vanilla essence is a poor substitute but if it's all you've got, go ahead and use it). Mix in an electric mixer for ten minutes. The mixture will now whiten considerably.
>
> Now, take 635 ml of milk, mix with the vanilla pods (you've used the seeds with yolks, so the pods should be left—assuming you've used real vanilla) and place on medium heat. When the milk boils, turn the heat to low.
>
> Return to your egg yolk mixture. Put an electric mixer on low and pour in a little of the warm milk. When this has been well incorporated, pour the mixture into the pot where your milk should still be warming on low heat.
>
> Keep stirring till the custard thickens enough to coat the back of a wooden spoon. When it's thick enough, pour it into a bowl sitting on another bowl of ice. Stir for five minutes till cool.
>
> And that's it. You now have a perfect custard that's never even been near a cornflour packet.

If Indian chefs have an aversion to real custard, then grant them this: they love jelly, the other great nursery dessert.

Or, to be more precise, it's not jelly that they are keen on, but gelatine itself.

At this stage, I suppose I better define my terms more closely. Jelly means different things on each side of the Atlantic. In America jelly is used to describe what you and I (and the Brits who taught us the term) call jam. In Britain, jelly describes a chilled dessert that is usually made by adding gelatine crystals to flavoured water and refrigerating. In America they call this jello.

The definition of gelatine is slightly less savoury. Gelatine is an organic substance made from collagen, the elastic protein that holds the body together. In scientific terms (and here again, my source is Heston Blumenthal), gelatine is composed of three protein chains that are happy to remain separate at above 40 °C. But once the temperature drops below that level, the chains bind together to create a substance that is solid but sticky, slippery and, well, jelly-like.

The trick with jelly, therefore, is to add gelatine to something, heat it, and then cool it so that the whole texture changes.

If you had jelly when you were young then you'll probably remember the process even if you didn't understand the science.

I recall that when I was young the cook would buy a packet of (synthetic) strawberry-flavoured Rex Jelly Crystals, add them to water and heat. The resulting mixture would be poured into a glass bowl and kept in the fridge for a while after which a luridly coloured jelly would emerge as a kiddie dessert.

Because it was so easy to make, jelly quickly became a favourite at children's parties. In vegetarian households it was accorded a special pride of place because it was an 'eggless pudding'.

Sadly for the vegetarians, nobody understood the science. Because collagen is an organic material, all gelatine came from the bones of dead animals. Perhaps the makers of Rex Jelly Crystals indicated this in small letters on the side of their packets, but nobody I knew ever bothered to read the fine print.

And so, vegetarian after vegetarian eagerly devoured a by-product of animal bones and hooves, pleased that this was, after all, an eggless pudding.

Then, in the 1980s, some enterprising manufacturer decided that the market was ready for taking, if only a synthetic (i.e. chemical) and therefore, entirely vegetarian, collagen could be introduced. Large ads appeared in the papers telling vegetarians (in effect) that the strawberry jelly they enjoyed so much was made from the bones of dead cows, and so on.

Since then, the consumer jelly market has never quite recovered.

However, all Indian pastry chefs use gelatine as a matter of course, whether or not they bother to inform their customers. For the sake of squeamish vegetarians, I hope they use synthetic gelatine, though frankly, I have my doubts.

For the talentless pastry chef, gelatine is the glue that holds his puddings together. Ever had that peculiarly Indian pudding: the cold pineapple souffle? The chances are that the chef threw in a packet of gelatine before cooking his so-called souffle.

Ever wondered why the cheesecakes at Indian hotels have the texture of marshmallows? Same reason. The pastry chef couldn't be bothered to make a proper, creamy cheesecake so he just doubled the quantities of gelatine to hold the damn thing together. Did he use synthetic gelatine? Is the cheesecake made from the shin bones of dead horses? Well, who knows?

If all this has put you off gelatine, then I make no apologies. That was partly the idea. I find that the Indian chef's reliance on gelatine is one reason why the Western desserts at most Indian hotels are so disgusting.

As for jelly itself, well, that's a taste that you are expected to lose once you are past the age of seven. Speaking for myself, I find it difficult to take any restaurant buffet seriously if I find that they have placed a large, wobbly jelly on the dessert counter.

There are, however, grown-up jellies (for non-vegetarians, that is). Many modern chefs love experimenting with the sensual texture of gelatine. Few, if any, will use it for desserts though. Most fancy chefs will use it for savoury dishes.

I think this is a valid culinary experiment but I'm still not totally convinced that 'grown-up jelly' is not an oxymoron like 'virgin prostitute' or 'Gujarati war hero'. (Or 'Punjabi intellectual', for that matter.)

Still, I'm intrigued by Blumenthal's recipe for a jellied Kir Royale (this is not as outrageous as it sounds, bartenders are forever making things like Bloody Mary jelly these days). If you really like jelly (and/or champagne), then it may be worth a try.

## blumenthal's kir royale jelly

This is interesting because it manages to keep the bubbles in the jelly itself. My friend, the chemist Len Fisher, devised the clever technique of preserving the bubbles more than in a regular champagne jelly. The crème de cassis and sugar seem to reduce the volatility of the champagne.

**750 ml champagne or sparkling wine**
**100 ml crème de cassis**
**7 leaves gelatine**
**150g sugar**

Well before you start making this, put six to eight champagne flutes in the freezer.

Soften the gelatine leaves in cold water. Pour out about 75 ml of the champagne into a small pan. Immediately seal the bottle. Add the sugar and crème de cassis to the champagne in the pan, and gently heat. Remove and squeeze the softened gelatine leaves, then add to the mix and stir until dissolved. On no account let the liquid come anywhere near the boil. As soon as everything is dissolved, remove from the heat and set aside.

Remove the glasses from the freezer, and divide the mix between them. Immediately pour reserved champagne over the mix, then freeze the glasses for one hour. After this time, remove from the freezer and store in the fridge until ready to serve.

But when it comes to kiddie desserts, give me custard over jelly anytime. It's sweet, it's wholesome, and it doesn't slink down your throat like an invading alien parasite.

# the enduring myths of pasta

When I was growing up in the 1960s the only pasta we found in the shops in Bombay was macaroni. Rarely, if ever, was it used for any dish other than the ubiquitous macaroni-cheese, in which macaroni, white sauce and cheese of dubious provenance (Aarey Milk Colony cheese, Ooty Cheese, smuggled processed cheese) were baked together to produce a food with the aroma and consistency of congealed vomit.

Needless to say, I was not a macaroni fan.

Calcutta was much the same with only the products of such macaroni producers as Licia gracing (I use the term loosely) the tables of Marwari households. But Delhi was much better, with spaghetti readily available and many housewives adept in the pasta arts. (A treat in my adolescence was the Spaghetti Bolognese made by the mother of my best friend at their Defence Colony home.)

By the seventies, most hotels had put three basic spaghettis on the menu: Bolognese (*keema* sauce), Carbonara (with egg yolk and bacon) and a tomato sauce (variously described as Neapolitan, Marinara, Arabiata or whatever took the chef's fancy). But it wasn't till about ten years ago that restaurants began serving a variety of pastas: rigatoni, fusilli, penne, farfalle, tagliatelle, etc.

Even so, most people of my parents' generation, who do not have the benefits of wide international travel, still call all pasta 'macaroni'. Before you smile patronizingly, I must tell you that they are not wrong. Macaroni may refer to a tubular pasta but it is also the generic term for all dried alimentary pastes made from hard wheat and water and eggs and cooked in broth or water. If you want to be pretentious, you can use the Italian generic (*pasta secca* or dried pasta), but macaroni is easier (*pasta fresco* is fresh pasta, but the two, as we shall see, are very different).

Pasta lends itself to legends and misconceptions. For instance, English food writers routinely go to Bologna in search of the perfect Spaghetti Bolognese. They always come back disappointed: the dish does not appear on any of the menus.

The truth is that Spaghetti Bolognese is an Anglo-Saxon invention, the creation of Italian immigrants who brought the *ragu* sauce popular in Bologna (where you are more likely to find Tagliatelle con Ragu alla Bolognese), threw out the sophistication (the classic Bologna *ragu* combines beef, veal, pork, chicken livers, prosciutto, mortadella and pancetta) and produced a simple minced meat sauce. (You will find the full story on page 332.)

But no legend about pasta is more enduring than the myth that Marco Polo returned to Venice in AD 1295 with the recipe for Chinese noodles, which intrepid Italian chefs then turned into macaroni, spaghetti and penne.

There are two problems with this story. The first is that when Polo described the food of China in his writings he used the words 'vermicelli', 'lasagne' and 'lagana'. This suggests that he was already familiar with pasta and was only making the point that noodles were similar.

The second problem has to do with wheat. *Pasta fresco* can be made with virtually any kind of wheat: *maida*, wholewheat, all-purpose flour, soft wheat etc. Typically it has a shelf life of a couple of days. *Pasta secca*, on the other hand, was always made with hard wheat (*Triticum turgidum*) in medieval times.

Even today, most dried pasta is made from durum (a hard wheat) which is similar (except for starch content) to our very own *suji* or semolina. The distinction was vital in medieval times because normal wheat (*Triticum aestivum*) did not last and the pasta began to spoil. Only after the large-scale cultivation of durum began did dried pasta become possible and popular. From most accounts, this happened in Europe around AD 1100.

But—and this is crucial—the Chinese (and the rest of Asia) did not know about *suji*/durum/semolina for centuries afterwards. The noodles that Marco Polo encountered (nearly two centuries after durum-based *pasta secca* was popular in Italy) were made from soft wheat and did not last.

So do not be fooled by claims that pasta is descended from Mixed Hakka Noodles or Chow Mein al la Bhatinda. Kublai Khan gave Marco Polo many gifts but no, he did not give him the recipe for Spaghetti alla Puttanesca.

Indians should have a natural affinity for pasta. It combines our classic food pairing (wheat and vegetables/meat or roti-*sabzi*) with the possibility of upping the spice content enough to appeal to local tastebuds.

Sadly, we don't treat pasta with the respect it deserves. We are a little more careful with the terms (Marinara means a seafood and tomato sauce, Arabiata needs tomatoes and crushed chilli) but we still treat pasta as a restaurant dish, which leaves us at the mercy of chefs who put cream and cheese in everything.

Here's a simple recipe for a pasta that no Indian can resist.

### fusilli con aglio olio e pepperoncino

Using a mortar and pestle (or a food processor, if you are rich and lazy), pound lots of garlic (six cloves or so), some *lavangi* chillis (around three) along with salt. Keep adding extra virgin olive oil till you have a paste that is to your liking. (You can vary proportions depending on your taste.)

Bring a large pot of pre-salted water to boil. Throw in a pound of pasta (this recipe is for fusilli but you can use spaghetti or tagliatelle) and cook till *al dente*. Once it is ready, mix with the sauce, add a little more olive oil and sprinkle with parsley.

Do not add cheese. Do not add anything else. Eat it as soon as it is ready. It will taste terrific and will be quicker to make than the average Indian meal.

# the heart of a salad is in the leaves

It is now impossible to go to a restaurant in America without being offered some variation on the Caesar Salad. Even if you remain in India and choose to frequent an American-style 'restaurant' (Thank God It's Friday comes to mind), you'll probably be offered some kind of Caesar Salad. Even in England the salad has a certain cachet, especially after Anton Mosimann produced his own variation.

All of this may lead you to believe that a Caesar Salad is a great staple of French cuisine (invented by Escoffier in honour of his boss Cesar Ritz, perhaps) or even that it dates back to the Roman Empire.

It is, in fact, of seedy Mexican origin.

We can pin down its provenance with some exactitude because it was invented only in the 1920s and we know the name of the man who did it: Caesar Cardini. In the 1920s, Cardini ran an Italian restaurant in the sordid Mexican border town of Tijuana (as in Herb Alpert and the Brass). Many Hollywood stars would go 'south of the border', to Tijuana for an illegal fix (a hurried abortion, supplies of drugs, etc.) and they became fans of Cardini's salad. They took it back to Los Angeles with them. And eventually, just like Hollywood, the Caesar conquered the world.

The reason for its popularity in the TGIF kind of chefless restaurant is that a) it is a recognizable brand name; b) it is relatively cheap to make; and c) it is so easy that any fool, even a 'cook' at an American fast food restaurant, can churn it out.

The most authentic Caesar Salad recipe comes from the great American cookery writer Julia Child who got it from Cardini's daughter. Child concedes 'you will hardly be a Caesar enthusiast if you've only dined on restaurant varieties made with cheap oil, store-bought croutons, garlic powder and bottled cheese.'

Child's claim is that the real thing—made with expensive ingredients—is terrific. I'm not convinced myself. But here's the basic recipe:

## caesar salad

Lots of ordinary lettuce leaves (Cos lettuce rather than iceberg), garlic croutons (i.e. croutons fried with garlic-infused oil), and boiled eggs. You mix all of these and season with a little salt, lots of pepper, olive oil, the juice of one lemon, a hefty slug of Worcestershire sauce and then grate some good quality Parmesan cheese on top.

Mosimann's recipe is not dramatically different but he uses anchovy paste instead of Worcester sauce which, in my view, marks no real improvement on Child's version. Lots of American restaurants now add grilled chicken and pass the salad off as a full meal. If you come across a version that includes tomatoes, cucumbers and mayonnaise, send it back to the kitchen. It is plainly not a Caesar Salad.

More famous than the Caesar Salad (at least in restaurants where they can be bothered to hire a chef) is the Salade Nicoise, or the traditional salad of Nice, the most important city in the South of France.

Most catering colleges teach a variation of Nicoise that any self-respecting Frenchman would vomit out, were it to be served to him. At its simplest, this bastardized Nicoise consists of boiled potatoes, boiled French beans, a few chunks of lettuce, leftover canned tuna, boiled eggs and any easily available salad oil.

In the 1980s, such chefs as Roger Verge made an attempt to reclaim the Nicoise but it was Nice's most famous mayor, an extreme right-wing, extreme crook called Jacques Medecin, who ruled Nice for twenty-four years and claimed to protect Nicoise values, who led the charge to spread the recipe for an authentic Salad Nicoise.

Because Medecin was such a charlatan (Graham Greene, who spent the last years of his life in Nice, ran a campaign against him) and ended up in jail for fraud, we are entitled to treat his version of Nicoise values with same scepticism.

## salad nicoise

For what it's worth, Medecin (along with most local chefs) insisted that a Nicoise must never contain cooked potatoes or french beans. His salad recipe called for small broad beans (or, if these were not available, small globe artichokes). These were mixed with lots of tomatoes, some cucumber, lots of spring onions, a couple of green peppers, a few black olives, a clove of garlic and either 12 anchovy fillets or tuna (canned was fine). The dressing was olive oil, finely chopped fresh basil, and salt and pepper.

This is probably how the real thing should be made—no lettuce, no beans, no vinegar, no potatoes, no herbs apart from basil (no rosemary or tarragon) and nothing already cooked—but even Nicoise chefs do make exceptions. (Verge's recipe differs from Medecin's.)

A more complicated recipe, which uses vinaigrette, lots of herbs, some lettuce and cooked potatoes plus both anchovies and tuna appears in Patricia Wells's normally authoritative *Food Lover's Guide to France*. But even Wells is sensitive to Nicoise sentiments. While most of her recipes are credited to the chefs who invented them, she is more circumspect about the authenticity of her salad recipe: 'This is my personal version of Salade Nicoise.'

Does it matter if a recipe is authentic? Does anybody really care if his or her Salade Nicoise differs from Roger Verge's recipe? Should you make a Caesar Salad the way that Cardini used to?

I have two answers to these questions. The first is for restaurants. If you are calling a dish Caesar Salad and it bears no resemblance to (or is sufficiently different from) the real thing, then you are, in effect, cheating the customer. It is like calling a dish a *sambhar* and making it with black dal, or describing something as spaghetti and then serving noodles.

So yes, it does make a difference for restaurants.

But for the rest of us, I don't think it matters very much. If you want to mix leftover boiled potatoes with beans, tomatoes and fish and make a variation on Salade Nicoise then it is entirely your own business, not Jacques Medecin's.

For my own part, I tend to shun restaurant-style salads and their recipes. Why bother to make a Caesar Salad at home or struggle to produce an authentic Nicoise when you can do so much more by using your own imagination?

The heart of a salad, it has always seemed to me, lies in the leaves. I have no great affection for lettuce or for raw spinach. The only salad leaves that really get me going are rocket (also called *aragula* or *ruccolla* or *rughetta*). These have a wonderful nutty taste that is hard to beat.

Fortunately, we've now started to get rocket at many *sabziwallahs*. If you are lucky enough to find some, forget about Verge, Cardini and the rest. Pair the leaves with some sliced raw mushroom, add a few batons of lightly blanched asparagus (sliced diagonally) and use a garlic-olive oil dressing. (Other options: a

Japanese sesame dressing or, if you are feeling rich, a little truffle oil.)

Take my word for it: you'll have made a better salad than anything Cardini or Medecin dreamt up.

As always, the best ingredients yield the best results—if you use them with imagination.

# the universal charm of omelettes

One of the great pleasures of food is that not only does it vary from place to place but it also takes on the flavours of its origins. A single bite of *bhelpuri* can transport you to Bombay; a good hot dog should remind you of a baseball game in New York; and the lemon grass and basil scents of a Thai curry will make Thailand came alive.

But there are some dishes that are truly universal, and the omelette is one of them. You can get omelettes anywhere in the world and though the basic recipe (lightly beaten eggs fried in a pan till set) rarely varies, there are as many regional variations as there are regions.

Railway station omelettes kept me alive during my train-travelling youth; you can still get excellent omelette-buns on the streets of most Indian cities. A classic French omelette is traditionally regarded as the test of a cook's hand. In Italy the related (but quite different) *frittata* is a staple. In Spain a tortilla (the word is not used for bread in Europe, the way it is in Central America) is one of the country's signature dishes (aka the Spanish Omelette). In Tunisia the *maquda* is a square of omelette used as a *mezze* or *tapas*-type dish. In Sri Lanka they make a curry out of cooked omelette. In South East Asia, they wrap fried rice in a paper-thin omelette.

In my experience though, there are three significant kinds of omelette. The first is the *masala* omelette of the sort that we in India love and devour. The first recorded recipe (as The King of

Oude's Omelette) appears in Eliza Acton's *Modern Cookery* (published in 1845). This included onion, chilli, fresh mint, cloves and leeks. As time went on the cloves and leeks were eliminated and replaced with tomatoes and fresh coriander (a touch borrowed from the Raj-loving Parsis of Bombay).

Today's masala omelette is broadly the same as the Raj-era version and it differs from the French original mainly in the style of cooking. For one, you add the flavouring to the egg mixture (the French add the filling as the omelette is cooking). For another, you beat the eggs like hell. (This makes them a little too tough for the French.) And finally, your omelette should be nearer the thickness of a chapatti or a pancake rather than the cylindrical French version.

It is this omelette that you find in every railway retiring room, canteen or *dhaba* all over India. If it is properly spiced, it should need no further flavouring but I've never come across an Indian-style omelette that did not improve when eaten with tomato ketchup.

Moreover, you don't have to be a great chef or a genius to make a *desi* omelette. The French, on the other hand, make a huge hoo-hah about their style of omelette-making. Much of the mythology associated with French omelette-making has always struck me as being old-fashioned rubbish. For instance, there is a huge mystique surrounding the pan: it must be a cast-iron skillet; it must never be washed, only gently wiped etc. Then, there's a lot of nonsense about technique: the chef should hold the pan with one hand while simultaneously making a circular motion with the other so that he stirs the egg mixture as it sets etc.

The truth is that omelette-making (at least in the classic French sense) requires practice. A French omelette is difficult to get right for a beginner because you have to learn to fold it into a cylinder while the top is still wet and then you must be able to slide it out of the pan while the insides are still runny. In more complex versions, you add the filling just before you start folding and this makes your task more difficult.

None of this is easy but considering that thousands of French catering students learn to do this every term, how difficult can it really be?

The Spanish tortilla (of which the Italian *frittata* is a close relative) is nearer our masala omelette than the French version. Basically, you first fry onions with vegetables (including potatoes). When they are cooked, you pour in the egg mixture and wait till the whole thing has taken on the shape and consistency of a pie. You also serve it like a pie by cutting triangular slices.

I have to say that the tortilla is my least favourite of the basic omelettes—thick, congealed egg with potatoes is not my idea of gastronomic excellence—but it has its adherents. In my view, if you are going to make a set omelette (rather than the runny French version), you are better off with our thinner railway station omelettes.

And if you want to be adventurous you can combine the *desi* and French techniques. To make this work, you need to get the filling right. In my experience, two fillings that work well are mushroom masala (cooked in advance) or some processed cheese to which you've added chopped green chillies and a few drops of Tabasco. Make the omelette the French way (it will have to be thicker than the *desi* version if it is to accommodate the filling) but don't worry about leaving the centre too runny. When the omelette seems about to set, spoon the filling into the centre and then fold. Masala mushrooms will blend nicely with egg while the chilly-cheese mixture will melt, providing the illusion of a soft-centred French omelette with a very Indian, spicy tang.

Of course, as with all omelettes, remember the basic warnings. No omelette is meant for keeping. It must be eaten fresh to be fully enjoyed. The exceptions are the Mediterranean omelettes made for *tapas* or *mezze*, the Sri Lankan omelettes that go into curries and perhaps, our own masala omelette whose life can be extended if you make it into masala omelette sandwiches. (Use wholewheat, untoasted bread and just before eating, slip a few potato chips or wafers between the omelette and bread—it helps with the texture of the dish.)

And in these days of super-health consciousness, be warned that the rare French omelette, with its runny centre, would be considered a salmonella risk. Remember also that doctors warn against the dangers of eating too many eggs though they can't explain why, in that case, the Parsis, who subsist on eggs, all live to be 120 or 130 years old. (Rusi Mody still brags about his twenty-egg omelettes and he's no spring chicken.)

One solution is to eliminate the cholesterol-rich yolk and eat the protein-heavy white. Most hotels will offer egg-white omelettes as a healthy option. I see the point, but frankly, if you are that worried about clogging up your arteries at breakfast, then you are better off giving the whole omelette thing a miss and eating a piece of grapefruit instead. It'll taste revolting but at least you'll feel healthy.

# the mostly accurate history of potato chips

As food legends go, the one about the invention of the potato chip (the crisp or wafer as distinct from what Americans call French fries) is unusual in two respects. One: it is a great story. And two: unlike most other legends of its kind, this one is probably accurate.

In the summer of 1853, a fancy restaurant called Moon Lake Lodge in Saratoga Springs, New York, employed a native American (in those days he would have been called an Indian) called George Crum as a chef. On Moon Lake Lodge's menu were fried potatoes, which had been popular in America for nearly a century since Thomas Jefferson brought the recipe back from France (hence the name: French fries).

In those days French fried potatoes had not acquired the thin long shape we now associate with them. Instead, they were thick and circular. So, when Cornelius Vanderbilt, the railroad tycoon, ordered fried potatoes with his main course, Crum was happy to send out a batch of thick, round fries.

Vanderbilt sent them back saying that they were too thick. Crum prepared a thinner batch but Vanderbilt sent these back too. An angry Crum then decided to teach him a lesson and cut a new batch of potatoes so thin and fried them so crisp that it was impossible to eat them with a fork.

To his horror, Vanderbilt loved the new kind of potatoes. The owners of Moon Lake Lodge realized that they were on to a good thing and quickly put Crum's super-thin fries on the menu, advertising them as a Saratoga speciality.

And thus was born the potato chip.

When the chips became a craze, Crum left Moon Lake Lodge and opened his own restaurant, calling them 'Saratoga Chips'. They would have remained a restaurant dish had a man called William Tappendon in Cleveland, Ohio, not had the bright idea of selling chips to local grocers in 1895. The demand was so great that Tappendon opened the world's first potato chip factory, and by the early 1900s, many others had followed his example.

Since then, the innovations have kept coming. In 1926 came the first potato chip bag (made from waxed paper). In 1929, the continuous potato chip cooker (the basis of all commercial chip production) was invented. Across the Atlantic, there were other innovations. A North London chip fryer decided in the 1920s to add a small blue packet of salt to each bag of chips. He called the product 'Salt 'n' Shake'. The product was such a success that the fryer, a man called Frank Smith, soon became the UK's leading manufacturer of crisps (as the English call them, preferring to use the term 'chip' for what the Americans call French fries) under the brand name Smith's. (Predictably, his company has since been bought over by Pepsi.)

The next major innovation was the introduction of the flavoured potato chip. Once marketers realized that they could flavour the chip according to the taste preferences of the target market, there was no stopping them. In the UK, ready salted chips have less than a third of the market. The rest belongs to such flavours as smoky bacon (my personal favourite), roast beef, cheese and onion and roast chicken. In the US, popular flavours include barbecue, sour cream and onion, and steak and onion.

Elsewhere, the range gets more complex. In Egypt they have ketchup-flavoured chips as well as such local favourites as chicken curry and kabab. In the Far East you get such flavours as smoked fish, prawn, and even durian and shrimp. We only got into the flavoured chip craze in India in the 1980s, so masala flavour remains ubiquitous. But as the market matures, expect to find more adventurous flavours: *bhelpuri* or tandoori chicken for instance.

Today, the potato chip is probably the most universally acceptable snack food in the world. Inevitably, as its popularity has increased, there has been increasing disquiet about the synthetic flavours and the methods used by the bigger manufacturers.

Take Pringles, pioneers of the stackable potato chip, the kind that you can buy in a package that resembles a tennis ball can. Market researchers at Procter and Gamble—the multinational owner of Pringles—determined that people cared less about taste than about looks. They wanted chips that were unbroken and identical.

This was impossible to do with conventional techniques. No two potatoes are exactly identical so how can a whole pack of chips be the same? Moreover, if you pack your chips in a polythene bag and then transport them, some are bound to break during the journey.

P&G's solution was the reconstituted potato chip. Pringles are not made from potatoes. Rather, they are made from potato flakes, which are then squashed together to create chips that are identical to each other—clone chips, as it were. The tennis ball packaging is to ensure that the chips do not break during transportation.

The problem with all this high-tech cloning is that the starchy chips that result from this process are not particularly tasty. Crazily, researchers claim that most consumers couldn't care less.

Fortunately there is now a gourmet segment in the market. The emphasis is on real potatoes (not reconstituted potatoes) and on chips that are batch fried. In 1982, a company called Kettle Foods revived the art of hand-cooking chips, and now the Internet is full of thousands of small manufacturers advertising their handmade chips. The synthetic flavours are on their way out and more natural flavours (Tabasco, balsamic vinegar etc.) are becoming popular.

Sadly, we seem to be going the opposite direction in India. When I was a child, companies with names like OK Wafers used to make their own chips. Now, the multinationals have taken over and virtually nowhere in the big cities can you find chips that are still handmade. All the five-star hotels buy them from multinationals, and Pringles are even considered the height of sophistication in some circles.

But give me a hand-cooked, slightly greasy, uneven potato chip anytime. It has a thousand times more flavour than the mass-produced variety. And it is closer to Crum's vision of his Saratoga chip than the latter-day clones.

# the hot dog less travelled

The internationalization of fast food is a funny business. Thanks to Ronald McDonald and his many local collaborators, the hamburger is probably the one fast food item that you can find nearly everywhere in the world (though oddly enough not in India, not since the goat burger died a well-deserved death). The American version of the pizza—which owes less and less to its Italian origins the more it travels—is nearly as ubiquitous. So is Kentucky Fried Chicken, an oily, rubbery substance created by a mysterious process in which a hormone-filled chunk of broiler chicken is dipped into a vat of boiling oil of such potency that all the chicken flavour is extracted from it with such miraculous effect that, within minutes, it is converted into a hunk of rubber suitable for re-soling your trainers or converting into tyres for your bicycle. (This too is no longer available in India after a rare outbreak of good taste afflicted urban consumers.)

But, try as you will, it is almost impossible to get a good hot dog outside the US these days. This is strange because, till the 1970s, at least, most of us spoke of the hot dog and the hamburger in the same breath, regarding them as equally important products of the American fast food culture.

But somehow, while the hamburger packed its buns and travelled the globe, the hot dog remained resolutely homebound. You'll still get it at every street corner in New York City and you are almost obligated to eat one if you go to a baseball game. But nope, you won't find it at McDonald's, Burger King, Wendy's, KFC, Domino's or any other international branch of the American fast food industry.

Nobody I've asked can explain why the hot dog never followed the hamburger on its travels. Logically, it should have been as successful as the burger. The basic principles of the fast food industry are: lots of starch (the bread), a low meat content centre (the hot dog sausage compares favourably with the hamburger patty in this respect), a recipe that even a moron can handle (you'd have to be a genius to screw up boiling a frankfurter), and a neutral taste that lends itself to commercially produced flavourings (a hot dog goes perfectly with mustard or ketchup).

My guess is that the hot dog missed the plane because of an accident of timing. As we all know, the original hamburger steak (i.e. a *keema* steak) was brought to America by immigrants from Germany who named it after the town of Hamburg. They also brought the long sausage that was a speciality of Frankfurt (in a much spicier form), called it a frankfurter and made it the centrepiece of the hot dog sandwich.

By the 1960s, however, the frankfurter had lost all contact with its Germanic roots. The original was made from a mixture of good quality beef and pork, seasoned with spices, and possessed of such flavour that you needed no mustard, ketchup, chilli or whatever, to tart it up. The US frankfurter, however, had no connection with the original. It was made—to put it crudely—from the sweepings of abattoirs.

Assume you were cutting pieces of beef. After you'd cut your rump, your fillet etc., you'd have lots of useless bits leftover. These would usually be minced to nothing and then packed inside a cylinder of sausage skin. If you were cutting up a pig: likewise. And if you were chopping up a chicken then the frankfurter offered you the additional benefit of being able to mince the gizzards, the beak etc.

It was not a pretty story but in the 1960s, Americans were

content to eat whatever rubbish was sold at the supermarket and so nobody minded.

Then, Ralph Nader got into the act. In the 1960s Nader was America's most famous consumer advocate (now he's just the joker whose misbegotten candidacy cost Al Gore the election). After taking on the auto industry and taming Detroit, Nader turned his attention to the hot dog.

As *Time* famously commented during that period, the word 'frankfurter' appears below 'Frankenstein' in the dictionary. In Ralph Nader's lexicon however, it appeared much below 'contempt'. Nader told Americans everything they had suspected but didn't really want to know: about the sweepings of abattoirs etc. Nationwide revulsion followed. Restaurants started dropping hot dogs from their menu. Frankfurter sales collapsed. And so on.

Thus, in the 1970s, when the US chains began expanding (McDonald's opened in England in 1973), they steered clear of the controversial hot dog, with its junk-filled frankfurters, and stuck to the all-American, all-beef hamburger.

By the time the frankfurter industry got its act together, it was too late.

Now, the hot dog only ventures abroad as a staple of coffee shop menus at American-style hotels. Few bother with the classic street-side US hot dog. To be authentic, the frankfurter should be made from beef, should have a vaguely all-American bland flavour (none of those spicy continental sausages, thank you) and should be boiled in hot water. The bun should never be toasted. It should be slit in half (lengthwise) and the frankfurter slid in. On the roadside, boiled onions are an acceptable garnish but you must then squirt the length of the sausage with a lurid yellow mustard (no Dijon-type stuff, please). At restaurants it is acceptable to coat the sausage with a couple of spoons of chilli con carne (the chilli dog) but as you are unlikely to rustle up chilli only as a garnish, this assumes that the restaurant already has chilli con carne on its menu.

Nobody in India does an authentic hot dog—the need for a

beef frankfurter more or less rules that out—and I'm always slightly dubious about the pork that most restaurants use for their sausages. (A useful rule of thumb is never to eat pork in India unless it is imported—that's what most people in the food business do and they should know.) Some restaurants use chicken frankfurters, which is less authentic but safer and matters less if you then slather chilli con carne on the sausage. In my experience, the best hot dog in India is at the American Diner at Delhi's Habitat Centre.

But if you do like hot dogs, go ahead and make your own—remember it is a dish that any moron can cook. The first thing you need to do is buy frankfurters from an Oberoi deli. They import their pork from Australia so it should be safe. I'm not sure what they put into their chicken frankfurters but no doubt the Oberois will claim that there are no gizzards, no beaks, and that Chairman Bikki personally pushes the finest supremes of corn-fed chicken into the sausage machine while humming the Eton Boating Song.

Hot dog buns are now easily available at most bakery/grocery stores but you may need to try a few brands before choosing what is best in your area. Squishy bottles of American mustard are also widely sold.

Here's my twist on the recipe.

Boil a pan of salted water. When the water is boiling, stick the franks in. (Do not pierce with a fork as some recipe books recommend.) After a few minutes, when they seem more or less done, pull them out of the water. In a frying pan, heat some olive oil over a gentle heat. When the oil is hot, put in the franks (do not raise heat) and slowly brown them.

Once they are brown, slice the buns and slide them in. I like to add long fried onions, and the mustard is essential.

The recipe is inauthentic (you shouldn't have to fry either the sausage or the onions). But yes, it works.

# deconstructing the sandwich

Ever since I was a child I have always been fascinated by the sandwich. I could be wrong but I get the distinct impression that in the 1960s, we were keener on sandwiches than we are today. My memories of growing up in Bombay always involve restaurant visits at which sandwiches were consumed. At the Khyber in Kala Ghoda (now recast as a trendy North Indian eatery designed by Parmeshwar Godrej), my usual treat was a milkshake and a grilled chicken and cheese sandwich. At the Sea Lounge at The Taj, the speciality used to be a toasted sandwich—the type you could make at home by putting the sandwich into one of those contraptions that you then held over the gas till you thought it was ready. And nearly everywhere you went—clubs, functions, more modest establishments etc.—they served chutney sandwiches.

However, the only bread available was your standard plasticky white *maida* bread. You couldn't get decent ham for a ham sandwich, the bacon for BLT (Bacon, Lettuce and Tomato) was always of dodgy quality (and usually unsafe). And the vast variety of cold meats .that you could put into a sandwich—which we now have access to, thanks partly to the Oberoi (Charcuterie)—were simply not available. Even the cheese (in the grilled chicken and cheese sandwich) was always of inferior quality.

So, now that we can get great bread, amazing charcuterie, wonderful cheese and fresh vegetables from all over the world, what do we do?

Well, to put it bluntly: we eat *channa* burgers.

Why should this be so? In almost all Western societies, the sandwich (or some variation thereof) is an integral part of the lunch ritual. In New York, they will feed you deli sandwiches—great big hulking monsters so full of heaps of cold meat that only Linda Lovelace could manage a full bite without choking. In France they'll make theirs with better bread and do strange, not always nice, things to the sandwich (the Croque Monsieur, for instance). In the north of England, they'll eat the disgusting Chip Butty (a sandwich made by putting French fries between two slices of white bread—I kid you not). And in London, an office lunch will usually consist of a sandwich bought from the nearby coffee shop and sandwich bar.

In India, however, we ignore the beauty of the carefully constructed sandwich, and stick to the worst excesses of the American fast food chains. Those who don't order dosas for lunch (and let's face it, they don't taste very nice cold) will phone for a takeout pizza or send for one of Ronald McDonald's newly Indianized offerings (variations of the *channa* burger, mostly).

Even when a great Indian sandwich has been popularized, it has happened abroad: the Chicken Tikka Sandwich is now one of the UK's best-sellers. But you'd have to search to find a decent version in Bombay or Delhi. (I wouldn't bother with the Barista variation—but then, it always seems to sell out first so perhaps it appeals to *some* tastes.)

By turning our backs on sandwiches and eating French fries and pizzas for lunch, we are probably walking the same road that Middle America took on its way to obesity. (Something like one-third of all Americans are now obese.)

My solution is simple. Don't give in to the tyranny of fatty fast food. Make your own sandwich before you come to work. It only takes five minutes, is cheaper than a takeout from a fast food chain, tastes much better, and is much, much healthier.

There are a few golden rules to sandwich-making. The first should be self-evident: buy good bread. Do not waste your time on cheap white bread. Buy good quality brown (or *atta*) bread, now available everywhere. Or, if you do like the taste of *maida* (you poor things!), then spend a little money on buying your bread from a bakery that makes fresh bread every day. If you want to splash out, you can go to a five-star hotel bakery for fancy breads, but this is not essential.

The second rule is simple but we sometimes lose sight of it: always combine flavours. A chicken sandwich is so-so. But a chicken and cheese sandwich is ace. Two flavours are always better than one, in every single case.

The third rule has to do with texture. All too often we forget that the complex phenomenon of liking food is only partly about pure taste. Texture plays a very important role in determining how enjoyable the experience will be. (So does smell, but we'll leave that for another time.)

If you get the three rules of sandwich-making right, it is difficult to go wrong with a sandwich. And once you've got the basics right, you can experiment with your own variations. Here are some of mine.

My take on the Chicken Tikka Sandwich is to take thin slices of leftover tandoori chicken (ideally, tear them off with your fingers) and some finely chopped vinegar onions (the things they send you along with tandoori food) and put them between two slices of lightly buttered brown bread. My trick is to first lightly toast the bread, to butter it while the bread is warm (so the butter melts) and to then apply a thin layer of pickle masala (the liquid part of any *achaar* that you like) on one of the slices. You can heat the chicken of course, but I find it always works, whatever you do.

I'm not wild about plain ham sandwiches and much prefer salami sandwiches. These are easy to make. Buy any pre-sliced salami (the Oberoi's Italian Farmer's Salami, for instance, or their

Pepperoni) and slice a fresh tomato into circles that are roughly the same size as the salami slices. Put both between two slices of bread (no butter needed), and you'll find it is a combination made in heaven.

The salami-tomato sandwich works because of texture. In my view, that's the problem with the classic Indian chutney-sandwich: there's nothing to bite into. The answer is easy. Put thin cucumber slices between the slices of chutney-smeared bread. It improves the texture, and the coolness of the cucumber sets off the chutney.

I love bacon, especially when it is really, really crisp, but am no fan of the BLT (Bacon, Lettuce and Tomato). In my view, crisp bacon needs something squishy to set it off. Two possibilities: either you put some mashed, ripe avocado between slices of toasted bread and stud it with nuggets and rashers of crispy bacon, or you take the easy way out—you make a fried egg the basis of the sandwich and then put the bacon on top.

My favourite restaurant sandwich these days is made by the Machan at the Delhi Taj. Tapas, the manager there, is himself a great chef, so he knows his food. He gets the kitchen to lightly sauté peppers, mushrooms and courgettes with oregano and basil in olive oil, and makes the sandwich with toasted brown bread. It's a wonderful low-calorie option, and easy to make at home.

What do you do if somebody gives you a horrible ready-made sandwich on white bread? You are hungry and have to eat it. Well, here's a trick: places that give you these sandwiches also usually give you potato crisps and tomato ketchup. Put a little ketchup inside the sandwich and then layer it with crisps. The ketchup will kill the disgusting taste of the original filling and the crisps will make up in texture for what the sandwich lacks in taste.

If you like chicken sandwiches and want a variation, here's a thought. Buy the Oberoi's Smoked Duck and tear off small pieces. Place the duck pieces on a slice of good (untoasted) bread. Top with sliced green olives. And then—this is the surprising bit—add a few thin slices of fresh green apple. It shouldn't work but it does. The secret is the sweetness of the apple which offsets the saltiness of the olives and the smoked duck.

Any other favourites? I've lots: pâté de foie gras with figs on walnut bread (if you are prepared to break the bank); scrambled egg with smoked salmon on toasted, buttered bread with the addition of a few capers and some squishy salmon eggs (easily available at upmarket groceries now); and masala mushrooms, cooked with lots of onion and served between toasted bread. But I'll keep these for later. Try the easy ones first.

# pulverize that potato

What do you suppose is, at once, the most boring and the most decadent side dish known to man?

Easy.

It's the mashed potato.

I don't have to tell you why it's boring. But decadent? Well, that's because such Michelin-starred French chefs as Alain Ducasse and Joel Robuchon now pride themselves on the fluffiness of their (overpriced) mashed potatoes—a fluffiness that comes, not so much from the humble potato itself, but from the gallons of cream and pounds of butter they add to the dish.

Truth be told, I'm not much of a mashed potato man. Even when confronted by dishes where mash is the required companion (sausages for example, as in Bangers and Mash), I always prefer chips (as in French fries) because I love the texture of a golden fried potato.

The trouble is that there's only so much you can do with the potatoes we get at our vegetable markets. In Europe you'll find a vast range of potatoes in the shops: Maris Piper for chips, Duke of York as delicate new potatoes or King Edward for baking. In India, alas, you'll only find one kind at most shops.

And they are nearly always useless.

Sometimes they'll cook unevenly (depending on time of year) and even when they don't have that problem, they'll be so full of sugar that they'll be no good for frying.

I don't deep-fry at home (though you can buy good quality, pre-cut frozen chips—made from imported potatoes—at most shops) but I do like to shallow fry potatoes, with a little onion, in goose fat. The potatoes take on such a wonderful flavour that all you need is a little good quality sea salt (i.e. Maldon) for the dish to overshadow any piece of meat you serve it with.

Sadly, it just doesn't work with the potatoes you get in the shops today—they are just too sweet and no matter how much you salt the outside of each piece, the centre remains annoyingly bland and sweet.

Lately, I've taken to buying potatoes when I go abroad (to the immense consternation of customs officers looking for 'electronics goods'), but as these run out relatively quickly (as, to be fair, does the goose fat), I'm usually left at the mercy of the local *sabziwallah* and his potatoes.

Hence my reluctant adoption of the mashed potato as the only way in which you can make an Indian potato edible.

The basic mashed potato recipe (as distinct from the Michelin-starred versions) is relatively simple.

You take a large pot filled with water, add some salt (and if you like, a couple of stock or bouillon cubes) and bring to the boil quickly. Once the water is boiling, you lower the heat to reduce the temperature. This sounds silly but there is a good scientific reason for it: if you drop potatoes into boiling water, then the starch breaks down unevenly, giving you potatoes that are underdone in places.

You add peeled and sliced potatoes and cook them uncovered for about half an hour till they are nearly done—the test is that they must not be squishy but that the tip of a knife should slide in.

Next, you take the potatoes out of the pot and wash them several times in cold running water. Once that's done, you put them in a pot and add enough warm water to cover. You bring the pot to a boil, lower the heat again, and simmer till the potatoes look like they are ready to be mashed (usually seven minutes).

After that, your ingenuity takes over.

The basic formula is that you combine lots of cream (about one cup for five large potatoes), lot of butter (five tablespoons), and (only if you like) some milk (in case you think the cream is not enough). You add salt and pepper to taste, and heat gently.

When the mixture is warm you add the potatoes and then mash with a hand masher. Once the potatoes are mashed and have no lumps, you beat the resulting mash with a whisk or even a fork, as you would an omelette mixture (i.e. you add air) till fluffy. Traditionally, French chefs sieve several times, but I'm not sure that's necessary for home-cooked mash.

Most people will regard this as enough. But I soon get tired of the taste of dairy products (basically, the recipe is potatoes and dairy fat) and look for more oomph in my mash. Chefs who keep adding more and more butter are just being lazy—there's lots more you can do.

In Gujarat, we add green coriander chutney and a little lemon juice to the potatoes (this becomes the filling for *batata wadas*). If you want an Oriental variation then you can add one full spoon of wasabi paste (best described, if somewhat inaccurately, as Japanese mustard), two spoons of toasted sesame oil and some finely chopped green onions.

Ritu Dalmia at Delhi's Diva restaurant does a deluxe mashed potato with bits of black truffle. If no black truffles are around (and let's face it, that's usually true) then you can achieve the same effect by using truffle oil and a good truffle paste (salsa truffina).

If you want a variation that's not so dependent on fancy ingredients then try chopped spring onions and English mustard (a Western version of the wasabi potato combination). Or, caramelize some onions and add them just before serving, to some warm mashed potatoes—more than the taste, it's the crunchiness of the texture that will work.

A vegetarian recipe book I got for my birthday (by the curiously named Crescent Dragonwagon) offers up Double Garlicked Mashed Potatoes. The trick here is to add raw garlic to the potatoes and then, just before serving, add little nuggets of caramelized garlic.

As you can see the possibilities are limitless.

You can eat mashed potatoes with pretty much anything but traditionally, they go with sausages (the wasabi version works brilliantly), roast or grilled chicken (the basic, buttery potato will do), or with gravy dishes such as Coq au Vin or Boeuf Bourgignon (the gravy is sucked up by the mash).

I eat them with steak, with lean pork chops, and with lamb cutlets. As a general rule, they go less well with crumbed foods (escalope Milanese, fried fish etc.) which need deep-fried accompaniments, but I guess you can experiment.

Do not, however, ever make the mistake of imagining that they are the healthy option. Good mashed potatoes should include enough butter and cream to induce a heart attack on the spot. Even chips are probably healthier than mash.

But then—what the hell!—everyone's allowed to indulge once in a while.

# making the oil flow

More nonsense is probably written about cooking fat than about any other gastronomic subject (with the obvious exception of wine which is a pseud's wet dream). If I read another pretentious article about olive oil, for instance, I'll probably throw up. Similarly, the whole debate about 'good' fat and 'bad' fat has now reached such levels that it is hard to make any sense of it. And it really annoys me when chefs brag about the tenderness of their kababs (the *kakori*, for instance) without ever admitting that the secret is simple enough: minced animal fat.

In case you are as confused as I am by the new fat orthodoxy or as bemused by the olive oil snobbery, I'm going to break from the usual format of this column and just give you a quick rundown of cooking food fats.

But first, a word about fat itself. If you've read articles telling you how bad fat is, pay no attention. Fat is an essential ingredient of nearly all tasty foods. If there's no fat in the food it won't taste very good.

I remember, years ago, at one of the very first Chefs' Conferences, listening to some foreign-returned Indian chef who told us how he made all his food healthy by removing all the fat. For instance, he said, when he served a *rogan josh*, he took care to skim off all the fat from the top of the gravy before serving the dish.

During the question-and-answer session that followed, Manjit

Gill, the doyen of ITC's chefs, got up to point out that you couldn't have a *rogan josh* without the fat. The *point* of the dish was the fat which floated to the top. Remove the fat and you'd have a mutton *korma*—possibly a good mutton *korma*—but you certainly wouldn't have a *rogan josh*.

This is true of many dishes and indicative of the power of fat to imbue dishes with taste. If you want your waffles to taste better pour a little melted butter on them. If you want to enjoy a great loaf of bread then the quality of the butter you eat it with is paramount. Any mediocre pasta (without a disgusting, cheesy, white sauce) improves dramatically if you drizzle a good olive oil over it.

Nor are the health objections always valid. Recent studies show that a high protein/low carbohydrate diet (such as Montignac or Dr Atkins) works best if you want to lose weight. The point of such a diet is that you can eat all the bacon fat and butter you like; it is the wheat and rice that make you fat.

Keep this in mind when you see foods packaged as 'low fat'. Usually the label is misleading. Low-fat foods are simply not tasty. So food companies get around this problem by adding more sugar.

Be suspicious also of 'fat alternatives', the most popular is something called Olestra. Research has shown that this leads to what its manufacturers call 'anal seepage'. (And what you and I call dirty underwear.)

## a guide to fats

**Butter**: Still the king, no matter what the olive oil snobs may tell you. There is no flavour to match the taste of fresh butter and you can't bake without good butter.

I'm not sure I accept all the health criticisms of butter (it clogs your arteries etc.) but to be on the safe side, I rarely cook with butter and even if I do, I use half butter, half oil.

Amul makes perfectly acceptable butter but there's no substitute for a good French butter.

**Olive oil**: Despite the snob value and pretension attached to the subject, I love olive oil and gallons of the stuff are used in my kitchen.

What you need to know about olive oil is simple enough. There are three broad categories: olive oil, extra-virgin oil and extra-expensive oil.

Extra-expensive olive oil is favoured by the sort of person who drinks the great Chateaus of Bordeaux. Its provenance is simple. It is estate-bottled and the argument is that each estate produces an oil of such distinctive character that an expert can identify the exact olive grove in Tuscany that it came from by merely sniffing its bouquet.

I'm sure this is true. But I'm no olive oil expert and can't tell the subtleties, so I steer clear of the extra-expensive oils unless somebody else is paying.

Extra-virgin, on the other hand, is a technical term. The old olive oil terminology—'cold-pressed' and 'first pressing'—dates from an era when olives were first crushed to extract extra virgin oil. The same olives were then pressed again or subjected to heat to extract ordinary olive oil.

These days, even modern industrial mills use hydraulic presses, so the olives are pressed only once and no heat is ever applied to extract oil.

So extra virgin now simply means oil with 1 per cent acidity while virgin has 2 per cent acidity. Oils labeled simply 'olive oil' have been refined to remove impurities and are paler than virgin and extra virgin.

The general rule is that extra virgin can be used for everything but tastes best uncooked (poured on pasta, as a dressing, eaten with bread etc.) while plain olive oil is only used for cooking.

In India the price difference is not huge so buy extra virgin for everything.

But remember: you can't deep-fry with olive oil.

**Mustard oil**: The Bengali oil. It now gets a bum rap as being heavy and unhealthy but it imparts a wonderful flavour to food and is perfect for pickles.

**Soyabean oil**: The best-selling oil in the world, but you wouldn't know it because nearly all of it goes into blended oil and margarine. A bit heavy on the palate.

**Sunflower oil**: Much used in India by people who know that it is healthier than, say, mustard oil. Pleasant but bland.

**Safflower oil**: Often confused with sunflower oil, it is actually even healthier. Made from the safflower plant, it is usually recommended to those on a low-cholesterol diet.

**Sesame oil**: It burns too early so the Chinese, who are its greatest adherents, use it for flavouring rather than cooking. You can add it to dips or dressings or to Chinese food when it is in the last stages of cooking.

**Flavoured oils**: When you see truffle oil or basil oil in the shops, don't be fooled into believing that these come from the truffle or the basil plant. Usually, these are just good oils that have been infused with the flavour of basil or truffle. You can't cook with them because this destroys the flavour. But they are great for finishing. A mushroom pasta drizzled with a few drops of basil or truffle oil will acquire a depth it wouldn't have on its own.

**Animal fats**: None of us (or few of us, at any rate) cook with animal fat in this country. But many animal fats offer superior flavour if used in the kitchen.

Pork fat is wonderful for flavouring stews, bean dishes, casseroles and the like. I use bacon fat a lot for its flavour, but of course, there are the usual health objections.

Goose fat is poultry fat so health freaks will consider it healthier than pork fat. It's not widely available but I use it for frying shiitake mushrooms, potatoes and onions. The flavour is unmatched.

Goat fat gives you a disgusting smell when used for cooking. But suet, the firm, white fat that surrounds goat kidneys, is much used by Indian chefs who wish to tenderize their kababs: lots of minced suet is the secret of the tenderness of the *kakori* kabab.

**Groundnut oil**: Widely available in India, it is much favoured by French chefs for deep-frying and it is the preferred oil of Chinese cooks because of its bland flavour. You can always use it for Indian or Thai food.

General Rule: I'm not one to lecture people but here are the principles I follow. Extra virgin oil for everything; sunflower for Chinese or Thai; butter when I'm using a really good bread; goose fat for special occasions; and bacon fat in small quantities every now and then.

It's not necessarily a healthy prescription, but by God, it makes for good food!

# saucing up the sausage

I've decided that I can live on sausages. Open my fridge and you will find it full of all kinds of sausage; torpedo-like garlic sausage from which you cut chunks each time you need to flavour a dish of lentils or beans; ready sliced salamis; old-style English breakfast sausages; spicy, slightly fermented Thai sausages; sweet Chinese sausage; and long hot dog frankfurters.

There are many things to remember about sausages. The first is that because the term encompasses any kind of mince meat in a casing, it covers a variety of foods from tiny Danish cocktail sausages to giant salamis. While I'm a fan of all kinds of sausages, my concern here is not with the ready-to-eat salami kind of sausage but with the sort you have to fry before you eat.

But even the cooking of sausages is a subject of controversy. Some sausages—say the frankfurters that go into hot dogs—need only to be boiled. But others require a rather more complex approach. Some cookbooks tell you that you must prick the sausages with a fork before you fry them—otherwise the skin will burst. Others advise plunging all sausages in boiling water for a few minutes before browning them in the frying pan later.

I've tried nearly all of the above approaches. But I'm now a fan of the style advocated by Matthew Fort, the sausage fanatic who reviews restaurants for *The Guardian*. I got Fort's recipe from a piece in the paper but it is also quoted by Nigel Slater in his best-selling *Real Food* (available at Delhi's Fact and Fiction and good bookshops everywhere).

The key to Fort's recipe is patience—lots of it. As he himself says, 'The proper cooking of sausages is a tranquil, almost meditative business. It involves no violence or agitation of any kind.' This may remind you of the sort of thing that Sri Sri Ravi Shankar says these days but I'm willing to bet that Fort cooks a better sausage than dear old Sri Sri.

In Fort's recipe (which I follow with slight variations) you put a frying pan over a very, very low flame. He doesn't use cooking fat but I put a little olive oil in the pan. Then, you place the sausages in the centre of the pan and go away.

According to Fort, you must leave the sausages 'gently cooking for a very long time—long enough to make a pot of tea, take it upstairs to your slumbering partner, rouse him or her, share a few agreeable moments of repose, wash, dress and slope downstairs again—anything from forty minutes to an hour.'

You must, he insists, never ever prick the sausages because this allows the juices to escape. And the point of a sausage is the juiciness of the meat. Fort's view is that only through slow cooking can you 'allow the meat to heat through slowly, and thoroughly, encouraging the polite transformation of flavours, the retention of juices and the fat to leach out through the semi-permeable skin.'

He is, of course, entirely right. But his recipe presupposes a good quality sausage—which is almost impossible to find in India. I loathe smooth, bland sausages in which the meat inside has been ground so finely that there is no sense of texture. A good sausage must be plump, the casing must be organic (a lot of synthetic substitutes are now used), and the meat should be both coarsely ground and flavourful.

The classic English breakfast sausage uses such herbs as sage, but many of us will probably prefer Continental sausages with their flavour of pepper, garlic and fennel.

The problem in India is that to be any good, sausages must be made from beef or pork or both. (Don't waste your time on chicken sausages and other such abominations. Pork in India is unsafe (which is why I'm reluctant to eat it) and beef poses its own problems. The only place I trust to make a safe sausage is the Oberoi deli where the pork is all imported from Australia and I assume the beef is well-sourced too, though, for obvious reasons, they are a little more shifty about advertising its provenance.

Oberoi sausages are not always great and are generally a little too Germanic for my taste (I prefer the French and Italian variations) but they are, nevertheless, acceptable enough. If you buy one of their better sausages and use Fort's recipe, then the results can be quite pleasing.

But what do you do if the quality of the sausage is not great or if you don't have the kind of time that Fort's recipe requires?

In such cases I find that the best way to proceed is to forget that the sausage has an Occidental origin and treat it like an Oriental ingredient: Indian, Chinese or Thai.

If I'm faced with a bland sausage I usually slice it into chunks and stir-fry (over high heat) with loads of chopped onion and sliced garlic. The flavour improves immediately and then, depending on what the sausage itself tastes like, I vary the seasoning. A dash of prepared Mediterranean-style herbs (the kind you get in a bottle) works well with all sausages; a little Tabasco never hurts; and if I have to cope with really bland frankfurters, then I rely on the a-good-hot dog-needs-mustard principle and throw some wasabi paste into the pan at the very end.

There are many advantages to this method: (a) it is quick, (b) the quality of the sausage doesn't matter so much, (c) you can pass it off as a proper dish even if you've used only three sausages—consider how strange it would be to bring a plate of three bland whole sausages to the dinner table and (d) I have yet to find somebody who doesn't like it.

You can of course get slightly more adventurous. In recent months the Oberoi has been mucking about with the recipe for its chorizo sausage (sometimes there are more peppercorns than meat) but I used to buy the chorizo regularly when the quality was consistent and then cook it as part of a Tex-Mex gravy dish.

My recipe was given to a chef who sophisticated it and got all the quantities right (I'm no good with numbers), so I have no hesitation in quoting it here—it is certain to work.

### chorizo sausage tex-mex style

Take a packet of Oberoi Chorizo, peel the skin off the sausages and cut into chunks. Chop two large onions finely. And take a third onion but cut it into large dice.

In a pan, heat olive oil and then add the finely chopped onion and one spoon of chopped garlic. When the onions are opaque, add two tetrapaks of tomato purée. Then add 50 ml (or a wine glass worth) of good red wine (Grover, Chantilly etc. will do).

As the gravy simmers, add a spoonful of roughly chopped garlic (or garlic purée), oregano (Mexican is better but the European variety will do), a little salt, and a quarter teaspoon of chilli.

As the dish begins to take on a Tex-Mex taste, add the diced onion.

Cook the chorizo separately in a pan (over high heat) and then add it to the dish. Let the whole thing simmer, let the flavours mingle, and watch the gravy get thicker. When you think the gravy is thick enough for you, add a dash of Tabasco.

You can serve this with rice but I find it works best with good, crusty bread.

Oriental sausages are a different matter altogether. The leading sausage of the Orient is the sweet, wind-dried pork sausage of Chinese cooking. Abroad, you'll find it nearly everywhere, but in India you have to search out places where real Chinese people go to buy groceries. In Calcutta I used to find it in Chinatown, and I'm sure that there must be equivalents of Chinatown in most big Indian cities.

The best way to eat a Chinese sausage is to slice it very thin and then quickly stir-fry the slices—you'll know they are done when they take on a goldenish hue.

Once the sausage slices are ready you can use them for pretty much everything. The best use is—in my view, at least—as a flavouring for fried rice. You fry cooked rice with onions, garlic and a little soya sauce and then at the very end, add cooked sausage slices. Toss for a minute, put off the heat and mix for another two or three minutes. That will be long enough for the flavour of the sausage to permeate the rice.

If you are not keen on rice you can use the sausage slices in salads (the Thais make an excellent Chinese sausage salad), stir-fry them with such vegetables as asparagus, or even serve them as a cocktail snack.

Sadly, Indian cookery is not big on sausages. Though the three examples I've quoted come from three completely different cuisines (the English breakfast sausage, the Mexican chorizo, and the Chinese sausage)—the charms of the sausage have left India behind.

There is, however, one part of India where they make great sausages. The spicy Goan sausage is a vinegary adaptation of the Portuguese chorizo, and I love it. Sadly, nearly all the pork in Goa is unsafe—don't forget that Goans used pigs before they had sanitation.

And so I have to always stop myself from ordering Goan sausages even though I'm repeatedly assured that they now farm pigs in Goa and that safety standards have improved.

If somebody—the Oberoi deli perhaps?—would do Goan sausages with clean pork, I would be overjoyed. So, I suspect, would anyone who tried them. In no time at all they would become India's best-selling sausage.

Now all we need is to find somebody who is willing to take on this task.

# bean to the wild west?

We know what the cowboys rode (horses). We know what they wore (Stetson hats and riding boots). We know how often they bathed ('rarely' is the official answer, though I suspect 'never' is closer to the truth). And we know what they drank (Bourbon usually, though the sissies—the Lone Ranger, Roy Rogers etc.—probably stuck to ginger beer).

But do we know what they ate?

Think about it. Cast your mind back to the days when Hollywood still made Westerns and Clint Eastwood still had hair. Do you remember any banquet scenes? Any shots of Buffalo Bill eating dessert; of The Man with No Name sprinkling salt and pepper on his fried eggs?

Short answer: no.

Westerns always had saloon scenes. In such scenes, our hero would enter a bar (or a saloon as it was called in those days) through swing doors (they had to be swing doors), stride to the counter and watch as a bartender poured out a shot of Bourbon. Usually one or two overmade-up, busty ladies of dubious moral character would enter the frame and in the long shot you could see that at least one table was occupied by a group of raucous individuals playing poker.

But before our hero could finish his drink and move on to the dining room (or to the bosomy ladies, for that matter), there would always be a shoot-out or a brawl.

And the scene ended before dinner was served.

If you ask people what they think cowboys ate, you'll get one of two answers. One: steak. And two: beans.

Of the two, beans is the one you'd expect to hear more often because baked beans have often been marketed on the basis of Old West associations (even though they were popularized by the citizens of Boston which is as far as you can get from the West). The only scene I really remember of a meal in a cowboy movie is the campfire dinner of beans in Mel Brooks's 1970s classic comedy *Blazing Saddles*. Of course, because this was a Mel Brooks film, the point of the scene was only to set up the next sequence, in which the cowpokes find their sleep disturbed by attacks of flatulence, captured with suitably gross sound effects.

But steak is right too. Except that the cowboys didn't eat cow meat. They would slaughter the American buffalo (no relation to our bovine, milk-producing water buffalo but a completely different animal called the bison), and cut its meat into steaks. Buffalo Bill, for instance, earned his name not from loving the buffalo but by killing it.

Sometimes, just sometimes, the two great frontier meals of meat and beans would come together in one single dish. And that was how Chilli Con Carne was born.

Of course, it wasn't called that in those days. Most cowboys preferred to call it a 'bowl of red'. Kit Carson, one of the most energetic explorers of the Old West, was so fond of what we now call Chilli, that his last words were: 'I just wish there was time for another bowl of red.' (Fortunately for him, he died without consuming the full bowl of beans and so there were no Mel Brooksian consequences in heaven.)

Most of us, of course, think of Chilli as being the national dish of Mexico. In fact, Mexicans loathe the thought of Chilli being seen as a representative of what they delude themselves into believing is a great native cuisine. Ask for a bowl of Chilli at a fancy Mexican restaurant and they'll probably show you the door.

As with all such dishes, the origins of Chilli Con Carne are obscure. We know that 'carne' means meat in Spanish and that Chilli uses herbs that were not much used in the rudimentary cuisine of the Wild West (cumin, oregano etc.). So, despite the sneers from top Mexican chefs, it seems reasonable to assume that Chilli has a Mexican origin of sorts.

The first use of the term 'chilli con carne' in print occurs in 1857 but most historians suspect that the dish was invented by Mexican cooks in the town of San Antonio (in Texas) in 1820 or so. By 1880, it had become the *bhelpuri* of San Antonio. Each night, women vendors would come to the downtown plaza with bowls of cooked Chilli and set up street-food stalls. They became famous as the Chilli Queens of San Antonio (dirty-minded readers may note that the term 'queen' did not have certain associations in those days and as for the possible significance of the Chilli in this context, don't even think about it...).

By 1890, the first recorded Chilli restaurant had opened in McKinney, a large town north of Dallas, and in 1893, there was a Chilli stand at the Chicago World Fair. Though the state of Texas officially declared Chilli as its State Dish only in 1977, it has been Texas's principal (and far as I can tell, only) contribution to the world of food for over a century.

But of course, nothing is ever that simple. Though Texas claims ownership of Chilli, there are many regional variations. In Cincinnati, where there were lots of European immigrants, they served Chilli with pasta, and used red kidney beans (*rajma*) while Texans insisted on pinto beans. In New Mexico, they used lamb rather than beef. Others argued about whether the meat should be minced or cut into chunks. (This is easy to answer. Do you suppose there were many meat grinders in the Wild West? They cut it into chunks, of course.) Then, there's the debate about whether you cook it with water or beer. And some purists even say that Chilli should never contain any beans.

These questions obsess Americans who have annual Chilli cookouts and compete for the perfect Chilli. For the rest of us, what we need to know is this: Chilli should be made with meat that is coarsely ground. If you use a fine *keema*, it won't work. (Though the fast-food version of Chilli gets its low-cost reputation from the use of poor quality, fatty *keema*.) The best meat is, of course, beef, but if you have religious hang-ups about that, you can use mutton. The classic recipes use buffalo meat anyway, which is nearer to venison than beef. Chilli made with chicken or pork does not work unless you use the trick of buying a packet of the Oberoi's Chorizo sausages, removing the skins and mixing the meat—this makes for an interesting pork-based Chilli. I'm told you can make Chilli with turkey but I've never tried it. And as for vegetarian Chilli, why not just eat *rajma* instead?

You should probably use pinto beans—the average American cook simply buys a can of cooked pinto beans and adds them to the meat. But in India, I think *rajma* makes an acceptable substitute and you soak it overnight as you would for dal. Americans use fancy, pre-packaged tomato sauces that we don't get here. But remember that you will need to use packaged tomato purée—this is not Mediterranean-style cooking that benefits from the flavour of fresh tomatoes.

There are as many Chilli recipes as there are Texans (yes, it's George W's favourite dish too but don't let that put you off) and so I've listed two contrasting versions. One comes from the fancy New York deli, the Silver Palate, the other won a prize at a Texas cookout and is probably more authentic.

But all Chilli recipes use the same basic principles. You brown the meat with onions, lower the heat, add the spices (often available pre-packaged in America) and mix with the meat. Then you add the (cooked) beans and the tomato and keep simmering for 20 minutes or so.

I love all kinds of Chilli and I've been making it at home for close to fifteen years now, so here are some hints: do not use cheap *keema*. Ask for good quality, roughly ground meat with as little fat as possible. Godrej and other packaged tomato purées work well. *Rajma* is fine but on occasion, when there's not been enough time, I've even drained the sauce away from two cans of Heinz Baked Beans and thrown them into the pot—there were no complaints.

Chilli is not haute cuisine. It was invented to feed men like Kit Carson and Wild Bill Hickock, not to win three stars from Michelin inspectors. So experiment with it. It'll take three or four tries to find your own variation. But when you perfect it, Chilli can be the ideal party dish to go with a good, chilled beer.

## the silver palate's chilli

(for 30 guests)

**½ cup olive oil**
**250 g (½ lb) coarsely chopped onions (the yellower the better)**
**1 kg (2 lb) sausage (meat) (I use Oberoi Chorizo)**
**4 kg (8 lb) coarsely ground meat**
**2 spoons freshly ground pepper**
**3 tetrapaks tomato puree**
**4 cloves minced garlic**
**3 oz cumin**
**4 oz red chilli powder**
**½ cup French (not English) mustard**
**4 tablespoons salt**
**4 tablespoons dried basil**
**4 tablespoons dried oregano**
**3 kg (6 lb) canned plum tomatoes (you can boil normal tomatoes and use them instead if the cans are a problem)**
**½ cup red wine (Grover Shiraz will do)**
**¼ cup fresh lemon juice**
**½ chopped fresh dill (or 3 tablespoons dried dill)**
**1¼ kg (2½ lb) *rajma* (first soaked overnight, then boiled till tender but not squishy)**
**1 lb pitted black olives**

Heat oil in a large wok. Add onions and cook over low heat till translucent.

Add the sausage meat and the ground meat. Cook over medium heat till brown. Remove excess fat. (If using Oberoi Chorizo, remove peppercorns, which are now added in liberal quantities to make up the weight.)

Over low heat, stir in the black pepper, tomato purée, garlic, cumin, chilli, mustard, salt, basil and oregano. Mix well.

Add tomatoes, red wine, lemon juice, dill, parsley and cooked *rajma*. Stir and simmer, uncovered, for 15 minutes.

Taste and correct seasoning. Add olives and simmer for another 5 minutes.

Serve.

## texas chilli

(for 10 guests)

**4 tablespoons vegetable oil**
**1½ kg (3 lbs) coarse ground meat or boneless steak cut in ¼-inch cubes**
**1 large onion finely chopped**
**5 cloves garlic finely chopped**
**1 tablespoon paprika**
**6 tablespoons red chilli powder**
**1 tablespoon cumin**
**1 teaspoon dried oregano**
**1 tetrapak tomato purée**
**1 cup water or beer**
**1 fresh red chilli, cut into small pieces**
**3 cups cooked rajma**

***For garnish:***
**minced onion**
**1 cup grated cheese**

In a covered saucepan over medium heat, cook the beef in the oil till it is evenly browned. Now add onion and garlic and cook for another 5 minutes.

Add the paprika, chilli powder, cumin and oregano and stir for 3 minutes.

Add the tomato purée, beer and salt. Stir to combine. Add the raw chilli. Bring to a boil, then lower the heat, cover and simmer for 2 hours, stirring occasionally. If the Chilli seems to be getting too dry, add more water as the process progresses.

Take four large soup bowls and put the cooked *rajma* at the bottom of each. Ladle the Chilli over the *rajma*. Garnish with chopped onion and grated cheese.

# such cold comfort

When I was a small boy in the early 1960s, ice cream didn't mean frozen white milk on a stick. It meant a creamy, yellowish substance, full of bits of fruit and hand-churned at my grandfather's home. At boarding school, the same ice cream reappeared. Twice a week, on special 'treat' days, the staff at the mess would pull out ancient wooden buckets into which they would pour a reduced milk mixture. All along the outside of the tub would be a second compartment into which the ice (along with saltpetre) would go. Then, it would be crank-crank-crank for ages till the milk inside the tubs miraculously turned into ice cream.

Even then, some boys at school were snobbish about this hand-churned, home-made ice cream. They longed, they said, for the milky smoothness of Kwality's or Joy. They were not impressed by the sensation of suddenly chewing into a bit of fruit or a chunk of pista. They wanted a uniform flavour.

I could never understand their longing for the commercial product. I loved the home-made version, and even when my grandparents sent out for commercial ice cream (from such Ahmedabad manufacturers as Havmore and Vadilal), they bought the same kind of fruit-rich ice cream that we were used to at home. (Sample: *sitaphal* ice cream—if any two flavours were meant to mix, it was creamy *sitaphal* and creamier ice cream.)

Moreover, ice cream was one of the few 'Western foods' that actually seemed to taste better in India than abroad. In London for my summer holidays, I would sullenly refuse all offers of English ice cream on the grounds that it was disgusting, till my bemused parents found a shop that made its own ice cream of a quality that I enjoyed (Marine Ices in Chalk Farm, London, which later went on to achieve a certain trendy status among ice cream lovers).

Sadly, I was never able to maintain the high ice cream standards of my childhood. By the 1970s, nearly everybody had stopped hand-churning his own ice cream. The smaller companies remained niche regional players (though Vadilal enjoyed a resurgence in the 1980s) and the Kwality monopoly took over all of India. Even my boarding school took to giving us paper cups filled with synthetically flavoured vanilla ice cream.

A love of good ice cream has remained with me from my childhood, and only now do I realize why my first instincts were correct. In the old days, all good ice cream was made from natural ingredients (fruit, *kaju*, *pista*, *kesar* etc.) Soon the factories took over and began to use cheap or synthetic ingredients. Hand-churning is time consuming and labour intensive but few people will prefer the taste of a factory-made ice cream to one hand-cranked with love and care.

And as for why I hated English ice cream, well, I worked that out in the 1970s too. For reasons that I never fully understood, most commercial English ice cream was made with congealed vegetable fat (not milk). This is why it tasted so disgusting. Even now, if you see a great British brand name like Lyons Maid or Walls, always check to see that you are being sold a dairy ice cream, not some nasty 'frozen dessert'.

Fortunately, like many other childhood passions (chocolate is another), ice cream grew trendier as I grew older. In New York in the 1980s I was pleasantly surprised to find ridiculously overpriced Häagen-Dazs ice cream being marketed as a sort of sex aid, with ads featuring an ice cream-licking couple making out. And for ageing hippies, there was also laid-back Ben and Jerry's owned by two self-consciously rock 'n' roll types whose signature flavour was called Cherry Garcia, after the Grateful Dead's bearded fatso.

Of course, much of this—like nearly everything else about the ice cream business—is pure marketing. Häagen Dazs was never Swedish. It had an American provenance and survives on the basis of multinational marketing. Ben and Jerry may have been really cool guys, but that didn't stop them from selling out to Unilever for a sum in excess of $600 million. In most of the world, the ice cream business is multinational-dominated. Walls (70 per cent of the UK's impulse-purchase market) is owned by Unilever. So too is our very own Kwality (the ice cream, not the restaurants).

There are still many small producers of quality ice cream, but in essence, the global ice cream market is controlled by giant corporations who, quite deliberately, divide their production into four categories, distinguished by price and fat content.

At the bottom are the economy brands, sold in supermarkets or in fast food outlets where you don't have a choice. These have a fat content of 10 per cent. Then there is the standard brand, marketed enough for you to recognize the name. This should have a fat content of 12 per cent. The premium brands (the so-called snob value ice creams) taste richer because fat content goes up to 15 per cent. And there's a tiny category called super premium, which could have a fat content as high as 18 per cent.

Alas, fat content is everything in the ice cream industry. At the premium end of the market they may worry about the things that foodies care about—quality of chocolate used; is it made with fresh fruit or is it a syrup, that sort of thing—but mostly, they spend more time worrying about 'building the brand' than they do about taste.

But even within this wasteland of brand-building and test-marketing, there is some room for originality. In 1983, some genius hit on the key to the future of ice cream texture. Cookies 'n' Cream ice cream made with real cookies (Oreos, which are useless for anything else) became the biggest hit in the history of ice cream, rapidly growing to become one of America's top five ice creams.

In 1991, some bright spark took the process back a stage and said to himself: 'If people like cookies in their ice cream then maybe they'll like the dough the cookies are made from.' And thus was born Cookie Dough ice cream, another flavour phenomenon, which combined vanilla ice cream with the raw dough for chocolate chip cookies and semi-sweet chocolate chips. (All this sounds novel, but there's been a traditional brown bread ice cream—made with bread crumbs—in England for nearly a century now. Only, you have to find a specialist maker because Walls won't touch it.)

All further advances in the ice cream business stemmed from this realization that texture was the way forward. Chocolate manufacturers who saw their sales plummet every summer decided to do ice cream versions of their most popular bars. So now you get a Mars ice cream (so-so), a Snickers ice cream (terrific) and even a Kit Kat ice cream (haven't tried it).

This seems to be the trend for the future too. Flavour scientists at Nottingham University have demonstrated scientifically what we already know intuitively. The brain quickly adapts to flavour change. It takes us eighty seconds to adapt to a persistent flavour, and in five minutes our noses lose the ability to smell a flavour at all. Take the example of chewing gum. Within five minutes we cease to taste the flavour. But if we were now to take the gum out of our mouths and resume chewing after, say, a ten-minute interval, we would find that it had just as much flavour. It wasn't that the gum had lost its flavour, only that we had lost the ability to taste that flavour.

So it is with ice cream. After a few mouthfuls of Kwality's vanilla a certain sameness sets in. But an ice cream that contains chunks of surprising ingredients jolts the brain. A strawberry ice cream has a single flavour. But if you put chunks of whole strawberry in it, the brain is jolted each time you bite into a new piece of fruit.

That's why ice cream with 'hot spots of flavour', such as chunks of cookie dough, chocolate chips or cookie pieces scores over single-flavour ice cream. An ice cream made with pieces of brandied cherries (like the famous Cherry Garcia) works on this principle; so too does that old favourite, rum 'n' raisin.

And so too, of course, did the ice creams of my childhood. The great thing about home-made ice cream was that it contained no essences. You would put a spoonful of ice cream in your mouth and suddenly, you would bite into a bit of custard apple, a piece of pista, or a whole cashewnut. That was what made it so much better than the commercially produced rubbish you get in the shops these days.

# lentil lament: where's the meat?

Indians should know all about lentils—after all, we eat them at nearly every meal in the form of dal. And sure enough, India has produced some great dals—the classic sour-sweet (gur and kokum) tuver dal of Gujarat, the terrific yellow dal fry of dhaba cuisine, the black dal of the Punjab, the world-famous sambhar of the South, and even that internationally renowned restaurant creation, the Bukhara-style dal with lots of tomato purée and home-made butter and/or cream.

Perhaps because these dals have become such staples of our cuisine we have been reluctant to experiment with lentils themselves. We do sometimes eat them dry, and in some parts of India—such as Gujarat—whole lentils are often preferred to dals (Gujaratis will cook sprouted moong as though it is a vegetable and will do interesting things with whole tuver) while Punjabi experimentation tends, alas, to stop with rajma-chawal or lobia-chawal. And of course, there's a long Indian tradition of cooking with channa, (chickpeas, gram etc.) which is nearly, but not quite, the same thing.

Sadly, the Hindu cuisines of India have been reluctant to match meat and lentils. That remains a Parsi speciality whose most famous expression is of course, dhansak. Parsis are so into dals that traditional Parsi cooks will even tell you which dal goes with which meat. And then of course there's dhansak's Muslim cousin, the dal-meat.

For reasons that have never been clear to me, fancy Indian

restaurants are loath to include dal-meat on their menus. (The exception is Delhi's Embassy where dal-gosht is a speciality and should be served with a strip of Gelusil as an added extra.) But dhabas do it all the time, and to get the best dal-meat you really have to go to the Muslim quarter of Bombay.

Muslims know what Hindus can only guess at—the secret of a dal is the quality of the water. If your water does not taste right then your dal will be a disaster. Many Muslim cooks take this a step further: if water is so important then why not go the whole hog and use stock instead?

Hindu cooks will cluck their tongues but some of the best dals I've had have been made from stock. A friend of mine (Hindu Punjabi, if you want to know) routinely makes dal with stock and smiles naughtily when vegetarian guests praise her cooking. (No, of course I don't approve of such subterfuge.) At many Muslim dhabas they take the trouble to warn diners that the dal is stock-based. My favourite warning is a board at a restaurant on Colaba causeway which reads 'Dal may contain pieces of bone', an unusual way of admitting that stock has been used.

Western cuisine, on the other hand, routinely mixes lentils with meat and chicken. Most French restaurants will use lentils as a garnish for meat dishes, and lentils are a staple of the peasant cuisines of Europe.

Alas, Indian chefs at Continental restaurants either shy away from using lentils or use them badly. The only time I've had a decent lentil dish in India was when Richard Neat used to cook at the old Longchamp at the Delhi Taj.

Neat's lentils were a counterpoint to his crisp *rosti*-wrapped duck, but their flavour goes well with any kind of meat—steak, rack of lamb, or even game. They are easy to make and both the chefs who worked with Neat at Longchamp (Tapas Bhattacharya and Pradeep Sharma) are now at Machan where they will turn them out on request.

Or, you can simply make them at home. When Neat cooked at

London's Pied à Terre (where he won his two Michelin stars) he used Puy lentils from France, but after a few months in India he switched to our local whole moong, with no loss of flavour.

The recipe (as recalled by Pradeep and Tapas) is easy enough.

You boil the moong till *al dente*. In a separate pan you sauté bacon, carrot and onion in quite a lot of butter. When the vegetables are soft you add the lentils and a spoon of chicken jus and cook for a while.

Stir well, take out the bacon (which has done its job by infusing the lentils with flavour), and top with a tablespoonful of chopped parsley. And that's it.

If you can't get chicken jus (and none of us has it lying around at home), don't worry. The dish still works. Some people put a cube of chicken stock in the water when they boil the lentils. My view is that the stock cube can't hurt.

That's lentils used as a garnish. But in Italy they use them as a main dish. One of my favourite Italian restaurant dishes (and I'm not alone in this given that it has survived several menu changes) is the Sausage with Lentils at London's San Lorenzo.

I don't know how San Lorenzo makes the dish but it is apparently a traditional Italian New Year's day favourite so there are lots of recipes and variations. This one is my adaptation of Nigella Lawson's version.

Cook finely chopped onion in olive oil over low to medium heat for five minutes. Add half a kilo of Puy lentils (or whole moong or whole tuver) and stir well. Cover with cold water and then bring to boil. Once it's boiled let it simmer gently for half an hour, by which stage most of the liquid will have been absorbed.

Buy two packets of strongly flavoured sausages from the Oberoi deli. Take eight sausages, add some mashed garlic, and cook them on both sides till brown. (Cooking times vary but I'm of the use-medium-heat-and-take-your-time school.)

When the sausages are ready add 100ml red wine (just over a quarter of a bottle; I use Chantilly) and a glass (50 ml) of water. Cover the pan and let it cook for 15 minutes.

By now you should have browned sausages in a thick wine-flavoured gravy. I add garlic purée at this stage and a dash of a pre-packaged Italian seasoning (but these are optional) to the gravy.

Remove from the pot, put in a bowl, and pour the lentils over the sausages and gravy. (In a restaurant you would do it the other way around—sausages over lentil—for purposes of presentation.) Garnish with parsley.

This is a peasant dish so don't expect haute cuisine, but in my experience, you can't go wrong with it. My quantities are for four people as a main course so you can adjust according to how many people you are cooking for. And of course, the way to do it is to make lots of the lentils at one go and keep them in the fridge. That way, you just have to cook the sausage with the wine each time and reheat the lentils when you need them.

At the end of the day of course, there's nothing to beat a good yellow dal with chawal, made at home. But that doesn't mean that we should ignore the potential of lentils. Pair them with steak or sausages and you'll end up looking at moong in a completely different way.

# spaghetti: twists in the tale

One of the curious things about the globalization of food is that many so-called ethnic dishes are actually unknown in their countries of alleged origin. Let's take the example of Indian food. The average Brit who goes to an Indian restaurant for a curry will usually order the following: Onion Bhaji (a variation on what we call a pakora or a *bhajiya*; Beef Vindaloo (meaning not the subtle Goan vinegar-flavoured dish but simply a very hot curry); Chicken Tikka Masala (not our dhaba Butter Chicken but a completely different gravy often based on a can of tomato soup); Prawn Patia (not the Parsi dish but the same basic curry as the Vindaloo with less chillies and more sugar), and Balti Chicken (Karahi Chicken as reassembled by a half-wit).

So it is with other cuisines. Nobody from China will recognize that Sino-Ludhianvi classic, Chicken Manchurian. The hamburger has nothing to do with Hamburg. Chilli Con Carne is unknown in Mexico. It was invented in Texas and Mexicans spit on you if you tell them that your favourite Mexican dish is Chilli Con Carne.

But in no case is the confusion more genuine or intense than with what must be the world's most popular pasta dish: Spaghetti Bolognese.

Unlike, say, Balti Chicken, this, at least, has the ring of authenticity about it. After all, spaghetti is Italian and why shouldn't the meat sauce come from Bologna—it is called a Bolognese sauce after all.

But the truth is that try as you will you simply won't find a single restaurant in Bologna that will serve you Spaghetti Bolognese. Oh, yes, you'll find the dish on practically every hotel coffee shop menu wherever in the world you go. You may even find Italian restaurants outside of Italy that will serve the dish.

But you won't find it in Bologna.

The reason for this is simple. Spaghetti Bolognese is as Italian as Winston Churchill. Or as Italian as Chicken Tikka Masala. As Fish and Chips. As Spotted Dick. As Toad in the Hole. As Roast Beef and Yorkshire Pudding.

Yes, that's right. It's a great British invention.

There are differing views on how Spaghetti Bolognese became a staple of British institutional catering and even of working men's caffs. But what is clear is that it is so much a part of life in England that they even have their own nickname for it: Spag Bol. If you've eaten Spaghetti Bolognese at a restaurant or a coffee shop, or if you've cooked it at home under the misapprehension that it was an Italian dish then you can place yourself in the same category as all the Brit yobs who think that India's national dish is Chicken Tikka Masala.

The British, it is well known, do funny things with pasta. Schoolchildren are fed such strange foods as pasta hoops with tomato sauce and Sonia Gandhi has written (in *Rajiv*, her first book) of being startled to discover, in Cambridge, that British people ate spaghetti on toast. (At least they've stopped doing that now because they've discovered Spag Bol.)

Institutional caterers like pasta because it's cheap and because it keeps for months without refrigeration. The appeal of Spag Bol is that the sauce is made from mincemeat so you can take any old rubbish, any piece of meat that's not good enough to serve on its own, mash it into *keema*, include large quantities of the fat (which is virtually free) and turn out a meat sauce at an amazingly low cost.

Unfortunately for Brits, until the River Café and all the fancy

Italian restaurants opened, the most successful Italian restaurants in London were always run by waiters (Alvaro, Lorenzo, Mario and Franco etc.), not by chefs. And if guests wanted to eat Spag Bol, well then, they would put it on the menu.

Less understandably, restaurants in other countries (though much less so in America where real Italians tended to eat in Italian restaurants) quickly picked up on the Spag Bol fad and it is today probably the best-known pasta dish in the world.

Most cookbooks have recipes for it and there's even a snob thing about the wine you add to the sauce. You and I would imagine that a dark gravy needs red wine but Spag Bol snobs will sniffily inform you that a real Bolognese sauce (whatever that is) needs white wine.

In Bologna, where the now world-famous Bolognese sauce allegedly originated, the closest relative that you can locate is the *ragu*.

Originally *ragu* did not have *keema* at all. Instead, the meat (usually beef) was cut into small chunks, cooked with chicken livers, bacon, onion, celery and wine. Later, when tomatoes became widely available (from America), a small quantity was added. Nor was this sauce used for spaghetti. Instead it was layered on to lasagna.

Over the years *ragu* has become more and more complex but nobody in Bologna eats it with spaghetti; tagliatelle is a much more suitable accomplishment. To make a proper ragu (of fancy restaurant quality) you need so many ingredients that you may be tempted to stop reading the recipe halfway through and order a Domino's pizza instead.

Here, according to one classic recipe, is what you need: pancetta, prosciutto, mortadella, porcini mushrooms, chopped lean beef sirloin, lean veal sirloin, chicken livers, heavy cream, dry red wine, beef stock, nutmeg, fresh celery . . . I could go on but life is too short.

Patricia Wells offers a (relatively) simpler recipe.

> Cook onion, celery, carrot and parsley with a little salt in olive oil over moderate heat for 4 minutes. Add sausage meat (i.e. remove the skins of good, spicy sausages and mash the meat together) and mix well. Cook over low heat for five minutes. Add fresh tomatoes plus a little tomato purée along with a little chilli (ideally, the kind of chilli flakes you see in pizza places). Cover and cook for 20 minutes.

I'm not sure if you can describe the result as a Spag Bol sauce but it has two great advantages. One: you can just use sausage meat which is easier than finding good *keema*. And two, you can refrigerate the sauce and pull it out whenever you want.

The typical English Bolognese sauce is slightly different.

> You cook mushroom, onion, carrot and garlic in a mixture of butter and oil for 4 minutes. Then you add *keema* and stir. Next you add beef stock (or any meat stock; a cube is fine), a glass of red wine, a bay leaf, and a few spoons of tomato purée. Bring to simmering point and cook for 40 minutes till the sauce thickens.

My own view is that neither sauce is terribly exciting and that both English Bolognese gravy and *ragu* are a bit boring unless you are cooking for small children who want to eat pasta or noodles.

If you do want to make pasta for guests or want to impress people then go for the other famous spaghetti dish: Carbonara. (You need to finish cooking this at the table to show off.)

> First, you fry small pieces of pancetta (you can use the Oberoi's bacon if you can't find pancetta). When this is done, you keep the following ready: a little warm dry white wine, a couple of spoons of cream and some raw beaten egg. As soon as the spaghetti is done you strain it into a bowl. Quickly add the cooked

pancetta, wine and cream. But before the spaghetti cools, pour the egg mixture over it and stir. The heat of the spaghetti will cook the egg and you'll have a rich pasta full of bacon flavour. Top with parsley (if you like) and Parmesan.

The dish has the advantage of theatre, is easier to make than a *ragu*, and tastes better especially to those who think of a Carbonara Sauce as a thick cream with a little bacon.

Is it authentically Italian? Well, yes and no. Italians like to claim that it is the traditional pasta of the Carbonari charcoal burners. But this is bogus. The truth is that during the Second World War, when victorious American troops occupied Rome, they had rations of eggs and bacon and wanted local cooks to do something unusual with them. Cooks from a restaurant called Carbonara invented this simple dish and the US army lived on it.

Typical, isn't it? Of the two most famous pastas in the world, one was invented by Brits. And the other was made to order for the Yanks.